general editor John M. MacKenzie

When the 'Studies in Imperialism' series was founded more than twenty-five years ago, emphasis was laid upon the conviction that 'imperialism as a cultural phenomenon had as significant an effect on the dominant as on the subordinate societies'. With more than seventy books published, this remains the prime concern of the series. Cross-disciplinary work has indeed appeared covering the full spectrum of cultural phenomena, as well as examining aspects of gender and sex, frontiers and law, science and the environment, language and literature, migration and patriotic societies, and much else. Moreover, the series has always wished to present comparative work on European and American imperialism, and particularly welcomes the submission of books in these areas. The fascination with imperialism, in all its aspects, shows no sign of abating, and this series will continue to lead the way in encouraging the widest possible range of studies in the field. 'Studies in Imperialism' is fully organic in its development, always seeking to be at the cutting edge, responding to the latest interests of scholars and the needs of this ever-expanding area of scholarship.

Ending British rule in Africa

Manchester University Press

Ending British rule in Africa

WRITERS IN A COMMON CAUSE

Carol Polsgrove

MANCHESTER UNIVERSITY PRESS
Manchester and New York

distributed in the United States exclusively by
Palgrave Macmillan

Copyright © Carol Polsgrove 2009

The right of Carol Polsgrove to be identified as the author of this work has been asserted by her in accordance with the Copyright, Designs and Patents Act 1988.

Published by Manchester University Press
Oxford Road, Manchester M13 9NR, UK
and Room 400, 175 Fifth Avenue, New York, NY 10010, USA
www.manchesteruniversitypress.co.uk

Distributed in the United States exclusively by
Palgrave Macmillan, 175 Fifth Avenue,
New York, NY 10010, USA

Distributed in Canada exclusively by
UBC Press, University of British Columbia, 2029 West Mall,
Vancouver, BC, Canada V6T 1Z2

British Library Cataloguing-in-Publication Data is available

Library of Congress Cataloging-in-Publication Data is available

ISBN 978 0 7190 8901 5 paperback

First published by Manchester University Press in hardback 2009

This paperback edition first published 2012

The publisher has no responsibility for the persistence or accuracy of URLs for any external or third-party internet websites referred to in this book, and does not guarantee that any content on such websites is, or will remain, accurate or appropriate.

Printed by Lightning Source

To my daughter, Cora Polsgrove, and my brother, William Claxon

CONTENTS

General editor's introduction—ix
Preface—xi
List of abbreviations—xviii

1	'Misery laid bare'	1
2	'Generals without an army'	23
3	Writing while the bombs fall	53
4	'A constant stream'	75
5	Strategist, publicist	96
6	Acts of betrayal	118
7	Their own histories	145

Select bibliography—175
Index—181

GENERAL EDITOR'S INTRODUCTION

In the era of printing, political movements have invariably sought to propagate their ideas through the published word. Printing gave oppositions a voice, initially through broadsheets, tracts, pamphlets, later through books and articles. But as the scale and complexities of print capitalism developed, notably in the nineteenth and twentieth centuries, small-scale production became increasingly difficult. Authors had to find outlets, willing publishers who controlled the means of print production and sought to limit damage to their reputations or their profits. Moreover, market and distribution shifted in scale from the local to the national and international. These developments moved the locus of opportunity and power from the author to the publisher. In many respects, this is one of the themes of this book. Finding outlets was the main problem that had to be surmounted by Black writers seeking from the 1930s to publish critical analyses of imperialism. Publishers, as well as editors of newspapers and journals, sometimes intimidated by state power, had to be convinced on ideological, social, marketing, and sometimes racial grounds before dissenting authors could get their words into the public domain. The writers were also soon frustrated by the exigencies of the Second World War.

Carol Polsgrove's study reveals the early and faltering attempts of writers such as George Padmore, C. L. R. James, and others to overcome these problems. Their movement was initially united by its high idealism, by a conviction that either communism or other Marxist solutions provided the necessary alternatives to imperial rule, by a powerful belief in moral rectitude, and by a common enemy in the imperial states of Europe. It is ironic, then, that as the publication opportunities for Black authors became more open, helped along by growing sales during and after the War, their sense of united effort declined. These writers represented a coalition of interests that came out of the West Indies, the United States, Africa, and Europe, a triangular trade in intellectual and political ideas. Such disparate origins began to reveal ideological and personal fractures as the flow of books and articles increased. The onset of divisions and distrust was also heightened as it appeared that decolonisation was about to become a reality.

What is striking about Polsgrove's work is the manner in which she has used a great range of sources from three continents, including material from hitherto little-used archives of publishers as well as security service documents from both Britain and the United States. By doing this, she has revealed the extent to which the spotlight, formerly on the big figures of the Black nationalist and Pan-African movements, should be shifted to accommodate the influential women, often white, who worked unceasingly as the literary advisers and facilitators of the authors. It is interesting that these women also communicated among themselves, discussing opportunities, advice, and the way ahead. They also participated in some of the growing divisions among them.

GENERAL EDITOR'S INTRODUCTION

By the time that the major authors of the first generation were coming to the end of their lives, high hopes for a particular type of socialist and transnationalist Africa were beginning to wither. Kwame Nkrumah, always central to their concerns as one of the first of the nationalist leaders, piloting Ghana to independence in 1957, swiftly came to disappoint them. African leaders seemed, in many ways, even less interested in press and authorial freedoms than their imperial predecessors. A new bourgeois nationalist elite destroyed (though not universally) the high idealism of the early days of the movements for freedom and independence. Ideologies of the left, often followed by lip service rather than practical policies, began to retreat. National boundaries generally stayed in their colonial forms. Power corrupted, in every sense, and African peoples remained victims to warfare and political violence, hunger and famine, wealth appropriation and repression. This book reveals in intriguing detail both the original ideals and hopes as well as the start of disillusion and disappointment.

John M. MacKenzie

PREFACE

'Blacks have no powerful press, control no broadcasting stations, sit in no parliaments of the world, and therefore have no means of voicing their grievances.'[1] So wrote George Padmore in *How Britain Rules Africa*, published in 1936, when Europeans still ruled nearly the whole of Africa. A Black Trinidadian, Padmore had already dedicated a decade of his young life to giving voice to Blacks' grievances. As a student in the United States, he had written and edited for communist publications. Relocating in Moscow and Hamburg, he had recruited Africans for the Communist International and edited the *Negro Worker*, publishing not only his own views but those of vigorous leaders from across the African continent: Johnstone (Jomo) Kenyatta of Kenya, I. T. A. Wallace Johnson of Sierra Leone, and Garan Kouyaté, born in the French Sudan and educated in Senegal. What Brent Hayes Edwards has written of Padmore's collaboration with Kouyaté could be said of them all: through 'print culture' they participated in 'a nascent discourse of black internationalism – spaces of independent thinking, alternative modes of expression and dissemination'.[2]

In the cities of Europe and America these Black men from the colonies found freedom of speech unavailable at home. Parting ways with the Comintern in 1934, Padmore lived at first in Paris, then the next year moved to London, where he became the centre of a shifting band of associates that for more than twenty years would mount a struggle for recognition, visibility, and the right to be seen as political agents of their own destiny. Publishing in the very headquarters of the British Empire, Padmore and his allies could speak directly to power, but they could speak also to readers in colonies that were often in closer communication with London than with each other. They wrote articles for an array of publications distributed on several continents. With the help of the English women in their lives, they wrote books and got them published. They produced pamphlets and short-lived periodicals that they smuggled into the colonies. On multiple fronts they challenged Britons' view of themselves as benevolent colonisers, carrying out a civilising mission in Africa.

An indefatigable networker, Padmore moved through time and place collecting talent for this anti-colonial publishing campaign: the young South African writer Peter Abrahams and the Gold Coast's Kwame Nkrumah, who would later lead his country to independence as Ghana; the African Americans W. E. B. Du Bois and Richard

Wright. Together, these writers struggled against marginalisation in what Jürgen Habermas has called the 'public sphere'. In Habermas's view, the bourgeois public sphere, as it developed separately in Great Britain, France, and Germany, was that arena of discourse where private citizens of a nation-state held 'public authority' accountable to the public.[3] Padmore and his associates were not true citizens of any nation-state – their very goal was to become citizens. Thus, ability to speak in a public sphere so defined was problematic. Like other groups that have battled their way into print, they found an entry point here, another there, working their way in from the margins of what amounted to a transnational public sphere.[4]

Did what they say make a difference? Officials kept watch on them as if it did, collecting their publications in London and sometimes banning them in the colonies. Whatever the effect their writing actually had on the readers they reached – and that is not easy to assess – the process of writing and publishing, especially against the odds, had an incalculable effect on the community itself.[5] Writing and publishing together shored up these nationalists' own faith that they could bring about – in Benedict Anderson's resonant phrase – their 'imagined community': a world free of European rule.[6]

For Padmore, at least, the imagined community was always larger than a nation-state, larger even than the West African union or the United States of Africa that Nkrumah pressed for. A West Indian who had journeyed far from home, Padmore imagined a world without empires, a postcolonial world. For rule over one particular country to be seen as illegitimate, rule of any country by another had to be seen as illegitimate. Commonly identified in years to come as a Pan-Africanist, Padmore had broader concerns: he ferreted out colonial rulers' misdeeds and news of revolt in virtually all corners of the imperial world, from India to the Gold Coast to Trinidad, and distributed these reports on several continents. He not only aimed to unite the colonised against the colonisers; he aimed also to undermine Western faith in the rightness and inevitability of colonial rule.

In his introduction to *West Indian Intellectuals in Britain*, Bill Schwarz has pointed out the absence among the photographs of West Indians arriving in Britain during the 1950s of 'reverse-shots, in which ... we see, through the eyes of the emigrant, the huddles of journalists and onlookers, police and social workers, white faces all'.[7] Padmore and his companions did not so much offer reverse-shots of the British people as of their Empire, presenting it from the point of view of the colonised. They who had been objects, spoken about, looked down upon, pitied, or maligned, had become subjects. Studies of social movements have highlighted this pivotal moment when those before rendered silent find their way to speech, asserting themselves as actors in the public sphere, agents of their own history. In her contribution to the collection *Recognition Struggles and Social Movements*, Anne Phillips writes, 'Oppressed or subordinated groups have to be able to find their own voice, to speak for themselves, to be recognised as active participants'.[8] The experience of the Padmore circle suggests how difficult that process can be.

Intellectual histories too often ignore the web of practical considerations that lead to published texts, for instance, writers' need for income and access to publishers, editors, and agents – all gatekeepers who may block the way or nudge the printed product this way or that according to their own predilections or worries about anticipated reviews, libel law, or political consequences, which in the colonial world could include bans on book sales. Writing from the political margins, members of Padmore's ragtag London community faced a particularly hard struggle to be heard beyond the alternative public sphere created through their own publications or the publications of other marginal groups. As Black writers, they were oddities; their racial identity could count against them, although sometimes it helped: authors' pictures, editors' notes, and book jackets signalled to readers that theirs were uncommon voices.

While they appeared to share a racial identity, their collective political identity was a work in progress. Unity within any movement is subject to negotiation; there is within any collective action, to use Alberto Melucci's terms, a 'plurality of possible meanings'.[9] Neither Kenyatta nor Padmore's old friend C. L. R. James was on the same political page as Padmore in the 1930s and both moved farther from him as the years wore on; Padmore eventually came to see his onetime ally Peter Abrahams as a political enemy. Partha Chatterjee's remark that revolutions proceed along a 'crooked line' applies to this political community as it moved through time. 'It is in the shifts, slides, discontinuities, the unintended moves, what is suppressed as much as what is asserted, that one can get a sense of this complex movement', Chatterjee writes in *Nationalist Thought and the Colonial World*,[10] as if movements were rivers with currents running above and below, eddying here around a rock, running off unexpectedly into a backwater.

To convey the intricate motion of lives and relationships behind this movement's published work, the narrative that follows draws on correspondence and other unpublished materials to discover not only what was public and generally known but also what was private or deliberately held secret. The story begins on the rocky stretch that Padmore's first post-Comintern book travelled towards publication and continues with the formal organisation of the International African Service Bureau in London before the Second World War. The London community dispersed during the war, although Padmore went on working in London, sending out news stories and writing books, while newcomer Peter Abrahams braved difficult wartime publishing conditions to make his way into print. After the war, with Abrahams's and Kwame Nkrumah's help, Padmore organised the Fifth Pan-African Congress, which energised London-based efforts for independence in Africa.

After Nkrumah and Kenyatta returned to Africa to build movements there, they knew that Padmore, back in London, would publicise their activities and any efforts to suppress them. Kenyatta found his way blocked, but Nkrumah emerged from prison to become head of what would, in a few years, become an independent government. Padmore sent regular London despatches to Nkrumah's party newspaper and wrote a book, *The Gold Coast Revolution*, meant to inspire nationalists elsewhere in Africa. He also encouraged Richard Wright to write his own book on the Gold Coast, *Black Power*. Although Padmore and Wright supported each other in their writing efforts, US State Department documents reveal that Wright became a secret informant for the United States government, providing information about Padmore's relationship with Nkrumah. Abrahams more openly went his own way, separating himself from the circle around Padmore and eventually writing a bitter *roman à clef*, *A Wreath for Udomo*. Published before Ghana's independence, it proved uncannily accurate in one respect: like the character for whom he served as a model, Padmore found himself beleaguered in the new Africa. By the close of his days in 1959, the union the members of his community had forged in London was ended, but so were the days of Empire as they had known it.

Documenting the twists and turns of the publishing path this political community took towards independence would have been easier if its most prolific member, George Padmore, had not published over such farflung territory. While I have explored publications where I knew that he published articles regularly, other scholars are likely to come across the Padmore byline in publications I have not mentioned, especially in African newspapers not yet available in searchable fulltext databases. Similarly, future scholars may put together a fuller picture of reader and reviewer response to the writings of his London-based community. Piecing together the informal relationships facilitating this community's publishing ventures would also have been easier if Padmore had not been so given to destroying his own records, as his longtime companion Dorothy Pizer lamented when she began collecting materials for a biography of him after his death. Substantial sets of letters from Padmore do survive, however, in collections of other people's correspondence, many of them made available since James R. Hooker brought out his early biography of Padmore in 1967 – *Black Revolutionary: George Padmore's Path from Communism to Pan-Africanism*.

With support from Indiana University, I was able to explore these collections in archives and libraries scattered across several continents. Padmore's and Pizer's detailed and intimate letters to Richard and Ellen Wright proved particularly helpful, and I am grateful to the Beinecke Rare Book and Manuscript Library at Yale University for making them available to me. The Kwame Nkrumah collection at the Moorland-Spingarn Research Center at Howard University contains letters from Padmore to Nkrumah that provide irrefutable evidence of Padmore's significance as Nkrumah's adviser. The St Clair Drake Papers at the Schomburg Center for Research in Black Culture enabled me both to understand Drake's role as the London community's first historian and to draw on his findings. Publishers' archives proved invaluable for tracing the publishing backstory. The C. L. R. James Collection at the University of the West Indies at St Augustine provided not only insights into James's activities but also material James collected for his proposed biography of Padmore. While I was writing this book, the Lilly Library at Indiana University purchased a small but useful set of James's correspondence in private hands, a reminder that more correspondence may turn up yet.[11]

The database of scanned Communist International documents and the microfilmed Communist Party USA collection at the Library of Congress enlarged my awareness of Padmore's communist years when he formed relationships that became important in London, sharpened his skills, and earned his permanent mistrust of communism. Although a full exploration of those years fell outside the scope of this study (as did a full exploration of Padmore's final service in Ghana), I did spend significant research time piecing together Padmore's pre-London life, the foundation on which he built his later work as a political writer. In his American communist publications and the *Negro Worker*, I saw the energy and skill that manifested itself later in London. I also saw evidence of American officials' early interest in Padmore. Surveillance, censorship, and other government attempts to silence him and his circle constitute a dominant theme in this book. Consequently, I mined Department of State records at the US National Archives and travelled to The National Archives at Kew to explore Colonial Office files, which included the Metropolitan Police's surveillance reports on the International African Service Bureau. A 2005 release of British intelligence records added further weight to the already ample record of official surveillance and concern about the influence of Padmore and his allies.

I thank all the archives and libraries for preserving these collections, and I thank their staff members for their courteous assistance. In a Sources section at the end of the book, I have listed those collections whose documents I used in the book, but I also appreciate the assistance I received from librarians at other collections which I explored but did not draw on in the book. I thank, too, those librarians at Indiana University's Herman B. Wells Library who handled countless interlibrary loan requests and helped me in other ways throughout this project.

I owe special gratitude to Padmore's daughter, Blyden Cowart (named for Edward Wilmot Blyden, the distinguished nineteenth-century diplomat and author), who provided information and copies of Padmore's family letters, now deposited at the University of the West Indies at St Augustine. I appreciate, too, her permission to quote from Padmore's unpublished correspondence. At the start of my research, conversations with several scholars already working in this field – Richard Rathbone, Marika Sherwood, and Hakim Adi – strengthened my confidence that this project was well worth the investment of time it would take. I am grateful, too, for the ongoing encouragement of Edwin Wilson, a Virginian who has shared with me his knowledge and artefacts of the African diaspora, including a tape of C. L. R. James giving a talk; from then on, when I read James's published words, I heard the measured lilt of his voice. At a 2003 conference on George Padmore at the University of the West Indies, St Augustine, where scholars and labour union members came together to honour his memory, Ed Wilson and I accompanied another attender to James's grave, its stone bearing the cautionary words, 'Times would pass. Old Empires would fall and new ones take their place ...'

Toward the end of my writing, Grace Lee Boggs, who knew several members of this community well and was involved in producing one of their publications, shared her recollections and helped me put into better perspective the limitations of James's and Padmore's understanding of Africa's future. Long before I began work on this book, the former Padmore and Nkrumah ally Joe Appiah and his wife, Peggy, gave me tea in their Kumasi home, providing another living link to the past I have reconstructed mostly from documents.

My reconstruction is, of course, partial. I have focused on some members of this community more than others and left out peripheral figures that I might have put in if I were writing a book of unlimited length. In crafting the narrative, I have tried to suggest the elasticity

PREFACE

of the topic: the events and conversations I describe are by necessity representative, implying rather than encompassing the dense network of relationships that sustained publication. For feedback on my narrative, I thank my Indiana University colleagues Radhika Parameswaran and Phyllis Martin; Clifton C. Hawkins, a thoughtful scholar of Black radicalism in the United States; my brother, William Claxon, a faculty member at the University of South Carolina Aiken; and my daughter, Cora Polsgrove. Finally, I am grateful to my parents, Emma and Neville Claxon, for taking me to Ghana in 1948, as Kwame Nkrumah was making his bid for power, and giving me an African childhood.

Carol Polsgrove
Bloomington, Indiana

Notes

1 George Padmore, *How Britain Rules Africa* (London: Wishart Books, 1936), pp. 390–1.
2 Brent Hayes Edwards, *The Practice of Diaspora: Literature, Translation, and the Rise of Black Internationalism* (Cambridge, MA and London: Harvard University Press, 2003), p. 265.
3 Jürgen Habermas, *The Structural Transformation of the Public Sphere: An Inquiry into a Category of Bourgeois Society*, trans. Thomas Burger (Cambridge, MA: MIT Press, 1989), pp. 25–6.
4 Nancy Fraser's 'Rethinking the Public Sphere', in Craig Calhoun (ed.), *Habermas and the Public Sphere* (Cambridge, MA and London: MIT Press, 1992), helped me see what they were doing in these terms.
5 For a study of how the process of publishing helps groups outside the mainstream forge their own identity see Susan Herbst, *Politics at the Margin: Historical Studies of Public Expression Outside the Mainstream* (Cambridge: Cambridge University Press, 1994), especially chapter 1, 'Politics, Expression, and Marginality'.
6 Benedict Anderson, *Imagined Communities: Reflections on the Origin and Spread of Nationalism* (London, New York: Verso, 1983).
7 Bill Schwarz, 'Introduction: Crossing the Seas', in Bill Schwarz (ed.), *West Indian Intellectuals in Britain* (Manchester and New York: Manchester University Press, 2003), p. 1.
8 Anne Phillips, 'Recognition and the Struggle for Political Voice', in Barbara Hobson (ed.), *Recognition Struggles and Social Movements: Contested Identities, Agency and Power* (Cambridge: Cambridge University Press, 2003), p. 265.
9 Alberto Melucci, 'Introduction', *Nomads of the Present* (London: Hutchinson Radius, 1989), p. 28.
10 Partha Chatterjee, *Nationalist Thought and the Colonial World: A Derivative Discourse* (Minneapolis: University of Minnesota Press, 1986), p. vii.
11 A C. L. R. James collection at Columbia University, not yet open to scholars when this book went to press, is likely to add useful insights.

LIST OF ABBREVIATIONS

CCF	Congress for Cultural Freedom
CIA	Central Intelligence Agency
CPP	Convention People's Party
IAFE	International African Friends of Ethiopia
IASB	International African Service Bureau
ILP	Independent Labour Party
ITUC–NW	International Trade Union Committee of Negro Workers
KAU	Kenya African Union
KCA	Kikuyu Central Association
NAACP	National Association for the Advancement of Colored People
NLM	National Liberation Movement
UGCC	United Gold Coast Convention
USIS	United States Information Service
WANS	West African National Secretariat
WASU	West African Students Union

CHAPTER ONE

'Misery laid bare'

It was the summer of 1934, and, in a village north of Paris, George Padmore wrote for hours, without sign of wearying, covering page after page with his nearly indecipherable scrawl. His hostess, the English poet and publisher Nancy Cunard, marvelled at his concentration, his ability to focus his mind while his political world was falling about his ears.[1] A year before, he had had the resources of the Soviet Union at his disposal. He had been 'the leading Negro Communist in Europe', in the words of the *Crisis*, an African-American magazine published by the influential National Association for the Advancement of Colored People (NAACP).[2] Now, he had lost the very foundation of his work, the institutional support of the Communist International.

Padmore had joined the communists after he left Trinidad in 1924 to attend university in the United States under his given name 'Malcolm Nurse'. Taking the political name 'George Padmore', he wrote for the *Daily Worker* and the *Negro Champion*, working side by side with fellow West Indians Cyril Briggs, Otto Huiswoud, and Richard B. Moore – older men who had thought long and hard about the relationship between racial oppression and imperialism.[3] He found other models when he transferred from Fisk to Howard University, where he particularly admired Alain Locke, a cosmopolitan scholar who set forth a plan for a corps of 'colored investigators' who would usher in a new age of research on Africa[4] – a plan Padmore, in his way, would help to realise. At Howard, Padmore planned a demonstration against the British ambassador with a Nigerian student named Nnamdi Azikiwe, who for many years kept a letter he received from Padmore even before they met. Introducing himself as 'your brother in a common cause', Padmore had invited Azikiwe to help form an organisation to launch a propaganda campaign against American economic imperialism in Liberia and elsewhere. Their model, Padmore said, would be the revolutionary Chinese Kuomintang Party. Padmore's letter inspired Azikiwe to correspond with other Africans abroad, and this correspondence, Azikiwe believed, 'ultimately crystallized into the struggle for the complete emancipation of the African colonial territories from European imperialism'.[5] The communists offered the sturdiest international support for that struggle at this point, and at a communist-backed League Against Imperialism conference in Frankfurt, Germany, Padmore came into contact with Tiemoko Garan Kouyaté of the French Sudan and Johnstone Kenyatta of Kenya, two men who, like himself, had been drawn into the communist orbit. Through all these relationships with men who had left their homes and families in the colonies to assert themselves in the wider world, Padmore glimpsed the potential power of the African diaspora. When he left New York for Moscow at the end of 1929, not long after the stock market crash signalled the possible end of capitalism, he was primed for the work ahead.

'Dear Cyril', Padmore wrote to a Harlem friend, Cyril Ollivierre, on 16 April 1930 on a ship bound to Africa, 'Just a few lines that should have been done long ago, but it was not safe to write before. I have been up & down across two continents.'[6] His letter captures the breathless pace of the life he was to lead for the next three years. Heading the International Trade Union Committee of Negro Workers (ITUC-NW), editing its periodical, the *Negro Worker*, Padmore quickly evolved into the Communist International's leading propagandist on Black affairs. He also became, in the estimation of scholar Edward T. Wilson, author of *Russia and Black Africa Before Second World War*, 'perhaps the keenest Comintern observer of the African scene'.[7]

In the spring of 1931 Padmore made a return trip to Africa, gathering information for the slender book he would produce on his return, *The Life and Struggles of Negro Toilers*. The volume made its way to the United States, and one copy fell into the hands of a British Guianan, George Thomas N. Griffith, who had taken the name T. Ras Makonnen the better to identify with Africa. Makonnen had known Padmore in the United States as Malcolm Nurse. Could Nurse and Padmore be the same man? Makonnen went down to the party office in New York to make inquiries. When an official offered him books by other writers, Makonnen thought they did not hold a candle to Padmore's. 'His language was entirely different, and a revelation to me with its new approach. It was almost as if he had invented a new dictionary of terms with which he could burlesque the chiefs and yes-men of the various colonial regimes ... [H]e seemed to have a magic weapon in his hands which I had not yet mastered.'[8]

Although Padmore was publishing under the aegis of international communism, his primary goal was ending imperial rule in Africa and the West Indies, as he wrote to Ollivierre on 26 September 1932. Of articles he had published in *Labour Monthly*, he said, 'I am not so interested in this kind of highbrow stuff as in getting rid of the damn white blood suckers from the W.I. [West Indies] & Africa, my fields of specialty'.[9] From Hamburg, Germany, he sent copies of the *Negro Worker* out to colonial ports in the hands of black sailors, evading bans imposed by colonial governments. Reflecting on this work, his longtime friend C. L. R. James later commented, '[A] movement, and there were scores of movements all over the world, needs an ideology. It needs a body of ideas and information to which its own efforts can be related, ideas and information in the light of which the daily grind can have some significance beyond that which is immediately visible … This *The Negro Worker* gave to the hundreds of thousands of active Negroes and the millions whom they represented.'[10] While James exaggerated the *Negro Worker*'s circulation (which probably never exceeded a few thousand), he stated here the political rationale for his and Padmore's lives as political writers.

Among Padmore's other publications during these years were his contributions to Nancy Cunard's monumental anthology, *Negro*. Of those who contributed articles (including Azikiwe and Kenyatta), none, she thought, was as important as Padmore. She had corresponded with him about the anthology before they met over dinner at a Montparnasse café-restaurant in the autumn of 1932. '[L]ong we sat over the meal talking, talking as if we knew each other well already – which, in a sense we did', she wrote later. They talked about the United States, where he had studied and she had recently visited, and they laughed at American racial ways. She was struck by his laughter, unlike any she had ever heard, and by his 'wonderful quick wit'. The next time she saw him was in spring of 1933 in London, when Padmore had been arrested in Hamburg, jailed, then deported to the United Kingdom.[11] While in London, Padmore spoke at a meeting in Gray's Inn Road where he met up again with James, who had known him when they were boys in Trinidad and, like Padmore, had left Trinidad hoping to find wider scope for his talents as a writer. Hearing only that the speaker was 'a great Negro communist', James was surprised to see before him his old friend Malcolm Nurse. 'He spoke to the audience about Negro struggles all over the world. George was a very good speaker, but not a great orator. What he had was authority. I was struck by the admiration and the awe with which the whole audience listened to him and looked at him.'[12]

As Europe moved closer to chaos, however, the ground under Padmore's identity as a leading international communist was shifting. He put out three more issues of the *Negro Worker* after his Hamburg office was closed; then, in the August–September issue, he published his 'Au Revoir'.[13] He was leaving his post, he implied, because of the *Negro Worker*'s weak financial position. There was more to it than that. Padmore's position in the Communist International had always been politically precarious. '[H]e was always accused of having a "black nationalist-deviationist" point of view concerning issues involving Africa and the West Indies', recalled the American anthropologist St Clair Drake, who got to know him well after the Second World War.[14] The threat Hitler posed in the West and Japan in the East further undermined Padmore's position as the Russians turned towards France as a potential ally. Of the major European powers, France had been the most hostile towards the Soviet Union; now, with Hitler on the scene, both the Soviet Union and France could see the advantage of rapprochement.[15] Padmore was in Morocco when he received an order to end his propaganda efforts in France's colonies and soften criticism of imperialism in the *Negro Worker*. 'Upon receiving the order', he later told Drake, 'I went down and sat on the beach on the Mediterranean and started thinking that if I were Stalin and I had one-sixth of the earth in my possession, I would cut my mother's throat, if necessary, to keep it. But I wasn't no Joe Stalin. I was just a West Indian darkie out here trying to help my African darkie brothers free themselves. And so I decided I wasn't going to stop my agitation.'[16]

American officials had been monitoring the activities of Padmore and the ITUC-NW, and on 29 December 1933 a memorandum from the American Embassy in London to the US State Department reported rumours that Padmore might face expulsion because the French party disagreed with a proposal he'd made 'for revolutionary activity in Liberia'.[17] About a month later, the Embassy reported that Padmore was being expelled from French, American and British parties.[18] George Padmore's career as a communist was over.

At her French home that summer, Nancy Cunard could see that Padmore's break with the Communist International was hard on him. This movement in which he had put so much faith had turned against him, unleashing an international assault on his character in an effort to undermine any future political influence he might have. He was living in exile, far from his wife, Julia, and his young daughter, Blyden, on the other side of the Atlantic. He even thought of retreating from politics for a while. 'It is time that I take a little holiday from this turbulent political life (a la Marcus Garvey) & look up my dear Julie & my child', he wrote to Ollivierre towards the end of July. 'I have been less selfish than most youth to have given these 5 years of my services to advance the cause of our Liberation, so they can give me at least a year's rest, after which, I shall return to the front! I have a loyal colonial army, which I might have to throw into battle against the white "Reds" – if they continue to be so disloyal to their allies.'[19]

The rest leave did not materialise, and Padmore's 'loyal colonial army' had already begun to assemble, as his former colleagues had feared it would: in a letter of 11 January 1934 to Arnold Ward of the Negro Welfare Association in London, the American communist William Patterson had warned that Padmore would try to join other 'renegades'. 'No internationalist could work alone; it is impossible. We would like to know what group he is attaching himself to.'[20] Indeed, Padmore had lost no time attaching himself to another 'renegade', his friend Garan Kouyaté, with whom he shared rooms in Paris. They had been publishing comrades in the Comintern, contributing to each other's publications, and for a brief period Kouyaté had served as managing editor of the *Negro Worker*. Now, both alienated from the international communist movement, they set about adapting familiar strategies to their new situation, raising funds for a new publication and making plans for a Negro World Congress. According to the French Préfecture de Police, Padmore and Kouyaté agreed 'that the freedom of blacks could and must be achieved outside the communist party and the I.S.R. (Internationale Syndicale Rouge)'.[21]

Padmore's close alliance with Kouyaté in Paris would end when Padmore moved to London the following year, but Padmore's goal would remain the same: creation of a Black socialist freedom movement beyond the control of the Soviet Union. The book Padmore was writing that summer of 1934 in Nancy Cunard's country home would be the cornerstone of that movement, laying claim to Africans' right to chart their own political course. Nnamdi Azikiwe was in London checking citations for his new book on Liberia when he heard news of Padmore's progress from Nancy Cunard. 'Our mutual friend, Padmore, is here now and we have spoken much of you', Cunard wrote from La Chapelle-Reanville. 'I am enjoying the typing out of his new book on British colonies in Africa. It is fine. What an indictment!'[22]

As Padmore explained to an agent Cunard recommended, the idea for *How Britain Rules Africa* came in response to a British Labour Party resolution promising colonial reforms when it came to power. 'So in order to arouse public opinion in Britain on behalf of the African peoples, my countrymen asked me to undertake the publication of a book giving the presentation of the situation from the point of view of the blacks, we think that the time has come for Africans to speak out for themselves.'[23] The point was well taken: all too few Africans had published books about Africa.[24] White Europeans and Americans had up to this point largely controlled Western readers' ideas of Europe's

African empires. For an African, writing a book – asserting his view of the world in a form that Europe had claimed as its own – was in itself a political act. A book had weight and heft. A book was a form of speech that Europeans would take seriously. Revolutionaries Padmore had admired – Lenin and Stalin – both wrote books that defined their movements, clarifying their goals for themselves and others. For his own book Padmore could make a special claim: because it was unusual for Africans to write books, a book by an African was likely to be noticed.

Some might quibble, of course, with Padmore's claim to African identity. He was, strictly speaking, a Trinidadian of African descent, though, for some in his generation, 'African' covered all those of African descent as a generic term, preferable to 'Negro' or 'Black'. However, he did write in this book as if he belonged to the colonised continent, speaking of 'we' and 'us'.[25] Claiming African identity, he claimed an authority he would not otherwise have had: he had no credentials as a scholar, and he had lost his standing as a leading communist. Beyond that, in claiming African identity, in using the term 'we', he laid claim to speak for a collective – all Africans.

His use of the term 'we' was not purely rhetorical. In his acknowledgements at the end of his introduction to the book Padmore thanked 'his many African friends and colleagues' for their 'unselfish co-operation and encouragement'. These, presumably, were the 'countrymen' who encouraged him to write the book. He mentioned several specifically. In addition to Kouyaté, he had help from Kenyatta, who had travelled to London in 1929 to present grievances over land rights on behalf of the Kikuyu Central Association. In Kenya, Kenyatta had edited the KCA's monthly journal, *Muigwithania*, and in England he had contributed letters to the editor and articles to the *Manchester Guardian* and *The Times*. Unable to budge officialdom on the land issue, Kenyatta fell in with the communists and wrote for the *Sunday Worker*, *Daily Worker*, and *Labour Monthly*.[26] He had studied in Moscow but like Padmore left in disillusion after the Soviet Union pulled back from its criticism of France and Britain in the face of Hitler's rise. In addition to Kenyatta, Padmore also acknowledged the assistance of Azikiwe, who by the time Padmore's book came out had published his own, *Liberia in World Politics* (1935), and was editing the *African Morning Post* in Accra, Gold Coast.[27] Padmore thanked Cunard for typing and preparing the manuscript for publication and James for proofreading and offering suggestions.[28]

The book that would come out under Padmore's name was then, as books often are, a collaborative work, an exercise in solidarity. Creating *How Britain Rules Africa* was, for these Africans and men of

African descent, an act of defiance of things as they were, a challenge to the idea that Africans were incapable of managing their own affairs, that they needed Europeans to educate and guide them. Around the act of publication, a political community had formed. As Europeans debated what changes to make in the colonial map of Africa, Padmore and his colleagues asserted their right to a seat at the table. As British and French politicians discussed how to respond to Italy's claim to Ethiopia, Padmore disputed the idea 'that Africa is the property of the white race, and that Africans can be bartered with impunity from one nation to another'. Europeans were not the only players. 'Today the coloured races do not intend to allow the white imperialist nations to trample over them as in the past.'[29] Four hundred and two pages long, *How Britain Rules Africa* defied the view that prevailed in Europe and even among some Africans themselves: that the British were caretakers, stewards, teachers, civilisers. Not so, this book's title asserted. They were imperial rulers, and the chapters laid out in detail the brutality of their rule: through forced labour, taxation, and co-optation of traditional leaders they had unravelled indigenous political, economic, and social systems – de-civilising, not civilising Africa.

Here Padmore and those who helped him had created what the Nigerian novelist Chinua Achebe would call a 'reconstitutive annal' – an attempt by the dispossessed 'to reclaim their history'.[30] They were performing a task that social movement theorists have seen as central to the task of building a movement: the struggle for recognition and redefinition by marginalised or disadvantaged groups. They were engaged in this struggle under circumstances common to the disadvantaged: they did not control the discursive machinery that defined them as powerless and undeserving of power. Thus, in producing a book at all with the expectation of publication, they challenged the status quo and their low place in it. Across the continent of Africa, a web of laws silenced African speech. '"Dangerous thought" is as much a bogey to the Nigerian officials as it is to those in India', Padmore wrote in his new manuscript. 'The country is ruled by a criminal code that makes for intellectual terrorism unsurpassed anywhere else in West Africa. The Press, one of the principal educational mediums in all civilised countries, lives in constant dread of the criminal code.'[31]

There was, for instance, a Sedition Bill imposed on the Gold Coast, motivated in part by colonial officials' concern that communists, and specifically Padmore, were stirring up discontent in the colony.[32] Enacted as Padmore was writing his book, the Sedition Bill made 'it a criminal offence for any Native to be found in possession of any newspaper, book, or document or any part thereof or extract therefrom, containing words or writing considered to be seditious by the

Governor'. Postmaster and police had 'absolute authority to open all letters, packages, etc., entering the country. They alone have the right to say what an African can or cannot read.'[33] In a book published in Britain, no such restrictive colonial laws would limit Padmore's ability to subvert British rule. In Britain, however, he ran into other obstacles as he sought a publisher for the book that was at this point titled 'Britannia Rules the Blacks'.

Governments are not the only gatekeepers of public speech nor, in a democracy, even the most significant. Book publishers and their auxiliaries – agents, manuscript reviewers, and book reviewers – have considerable power to block challenges to prevailing paradigms. As Padmore explained to Otto Theis, the London agent Cunard had suggested to him, he had thought he had a commitment from Wishart, the publisher that had brought out Cunard's *Negro*. However, Wishart had insisted that before publication could proceed Padmore needed to find an American publisher who would buy 'sheets' for an American edition. Several American publishers were interested, but none who would commit themselves without seeing the sheets.[34] Since Wishart would not produce the sheets without the American commitment, Padmore was at an impasse.

Theis responded promptly, asking Padmore to tell him about himself. 'This is so embarrassing,' wrote Padmore in reply, but he did provide a paragraph of information that rendered nearly invisible his connections with the Communist International.

> I am the son of middle-class intellectuals, my father was a Naturalist by profession and at one time H.M. Inspector of Schools in the West Indies. I was educated by the Jesuits at St Mary's College and later studied at Howard University in the USA, and Anthropology at Hamburg University in Germany. I have written much on the colonial and Negro problems, and edited the 'Negro Worker' for some years. My first book, 'Life and Struggles of Negro Toilers' appeared a few years ago and enjoyed quite a good reception in left and liberal circles.

Concluding, he identified himself firmly as a writer: 'Profession, Journalist. Now European Correspondent for American and West African Negro Press'.[35] Here, as elsewhere in his correspondence with Theis, Padmore attempted to avoid identification of his own attack on capitalism with the international movement directed by Moscow. He discreetly made no mention of his work with the International Trade Union Committee of Negro Workers (although his mention of the *Negro Worker* would have given that connection away to anyone who knew the *Negro Worker*). He presented himself, simply, as a serious journalist with an academic streak. He had begun the task of rebuilding his political identity as a non-communist – a strategic move.

If he wanted to reach a larger, non-communist British audience – the leaders and members of the Labour Party, for instance – he needed to distance himself from the movement in which he had lately played a leading role.

His letter was carefully calculated in other ways: a model blend of diffidence and confidence. He understood 'how reluctant publishers are in these days' to publish books like his; on the other hand he was confident it would soon be published. He suggested several publishers who had recently published other books on Africa: Cambridge (University) Press, Routledge, and Kegan Paul. He also pointed out that the typescript Theis had in hand was uncorrected. Padmore was apparently still in France, and he had asked Kenyatta to pass on to Theis the manuscript in his possession after he reviewed the chapter on Kenya. A final draft was considerably altered, but Padmore hoped the version Kenyatta had delivered to Theis would suffice to give publishers 'an idea of the scope of the book, and my point of view'.

That would prove to be a misstep on Padmore's part – better to have waited until he could get the final draft into Theis's hands – but in other respects Padmore was a savvy author. In his next letter he described the book's audience as he saw it: not Blacks, who knew their problems well enough and lacked the resources to buy books, and not British workers, who were also poor and did not have time to read, but the British middle class. 'For when all is said and done, they are the ones really responsible for all that goes on in Africa, for as voters they control Parliament and therefore Whitehall and its officials … [I]f the British middle classes and the leaders of the Labour Movement want to know about the colonies, then they will have to read, not what Whites think about blacks, but what blacks think about their "civilisers".' Recognising the distaste the book's rhetoric might arouse in non-communist publishers, he had toned the manuscript down in the corrected version. 'I hope the publishers will not get alarmed with the copy I sent you (laughter). We are not yet on our way to Moscow!' Theis had suggested that Padmore find someone well known to contribute a foreword to the book, and Padmore thought he could get 'a certain British professor' not as paternalistic as some to do it.[36] He was doing what he could to oblige his new agent.

At the same time, Padmore did not rely wholly on Theis. After he approached Theis, a 'Miss Radford' (not, apparently, anyone from Theis's office) showed George Routledge and Sons a 'contents list' of 'Britannia Rules the Blacks', and Maurice Richardson of Routledge asked Padmore if he could have a look. Responding to Richardson's letter, Padmore said he was indeed working on a book 'from the point of view of a black speaking on behalf of millions of inarticulate members of a race'. His approach, he acknowledged, was from the left, though he did not belong to either communist or socialist movements. That was worth mentioning, he thought, since he knew some publishers were 'prejudiced against anything which is not reactionary'.[37]

Padmore had reason to be concerned. Although he was no longer part of the international communist movement, he had not abandoned the Marxist view that imperialism was the offspring of capitalism, an analysis honed by Padmore's reading of the three books that most influenced his views of colonialism: J. A. Hobson's *Imperialism*, Lenin's *Imperialism: The Highest Stage of Capitalism*, and Parker Thomas Moon's *Imperialism and World Politics*.[38] Padmore's very first paragraph announced his intention to show 'the effects of the capitalist economic system upon the Native populations' of Africa. His rhetoric warmed up as he went along: 'The English capitalists have their tentacles in every nook and corner of the world. And in this period of declining capitalism they tend to draw more and more of their strength from the Colonies, especially India and Africa.'[39] Far from preparing Africans to take their place as equals in the modern industrial world, the British were exploiting African labour and resources to maintain their own position in the international capitalist system. So long as capitalism survived, Padmore maintained, so would colonialism. Although he had told Theis that British workers would not read his book, here he appealed to them – as represented by the Labour Party (whose leaders might read the book) – to make common cause with the 'wage-slaves' of Africa.[40]

As it turned out, Leonard Woolf, the reader Routledge asked to write a report on Padmore's manuscript, was sympathetic. Having Woolf as an outside reader was something of an honour. Woolf and his wife, Virginia, were part of the Bloomsbury circle, an informal community of writers, artists, and intellectuals in London. The Woolfs had started their own little Hogarth Press in 1917 as a form of relaxation for Virginia, but by the early 1930s Hogarth Press had become a good deal more than a sideline. The Woolfs published leading literary and cultural figures, from the poet T. S. Eliot to the psychologist Sigmund Freud, as well as political books and pamphlets. Whether political or literary, Hogarth Press's publications were meant to challenge conventional thought and prevailing practice; the Woolfs published books and pamphlets that might otherwise not be published at all.[41] Just a couple of years before Woolf read Padmore's manuscript they had brought out a slim book by Padmore's friend James, *The Case for West-Indian Self Government* (1933).

Leonard Woolf's personal experience predisposed him to like Padmore's work. Serving in Ceylon as a colonial administrator had led

Woolf to doubt the assumption of European superiority on which the Empire was based. He had learned to speak the languages of the people he governed, and he appreciated their cultures. The English colonial culture, on the other hand, seemed ridiculous to him: rounds of tennis, drinking, and tea. He wrote a novel, *The Village in the Jungle*, which focused not on the Europeans but on the indigenous peoples themselves and the jungle in which they lived.[42] Back in England, Woolf became a spokesman for independence for the colonies. In a 1926 memorandum submitted to the Labour Party, he wrote that independence ought to be 'granted immediately' to all Crown Colonies – except those in Africa, where he feared that immediate independence would result in rule by white settlers.[43] He wrote two books that Padmore included in his bibliography for his own book: *Empire and Commerce in Africa* and *Imperialism and Civilization*. Parker Thomas Moon, one of the scholars on whose work Padmore relied, described Woolf as a 'keen British critic of imperialism'.[44]

Padmore was fortunate to have Woolf as a reader: Woolf found himself 'in complete sympathy with the author's opinion of white rule in Africa. The case against European and British methods of acquisition and administration is overwhelming.' The book seemed to him 'extremely interesting, particularly as giving an American Negro's view of the effects of white rule in Africa'. He recommended publication, but he had one serious criticism: he did think Padmore often exaggerated, selecting facts that supported his views and ignoring those that did not. He offered eleven examples. Routledge sent Padmore a copy of the reader's report, identifying its author only as a 'liberal intellectual'. If Padmore would make the changes Woolf suggested, Routledge would 'reconsider the manuscript'.[45]

Reading the critique, Padmore was stung. He tried to give his unidentified critic his due for agreeing with him fundamentally but protested that 'the gentleman has not quite done me justice'. This book presented 'the colonial question from the point of view of an African. Surely no intelligent person [would] expect an African intellectual to view the conditions of his life from the same point of view of say, Lord Lugard, Sir Donald Cameron, etc.' Still, though Padmore thought the criticisms were unfair, he went down the list of suggestions, either making corrections or responding to the criticisms, at one point, out of patience, saying, 'Evidently he did not read the first chapter'. Since there were no serious differences, he hoped publication could proceed, 'as I must hold myself in readiness to leave for Africa at any moment'. Storm clouds were gathering over the north-east corner of Africa – a developing story Padmore hoped to report in person.[46]

In search of new territory for Italy, Mussolini had fixed his dictatorial eye on Ethiopia, nearly the only self-governed spot on the continent. Padmore did not in the end go to Ethiopia, but he laid out the situation for readers of the *Crisis*, the American magazine published by the NAACP, in May 1935. With Hitler threatening a military strike in east and central Europe, Mussolini meant to take advantage of this moment, offering his support in the coming war to whichever side would let him have the territory he reached for now. This was the background of French Foreign Minister Pierre Laval's agreement with Mussolini, essentially giving Mussolini 'a free hand to grab as much of Ethiopia as he can'.[47] The larger message here, as Padmore spelled it out for *Crisis* readers, was '[t]hat white nations, regardless of their political systems, have no scruples in joining hands in assigning parts of Africa to whichever one stands most in need of colonies'. In the current fearful times, the European press was arguing 'that it is better to sacrifice Ethiopia than to disturb the peace of Europe'. Even liberal and democratic papers offered the argument that Italy would bring civilisation to Ethiopia, which was seen as not yet fit to rule itself. '[T]he most liberal whites can adopt a hostile attitude towards colored peoples when it suits their purposes', Padmore wrote.[48] His article was 'well read' in London, according to a Negro Welfare Association letter in Comintern files, and shed a harsh light on other organisations (including the Communist Party) that were inactive on the Ethiopian issue.[49]

In Padmore's view, the nineteenth-century 'scramble' for Africa was being re-enacted in Ethiopia and in South Africa, a self-governing dominion that wanted control over nearby British protectorates. Meanwhile, he wrote to Theis on 7 July 1935, 'the British public, especially the workers and middle classes know as much about Africa and its problems as the man in the moon. It is to supply this want that I have written, but it seems that there is a conspiracy among publishers to keep the public as dumb as possible. I hope that I am wrong, but it seems so.' American publishers seemed to him more responsive than the English. Padmore himself had heard from Putnam's, he told Theis, and Putnam's believed there was an American market for the book. Padmore had a friend who had just published a book indicting 'missionary practices in Africa'; five thousand copies sold the first week after publication and the book had become a Book of the Month Club selection. 'I think English publishers are sleeping. People are tired reading what whites write about blacks; they want to hear from the Africans themselves, that's why they are buying my friend's book.'[50] The next week he wrote expressing regret that Allen and Unwin was seeing the unrevised manuscript (since Wishart had held on to the revised copy for the last year); in the revision he had 'toned down' some of his 'too sharp formulations so as to make it a more palatable book for the middle classes'.[51] His fears were well founded.

The critique by Leonard Woolf turned out to be mild compared to the report by the Allen and Unwin reader, who had seen the unrevised manuscript, and slashed and burned a path through it.

> This MS. of some 91,000 words, is a very uneven production. The XIII chapters, typed on different machines with widely varying degrees of accuracy and skill are almost certainly not the work of one writer solely. G. Padmore acknowledges the help of numerous African friends and of Miss Nancy Cunard and it may well be that considerable passages were supplied to him in a form ready for incorporation.
>
> Although in one chapter the writer manages to include derisory comment on the Red International, the MS. may well be considered to have been from the Communist angle.[52]

The reader's report went on in that vein, supercilious and insulting for three full double-spaced pages. A belief that the manuscript was communist permeated the report. Even Padmore's lack of documentation (although he did provide bibliographic notes) was for this reader a telltale sign: to acknowledge that other writers had already said these same things would invalidate 'the Communist gospel that the ruling classes contain nothing but exploiters, and that the toiling masses have no hope of salvation from their woes except only from their Communist comrades'. The unidentified reader noted the book's uneven tone – 'bursts of indignation ("What rascality! What downright robbery!")' while other chapters were 'soberly worded essays ... written by a different hand, no doubt'. The reader pointed out factual errors in the chapter on Kenya, a country whose history he claimed special familiarity with. Noting infelicities in grammar and sentence construction, the reader concluded with a parting salvo aimed at Cunard, who 'is said to have "prepared [the manuscript] for publication" but she has done it either with insufficient care or inadequate knowledge'.

Padmore was not having an easy time of it. Leonard Woolf's comments had been gentlemanly compared to these. Padmore wrote an impassioned response.

> Messrs Allen & Unwin, if they are only to depend upon his report, would believe that I am an agent of M. Stalin or Mr Pollit, trying to introduce bolskevism [sic] into their firm. If my political view [sic] are important to determine whether or not a MSS on Africa can be accepted, then, I have no objection saying that I am an African Nationalist, and an uncompromising believer in 'Africa for the Africans'.

He said, further, that he had drawn his evidence from 'official statistics, documents, quotations from the speeches of officials', and it was possible 'a few errors have crept into the script'. This was an unedited draft – 'unfortunately' – and 'a more sympathetic' reader would have realised that. As for the other writers who have taken up this topic, 'we, Africans, do not consider the authors referred to as our spokesmen. Why, some of them are even hostile to our fundamental interests, while others, reflect that old missionary, paternalistic, condescending attitude, which we New Negroes, resent even more that [sic] the die-hard Tory jingoism ... I often wonder when will the whites begin to understand the point of view of the coloured races.' As for the alleged 'uneven style' – Africa is a big place and one place in it differs from another. 'Surely I cannot write with the same indignation about say, Gold Coast as South Africa.'[53]

Padmore took up the allegations of error in detail, accepting correction on some, but argued that the manuscript reader could not speak on Kenya with the authority of Kenyatta, who had gone over the Kenya chapter. 'He might be able to express what he knows better than us, for English is not an African language, but he cannot interpret to the world the hopes, aspirations and feelings of blacks as we can.' He returned to that note later: speaking of the 'errors in construction', he said (disingenuously, given the fact that English was his own first language), 'For what Englishman writing a book of 91,000 words in an African language would not make such mistakes?' He defended Cunard: 'she had to hurriedly type the MSS. and had no time to read over the copy which was submitted to Messrs Allen & Unwin'. Forwarding Padmore's heated response to Unwin, Theis noted that he might have made a 'tactical error' in showing the reader's report to Padmore. 'These young African Nationalists ... can neither see things in an historical perspective nor objectively.' Theis wasn't sure that mattered. '[I]n purely propaganda books there is always a certain amount of "cooking" of facts ... [D]on't you think it is rather important that we should know something of their ideas and activities?'[54] Theis failed in his attempt to talk the publisher into accepting the book for what it was.

The process by which any book makes its way into the public sphere is more complex than readers often know; Padmore's experience suggests the roadblocks that face an author who challenges the prevailing paradigms of political rule. Hard as he tried to redefine his identity and frame his message in acceptable terms, he ran up against what must have felt like a stone wall of manuscript reviewers' resistance. He was fortunate in finding an agent who persisted. *How Britain Rules Africa* finally appeared in 1936, published in Britain by Wishart and in the United States by Lothrop, Lee and Shepard. Wishart had an arrangement with Victor Gollancz's Left Book Club to offer Wishart books to the club's members at reduced prices, and a special Left Book Club edition was also printed up. Typical Left Book Club sales had climbed to thirty thousand copies or higher by the end of 1936, the club's first year; even a fraction of that number could have given the book significantly higher sales than it otherwise would have had.[55] Given Padmore's break with the communists, there was an irony here, or a mystery, since Wishart had communist leanings and, as Padmore himself said, 'the Left Book Club was the most effective instrument of the Communist Party during the period up to the Hitler–Stalin pact'.[56]

Stranger bedfellows than Wishart followed, when Germany, which had so recently put Padmore in jail, became a market for the book. Changes made by the Swiss publisher who distributed the book in Germany and Switzerland suggest how the delicate political realities of the moment shaped what could be said. Retitling the book *Afrika unter dem Joch der Weissen* (*Africa under the Yoke of the Whites*), the publisher cut out Padmore's references to the Nazis and unflattering references to Mussolini. The cuts were substantial: the thirteen pages of introduction in the British edition shrank to eight. Gone were entire sections comparing colonial administrations to Nazi Germany, comments critical of Italian and Japanese expansion, references to German demand for colonies in Eastern Europe and Africa. Cuts were also made in the Epilogue – paragraphs on Mussolini's domestic record and efforts to annex Ethiopia, along with positive comments on the Soviet Union's treatment of its own national minorities. The links Padmore had made between imperialism and European fascism simply vanished. No longer were sympathetic whites 'struggling against the new slavery – Fascist-Imperialism'. In the German edition, these whites were fighting 'die neue Sklaverei - den *Imperialismus*' ('the new slavery – imperialism').[57] Demonstrating a practical bent, Padmore did not apparently protest against the cuts – they would improve the book's chances of sales in Germany, he told Theis. 'I note that Hitler is pressing forward claims for the return of the German colonies, and I presume that if the Swiss publisher cuts out the references which I made about the Nazies [sic] the book stands a chance of finding a good market in the Third Reich.'[58]

In addition to the cuts, Rotapfel-Verlag also added an unsigned preface to the German edition, proclaiming in the opening paragraph that the book's author was an African and repeating the claim later on, referring to Padmore as an 'inhabitant' of Africa. The German edition, unlike the English, underlined Padmore's identity with a glossy photo

– a handsome young black man wearing a European suit and tie, with a cigarette dangling from his lip. Having established Padmore's claim to authority – his African-ness – the publisher went on to say in the second paragraph of the added preface: 'It would be a great misunderstanding of the publisher's purpose, however, if someone wanted to exploit this book for political purposes.' Apparently concerned about the response of the British foreign office (a concern that may have contributed to the German title, replacing 'Britain' with 'whites'), the publisher suggested that all colonising nations had behaved badly. In a statement that ran counter to the German behaviour the world was about to see, the publisher proclaimed (in German), 'The true needs of the national inhabitants there must be considered. The practice of ignoring of their rights and suppression by force is not in the generally understood material interest of whites.'[59]

For the German-language edition Padmore received an advance of £25 (his agent got £3 15s of that), and was pleased with the way the book came out. He wrote his former Howard University professor Alain Locke on 17 December 1936:

> I just received a copy of the German edition of my book on Africa. They made a splendid job of it, & strange as it might sound it's doing well in Germany. It is all the more ironical when it is recalled that the Nazis expelled me from there after Hitler came to power. The Germans are making a drive for colonies & no doubt feel that a book indicting their opponents – the British imperialists, by a Black would help to prove that they are not the only villains. It is all a game of Realpolitics.[60]

For a while, Theis thought he might be able to sell the book to Germany's fellow fascists, the Italians. Making his pitch to a prospect, he wrote, 'It seems to me that it has a great deal of topic interest in view of the situation in Abyssinia ... The book is written from the point of view of a Negro intellectual [he wrote African, first, then struck it out] who is extremely critical of the methods of British imperialism.'[61] He told Padmore he doubted an Italian edition would materialise, though, since the Italians were responding to League of Nations sanctions by 'boycotting everything English'. He understood that the Italian Ministry of Propaganda would have published the book 'only they were afraid that if they gave it their official approbation it might have had diplomatic difficulties'.[62] The publisher of the German edition had been worried about that, too, but in the end the English had proved their willingness to tolerate dissent: after the English edition came out, Padmore pointed out to Theis that even some semi-official British media – the BBC's *Listener*, for instance – had treated the book well enough. He sent along reviews to Theis to forward to the German publishers. 'Perhaps the Nazi papers might be induced to insert excerpts from them in the form of adv[ertisement]s.'[63]

The reviews that appeared in the summer of 1936 were actually mixed. The *Times Literary Supplement* review was rough. 'The case for the African native is strong enough in all conscience. If it could be weakened, Mr Padmore's handling of it would be fatally certain to have that effect.' Getting his own facts wrong (Padmore 'is apparently an African native himself'), the reviewer scored Padmore for factual errors. He also took aim at the publisher's claim that the book was anchored in 'economic realities'. 'If persistent representation of everything the white man has done in Africa as wickedly calculated to put money into the pockets of the European "capitalist" at the expense of the native is consistent with "economic reality" these statements are justified; not otherwise.'[64] C. L. R. James, who had checked the manuscript, signed only his initials to a review to the Independent Labour Party's *New Leader*, praising the book as 'a masterpiece of reliable information, knowledge and understanding' but noting it was 'not easy reading'. He also criticized Padmore for imagining that enlightened members of the European ruling class would make common cause with Africans. 'How does the lion co-operate with the lamb?'[65] Padmore had thanked James in his acknowledgements for offering suggestions but perhaps had not taken them.

The Spectator gave Padmore's book to a leading expert on British Africa – Margery Perham. A fellow at an Oxford college, Perham had travelled widely in Britain's African empire, spending hours poring over documents, talking with colonial officials and chiefs, and observing local courts. Her diaries of these journeys display her real sympathy for native peoples and an understanding of how harmed they had been by the colonial system.[66] Azikiwe had met her while he was in England – she had invited him to spend the weekend at her country home, and, although sceptical of her enthusiasm for Lord Lugard, architect of indirect rule, he respected her scholarship and common sense.[67] Given her experience of Africa and the esteem in which other Africanists held her, Padmore could not have asked for a reviewer more knowledgeable or influential. He would have known her work – she had written articles for *The Times* opposing transfer of three British protectorates (Basutoland, Swaziland, and Bechuanaland) to South African control, a position Padmore himself held. These articles had subsequently appeared in a book Padmore cited in his bibliography. Nevertheless, Perham turned out to be an unsympathetic reader. Interested in hearing 'a Negro's opinion' of Empire's spread across the continent, Perham pronounced herself disappointed.

> [T]he criticism of this book is not that it contains the full list of our sins in Africa, but that it presents them against a standard so far above that of this world that hardly a fact is given to explain, still less to compensate. We do not learn in these pages of the backwardness of Africans, their social atomisation and savagery. We seem to see a number of potentially democratic nations held back by nothing but the greedy determination of the British to monopolise all power. Minor inaccuracies and exaggerations abound.[68]

While Perham was sympathetic to native African peoples and sometimes critical of colonial administration, she saw British rule in Africa as, on balance, good for Africa. As Azikiwe put it, she favoured self-determination but 'if and when the Africans themselves had proved their political capacity'.[69]

For an author trying to earn credibility in British political circles, Perham's review was a harsh blow. A more favourable review of *How Britain Rules Africa* appeared, however, in *The Economist*. The anonymous reviewer recognised Padmore's point of view as a natural bias, which did not undermine the worth of his book. 'Being of African descent himself', the reviewer said, 'he not unnaturally has a strong bias against imperialism as such, and in particular against the British colonial system, for which indeed he has scarcely a good or civil word to say'. Briefly, but accurately, the reviewer summed up several of Padmore's key political points: his criticism of trusteeship, indirect rule, and the Labour Party's proposal to put British protectorates and colonies under League supervision. 'That whole question Mr Padmore sees as a discussion among the members of a gang of racketeers about the disposal and division of colonial swag. As an African, and in a sense therefore as part of the swag himself, he considers it prejudicial as well as undignified to join in any such debate.' The reviewer managed to put forth Padmore's perspective fairly, even respectfully, without necessarily sharing it. '[I]t is no surprise', the reviewer said, 'that for Mr Padmore the only way of escape from an intolerable situation lies along the path of independence and self-determination for coloured peoples'. He concluded with what turned out to be an accurate forecast: 'Our professional patrons of the Empire and indeed respectable members of society in general will be tempted to ignore this book. They will make a great mistake if they succumb. It has its faults – but for all that it may mark the turn of a tide.'[70]

Despite the notice paid by these reviews in prominent periodicals, sales for *How Britain Rules Africa* moved at a trickle. It was not easy to build an audience for an unknown author, especially one with discomfiting views. Only 165 copies were sold the first six months the book was out; sales slowed by the first half of 1938 to eighteen copies.[71]

Not many copies of the book could have made their way to Africa, where bookstores were few and not many readers could afford a book that sold 12s 6d, more than even skilled workers made in a whole day. However small the book's African readership, to Ras Makonnen the book's most significant audience was its African readers, for whom its impact was 'crucial'. By the time the book was published, Makonnen had moved to London and joined Padmore in what became a long political alliance. Looking back from the 1970s, he said that the book's ideas 'continued to guide many of us for years afterwards ... [H]ere was the anatomy of our misery laid bare.' He recalled letters from students in Africa who said that 'up till their reading of this thing, they had been in darkness; but now they had a Magna Carta'.[72] As late as 1947 *How Britain Rules Africa* would appear on a *New York Amsterdam News* list, 'Selected Reading for Negro History Week'.[73] In the language of social movement theory, *How Britain Rules Africa* contributed to 'cognitive liberation', that perception of injustice which precedes collective action.[74]

Padmore closed the book with a vision of the future that contrasted sharply with the picture of the present he had laid out for nearly four hundred pages. Melding Marxism with nationalism, he wrote, 'The future belongs to the oppressed. The future of Africa belongs to the Blacks, for they are the most oppressed of the Earth.'[75] While thoughtful British observers could imagine an Africa belonging to Blacks, even the most sympathetic thought it would be a good while coming. They were to be surprised. Africa would be ruled by Africans far sooner than they imagined, and Padmore and his colleagues would help bring that future about. The *Economist* reviewer had it right: *How Britain Rules Africa* marked 'the turn of a tide'.

Notes

1 Harry Ransom Humanities Research Center, University of Texas at Austin, Nancy Cunard Collection, Box 17, Folder 10, carbon typescript, Nancy Cunard, 'For Dorothy', mid-November 1959.
2 Editor's note to 'Ethiopia and World Politics', *Crisis*, 42: 5 (May 1935), 138, 157.
3 Scholars interested in this period of Padmore's life will find useful documents in the microfilmed Records of the Communist Party, USA (CPUSA), Library of Congress, Washington, DC.
4 Clifton Hawkins, '"Race First Versus Class First": An Intellectual History of Afro-American Radicalism, 1911–1928' (Ph.D. dissertation, University of California, Davis, 2000), p. 528.
5 Nnamdi Azikiwe, *My Odyssey* (London: C. Hurst and Company, 1970), pp. 139–43.
6 Schomburg Center for Research in Black Culture, New York Public Library, George Padmore Papers [Padmore's correspondence with Cyril C. Ollivierre], Padmore to Ollivierre, 16 April 1930.

7 Edward T. Wilson, *Russia and Black Africa before Second World War* (New York, London: Holmes and Meier, 1974), p. 194.
8 Ras Makonnen, *Pan-Africanism from Within*, recorded and edited by Kenneth King (Nairobi, London, New York: Oxford University Press, 1973), pp. 102–3.
9 Padmore Papers, Padmore to Ollivierre, 26 September 1932.
10 C. L. R. James, 'Notes on the Life of George Padmore', carbon copy, typescript with author's corrections, microform (Chicago, IL: Center for Research Libraries, 1959), p. 16. The original carbon copy is available in the Northwestern University Libraries, where it was placed by Walter Goldwater, a New York bookseller who acted as James's agent. (See Lilly Library, Indiana University, James Mss, Folder 1, James to [Goldwater], [November 1949] and [Goldwater] to CLR [James], 4 December 1969.) This manuscript incorporates material from and postdates the eleven-part series by the same title that James published in the *Nation* (Trinidad and Tobago), October 1959 to January 1960, after Padmore's death. Anna Grimshaw (ed.) excerpted the *Nation* series in *The C. L. R. James Reader* (Oxford and Cambridge, MA: Blackwell, 1992), pp. 288–95.
11 Cunard Collection, Cunard, 'For Dorothy'; for information on his imprisonment and deportation see 'George Padmore: Mr Pan-Africa', *Contact* (21 March 1959), 15.
12 James, 'Notes', p. 12.
13 'Au Revoir', *Negro Worker*, 3: 8–9 (August–September), 18.
14 St Clair Drake in George Shepperson and St Clair Drake, 'The Fifth Pan-African Conference, 1945 and the All African People's Congress, 1958', *Contributions in Black Studies*, 8 (1986–87), 54. This is a transcription of remarks made to the Five College community in Massachusetts on 11 May 1987.
15 George Padmore, *Africa and World Peace*, with a new introduction by W. M. Warren (London: Frank Cass, 1972; originally published London: Secker and Warburg, 1937), p. 79; a caption under a photo of Padmore in the *New Leader*, 20 October 1939, 2, says that Padmore resigned from the Executive of the Communist International 'when ordered by Moscow to tone down his anti-Imperialist activities in order not to prejudice the Franco-Soviet Pact and the Liberal elements in the French Popular Front'.
16 Quoted by Rukudzo Murapa, citing a 1970 interview with Drake, in 'Padmore's Role in the African Liberation Movement' (Ph.D. dissertation, Northern Illinois University, 1974), pp. 66–8. Drake also told this story at a presentation in Shepperson and Drake, 'The Fifth Pan-African Conference', p. 55.
17 United States/National Archives at College Park, MD (US/NA), General Records of the Department of State / Central Decimal File / RG 59/800.00B-Padmore, George / 16, Memorandum, London, 29 December 1933. Subsequent notes to Central Decimal File documents will include only the file number.
18 US/NA, US Department of State, 800.00B-Padmore, George / 17, typed copy, letter from William Patterson, International Labor Defence, New York, to Arnold Ward, Negro Welfare Association, London, 11 January 1934, attached to Memorandum from US Embassy, London, 30 January 1934.
19 Padmore Papers, Padmore to Ollivierre, 28 July 1934.
20 US/NA, US Department of State, 800.00B-Padmore, George / 17, typed copy, letter Patterson to Ward, 11 January 1934, attached to Memorandum from US Embassy, London, 30 January 1934.
21 University of the West Indies at St Augustine, C. L. R. James Collection, Folder 194, Jean Confida, Le Préfet de Police, to C. L. R. James, 4 June 1968, quoting a note from police archives, dated 5 June 1934. James collected this and other materials for a biography of Padmore he never completed.
22 Azikiwe, *My Odyssey*, pp. 200, 198.
23 Beinecke Rare Book and Manuscript Library, General Collection, Louise Morgan and Otto Theis Papers, Series I, Box 13, Folder 291, Padmore to Otto Theis, 1 May 1935.
24 In his bibliography for *How Britain Rules Africa*, Padmore includes D. T. T. Jabavu's *The Black Problem*, Prince Nyabongo's *The Story of an African Chief*, P. M. Makerie,

'MISERY LAID BARE'

An African Speaks for His People, A. K. Ajisafe's History of Abeokuta, Nnamdi Azikiwe's Liberia in World Politics, J. B. Danquah's Akan Laws and Customs, Casely Hayford's Gold Coast Native Institutions.

25 George Padmore, How Britain Rules Africa (London: Wishart Books, 1936), p. 379.
26 Bruce Berman, 'Ethnography as Politics, Politics as Ethnography: Kenyatta, Malinowski, and the Making of Facing Mount Kenya', Canadian Journal of African Studies, 30: 3 (1996), 315–16, 320–4.
27 In his 28 July 1934 letter to Ollivierre, Padmore mentions hearing from Azikiwe when Azikiwe stopped in London on his way back to Nigeria.
28 Padmore, How Britain Rules Africa, p. 17.
29 Ibid., pp. 8–9.
30 Chinua Achebe, Home and Exile (Oxford and New York: Oxford University Press, 2000), p. 60.
31 Padmore, How Britain Rules Africa, p. 227.
32 Stanley Shaloff, 'Press Controls and Sedition Proceedings in the Gold Coast, 1933–39', African Affairs, 71: 284 (July 1972), 242–5; Leo Spitzer and LaRay Denzer, 'I. T. A. Wallace Johnson and the West African Youth League', International Journal of African Historical Studies, 6: 3 (1973), 428.
33 Padmore, How Britain Rules Africa, p. 377.
34 Morgan-Theis, Box 13, Folder 291, Padmore to Theis, 1 May 1935.
35 Ibid., Padmore to Theis, 12 May 1935.
36 Ibid., Padmore to Theis, 17 May 1935.
37 Reading University Library, Routledge and Kegan Paul Ltd Records, [Maurice Richardson, unsigned] to Padmore, 27 May [1935]; Padmore to Richardson, 29 May 1935; Padmore sent the manuscript off with a letter on 4 June 1935.
38 In Pan-Africanism or Communism?, Padmore lists all three writers as the ones having 'the greatest influence' on his views of colonialism (London: Dennis Dobson, 1956), p. 300, n. 7.
39 Padmore, How Britain Rules Africa, pp. 1, 4.
40 Ibid., pp. 395–6.
41 Frederic Spotts (ed.), Letters of Leonard Woolf (San Diego: Harcourt Brace Jovanovich, 1989), p. 268.
42 Ibid., pp. 60–1.
43 Woolf, 'Memorandum to the Trades Union Congress and the Labour Party', Letters, p. 393.
44 Parker Thomas Moon, Imperialism and World Politics (New York: Macmillan Company, 1926), p. 512.
45 Routledge, [Richardson] to Padmore, 2 July [1935].
46 Ibid., Padmore to Richardson, 3 July 1935.
47 Padmore, 'Ethiopia and World Politics', p. 139.
48 Ibid., pp. 139, 157.
49 Library of Congress, Washington, DC, Incomka, a selection of digitised files of the Communist International at the Russian State Archives of Socio-Political History (RGASPI), Moscow, F495, op. 155, d. 157, p. 15, from W., 16/6/35
50 Morgan-Theis, Box 13, Folder 291, Padmore to Theis, 7 July 1935.
51 Ibid., Padmore to Theis, 13 July 1935.
52 Ibid., reader's report, accompanied by a letter from Allen and Unwin (signature indecipherable) to Theis, 16 July 1935.
53 Ibid., Padmore to Theis, 4 August 1935.
54 Ibid., [Theis] to Unwin, 6 August [unclear], 1935.
55 Peter Gaunt, 'The Left Book Club at the Cross Roads', Left, 51 (December 1940), 351.
56 Pan-Africanism or Communism?, p. 331.
57 Padmore, Afrika: Unter dem Joch der Weissen (Erlenbach-Zürich/Leipzig: Rotapfel-Verlag, n.d. [1936]), p. 451.
58 Morgan-Theis Papers, Box 13, Folder 291, Padmore to Theis, 1 July 1936.
59 Padmore, Afrika, pp. 9–10. Padmore mentions the concern that the German edition

[21]

might ruffle the feathers of the British foreign office in a letter to Theis, 7 January 1937.
60 Moorland-Spingarn Research Center, Howard University, Alain LeRoy Locke Papers, Padmore to Locke, 17 December 1936.
61 Morgan-Theis, Box 13, Folder 291, Theis, apparently to the Ministry of Propaganda, 14 October 1935; a reply from the Italian London embassy, referring to a letter to the 'Ministero per la Stampa e Propaganda' and dated 2 November 1935, follows in this file.
62 *Ibid.*, Theis to Padmore, 7 December 1935.
63 *Ibid.*, Padmore to Theis, 7 January 1937.
64 'Miscellaneous', *Times Literary Supplement* (27 June 1936), 546. Padmore did not identify himself in any way in his introduction to the book; but he did dedicate it to 'The Youth of My Race / The Vanguard of the New Africa'.
65 James,'"Civilising" the "Blacks"', *New Leader* (29 May 1936), 5.
66 Margery Perham, *African Apprenticeship: An Autobiographical Journey* (London: Faber and Faber, 1974); *East African Journey: Kenya and Tanganyika 1929–30* (London: Faber and Faber, 1976); *West African Passage: A Journey through Nigeria, Chad and the Cameroons* (London and Boston: Peter Owen, 1983).
67 Azikiwe, *My Odyssey*, pp. 206–9.
68 Perham, 'European Civilization in Africa', *The Spectator* (12 June 1936), 1089. Her book on South Africa was *The Protectorates of South Africa: The Question of Their Transfer to the Union* (London: Oxford University Press / Humphrey Milford, 1935).
69 Azikiwe, *My Odyssey*, p. 209.
70 'Books and Publications', *The Economist* (26 September 1936), 564.
71 Beinecke Rare Book and Manuscript Library, Yale University, Lawrence and Wishart Archive, [no signature] to Padmore, 8 July 1938.
72 Makonnen, *Pan-Africanism*, p. 194.
73 'Selected Reading for Negro History Week', *New York Amsterdam News* (8 February 1947), 20.
74 David A. Snow, E. Burke Rochford, Jr, Steven K. Worden, Robert D. Benford, 'Frame Alignment Processes, Micromobilization, and Movement Participation', in Doug McAdam and David A. Snow (eds), *Social Movements* (Los Angeles: Roxbury Publishing Company, 1997), p. 236.
75 Padmore, *How Britain Rules Africa*, p. 396.

CHAPTER TWO

'Generals without an army'

By the time *How Britain Rules Africa* came out, George Padmore had moved to London and joined C. L. R. James in speeches at Hyde Park and Trafalgar Square. They were a powerful duo, these two Trinidadians – 'unquestionably,' in James's mind, 'the leaders of the struggle against imperialism in London on behalf of the African people and people of African descent'.[1] Their immediate target was Italy's assault on Ethiopia, but their ultimate aim was larger: undermining imperial rule, specifically British imperial rule, which had limited their own prospects in Trinidad. Growing up in Trinidad, Padmore and James had shared both a Western education and a very restricted opportunity to use it in a colonial society firmly controlled by the British government and a small white business elite. Padmore's father, James Hubert Alfonso Nurse, son of a slave, had risen to a position rarely granted to non-whites: he taught elementary teachers agriculture for the Department of Education. James's father, a schoolteacher in Tunapuna, knew the elder Nurse and would take C. L. R. along when he visited him. James recalled Nurse living 'almost entirely surrounded by books from floor to ceiling ... I had never seen so many books before in a private house'. Outside his home, the elder Nurse had to display his erudition with care. Once when he actually signed a paper he had written for a meeting, the head of his department was infuriated.[2] In his retirement, he wrote a book on West Indies geography; it was never published.[3] Whatever hopes he had as a scholar were largely disappointed.

Hopes for a Trinidad writer with political inclinations were if anything more bleak. Among the obstacles in the early 1920s was a new Seditious Publications Ordinance that enabled the government to fine and imprison anyone who published criticism of either the British or the Trinidadian government. Approved in 1920 just after a series of strikes, the ordinance actually seems to have been a response less to that local upheaval than to African-American publications coming into the country from the United States. According to the radical paper *Argos*, the government was especially worried that Trinidadians might be stirred up by Jamaican Marcus Garvey's *Negro World*. Within months of the ordinance's passage, *Argos* itself ceased publication, possibly, a historian has written, 'one of the first casualties of the ordinance'.[4]

The newspaper for which Padmore worked opposed even small official steps towards local democracy. As the loudest voice of the business class, the *Guardian* preferred that things remain as they were.[5] One editor in particular struck Padmore, he later said, as 'one of the most arrogant agents of British Imperialism I have ever encountered. I held him in utter contempt, and had hoped to use my pen in exposing his role before the colonial workers and peasants whom he oppressed through his dirty sheet the Guardian.'[6] In later conversations with James, Padmore would recall bitterly the way a young black assistant editor emerged chastened from the white editor's office. The scene stuck like a burr in his memory, symbolising to James the reasons Padmore would 'shake the dust of the Trinidad of those days from off his feet'.[7]

Many years later James would say that for West Indians during those years '[t]he first step to freedom was to go abroad'.[8] Padmore had taken that step in 1924 when, like Edward Wilmot Blyden the century before him, he left for the United States. For his part, James had arrived in England in 1932 after Trinidadian-born cricketer Learie Constantine, living in the Lancashire town of Nelson, encouraged him to come to help him write a book at a time when James knew no one in the West Indies who 'was writing books at all; certainly none was being printed abroad'.[9] Living with Constantine, James helped write *Cricket and I*, and Constantine, in turn, underwrote publication of a political manuscript James brought with him to England, *The Life of Captain Cipriani*. James sent copies back to the West Indies, and Leonard and Virginia Woolf's Hogarth Press republished the book in shorter form under what James regarded as its 'real' (and more provocative) title, *The Case for West-Indian Self Government*. Meanwhile, James also reported on cricket for the *Manchester Guardian*.[10]

As Padmore had found a new ideological frame in the United States, James, too, moved leftward in England, joining a Trotskyist group in London. Trotsky, the Russian revolutionary exiled by Stalin, upheld the goal of world revolution at a time when Stalin maintained that socialism could be established first in one country, the Soviet Union, and spread from there elsewhere. The Trotskyist group James belonged to spent hours talking over Trotsky's writings in James's dingy room near Gray's Inn Road. It was a room like the one James recalled Padmore's father living in. 'There were books everywhere: books up the walls, books on the floor, books and papers on the table', group member Louise Cripps later wrote. Cripps was attracted to the group by her own reading of Trotsky's *History of the Russian Revolution* but also by James – 'very tall, lean, handsome' and a dynamic talker.[11] Cripps had studied journalism at University College, London, edited at a magazine, *Nursery World*, and written for London newspapers. When James proposed bringing out a paper expressing the group's ideas, she volunteered to help. 'We were all young and idealistic', she wrote in her memoir of James. 'We felt our work could contribute to the time when we would see Socialism spreading, when the poor would not be starving, when the homeless were given shelter, when the unemployed would be guaranteed jobs. Most of all, we believed, we could help working people of all nations realise that they had no interest in fighting in imperialist wars.'[12]

Another imperialist war seemed perilously close when Padmore moved to London in 1935. Anticipating Italy's attack on Ethiopia, James had started the International African Friends of Ethiopia (or Abyssinia, as it was sometimes called). Meeting at the Oxford Street restaurant operated by Marcus Garvey's former wife Amy Ashwood Garvey,[13] the IAFE sent out speakers and articles to rouse British sympathies with the Ethiopians. West Indians formed the core of the IAFE, their interest in Ethiopia explained by James's later comment that West Indians focused on Africa in the years between the First and Second World Wars because '[b]efore they could begin to see themselves as a free and independent people they had to clear from minds the stigma that anything African was inherently inferior and degraded'.[14] Among the few Africans at the core of the IAFE was the Kenyan Johnstone Kenyatta, who had known Padmore in Moscow and advised him on *How Britain Rules Africa*. 'We had little African support', James would write later, 'and but for George's contacts we would have been in a bad way'.[15]

The West Indian Ras Makonnen, the British Guianan who had known Padmore in the United States, soon joined them, bringing valuable experience as an organiser and player on an international field. In the United States, Makonnen had worked for the Young Men's Christian Association, at that time one of the white-dominated institutions most dedicated to advancing racial equality. He had also studied at Cornell University and mingled with American socialists, who had helped him arrange studies at the Danish Agricultural College. On his way to Denmark, Makonnen stopped in London, and there he attended a rally on Ethiopia at Trafalgar Square. After the rally, he retired with some of the IAFE group to Lyons Corner House where, over tea, they talked further. A few days later, he went on to Denmark. Visiting

Sweden and Norway as well, he formed connections with radicals throughout Scandinavia. Denmark had become a haven for Europeans fleeing fascism, but there were, as it turns out, limits to Danish tolerance. Makonnen wore out his welcome when he suggested that Danish farmers should stop exporting mustard to Italy since Italy could turn the mustard into mustard gas to be used against Ethiopians. He was promptly deported.[16]

Makonnen arrived in London again in time to welcome the Ethiopian Emperor Haile Selassie, who fled his country after Italy invaded in October 1936, pounding villages that had never seen planes and raining poison gas on a pastoral people.[17] Despite the mismatch in power the Ethiopians continued to resist, and the Italian conquest of Ethiopia did not put the Ethiopian issue to rest. For Africans and African descendants worldwide, this was one of those galvanising issues that allow movements to take leaps forward. The members of IAFE seized the moment of opportunity and made the most of it. Makonnen joined in the speechmaking, and he and Padmore went to the British Library together to study Ethiopian history. They also roomed together, renting a basement flat at 2 Calthorpe Street, off Gray's Inn Road. They kept a coffee pot hot and the door open, and their flat became an informal meeting ground for Africans and West Indians.[18] Ivar Holmes, a visiting Norwegian, would later recall a wonderful evening of conversation with them over beer and whisky, talking about Comintern policy. That was the night Holmes met Padmore for the first time, at an Indian political congress, when criticism of Comintern acceptance of Italy's assault on Ethiopia was rife. The communists tried to defend the policy but, Holmes wrote in his diary, 'they were completely defeated by the coloured speakers who were excellent speakers'.[19]

If the Comintern had proved once again its unreliability as an ally for Africans, Padmore believed that the European left, as a whole, had failed Ethiopia. 'Not even the organised labour movement of Western Europe – England and France, which is supposed to be passionately anti-Fascist, did more than express pious words of sympathy', he wrote in a new book he was working on, *Africa and World Peace*. '[O]ne cannot help feeling that had it been Abyssinians raining death from the air upon a white people ... European Socialists would not merely have passed pious resolutions on behalf of the victim, but would have aroused the working classes into action.'[20] That they did not was due, at least in part, to a feeling by some on the British left that Ethiopia, as a feudal autocracy, did not deserve defence by socialists, the prevailing opinion in the Independent Labour Party, although the ILP's paper, the *New Leader*, under the editorship of Fenner Brockway, had earlier argued for taking Ethiopia's side.[21]

Padmore, James, and Kenyatta had found something of a political home in the *New Leader*, its anti-communist democratic socialism compatible with their own political views. Although the ILP was itself only a marginal political player with a membership dropping rapidly (from 17,000 in 1932 to 3,500 in 1937), by publishing in the *New Leader* they could draw on another organisation's resources – a common strategy for social movements – and speak to a sympathetic audience that already existed rather than having to mobilise their own audience from scratch.[22] The *New Leader*'s editor, Fenner Brockway, became a significant ally. Born in India where his English parents were missionaries, Brockway had long been involved in both the ILP and the international anti-colonial movement, where his path had likely crossed Padmore's even before Padmore moved to London. Now he not only provided a periodical publishing venue but he also found a book publisher, Fredric Warburg, who helpfully opened his door to James, Padmore, and Kenyatta, raising their visibility on the British literary and political scene.

Formerly employed by the publisher Routledge and Sons, Fredric Warburg had bought out the old firm of Martin Secker, Ltd, to start a new house publishing iconoclastic books that would pronounce a plague on both fascism and communism; he intended to make Secker and Warburg 'radical, anti-conservative and unorthodox'.[23] Brockway convinced him that ILP writers could help him create that identity. Following Brockway's advice, Warburg published a novel James had brought with him from Trinidad, *Minty Alley*. Then in 1937 he published James's *World Revolution 1917 to 1936: The Rise and Fall of the Communist International*, which was promptly banned in India.[24] An indictment of the Soviet Union's betrayal of working-class revolution, *World Revolution* was also a blueprint for action at a time when James and his Trotskyist group believed revolution was imminent. Just as Kenyatta and the others had earlier helped Padmore with *How Britain Rules Africa*, members of James's Marxist Group helped him research *World Revolution*, clipping articles from newspapers and magazines and ferreting out other useful information. Looking back on their lives together, Louise Cripps, James's collaborator and lover, described the passion with which they believed they could change history. 'It is sad and may now seem pathetic', she wrote in a 1997 memoir, 'that this small group formed by C. L. R. James, sitting around that table in that dusty room, could have hoped to have an effect not only in England, but with others internationally. It was not that we were intellectually arrogant but lost in the excitement and camaraderie of high visions that perhaps only the young can aspire.' James – 'our leader, the born talker' – inspired them all.[25] 'Turn the imperialist war into civil war', James urged the readers of *World Revolution*. 'Abolish capitalism. Build international Socialism.'[26]

Padmore mirrored James's views in his own book published the same year by Secker and Warburg: *Africa and World Peace*. If war was caused by capitalists competing with each other for markets, resources, and targets of investment, then the only way to end war was to bring down capitalism. The coming war presented an opportunity to do just that in capitalist countries and colonies alike. 'Comrade-workers, hold high your revolutionary banner!', Padmore exhorted his readers, sounding very much like the Comintern propagandist he had been.[27] In retrospect, the idea that while Hitler's planes rained down bombs English workers would storm Buckingham Palace seems far-fetched, but at the time the belief that war could provoke revolution was not uncommon on the left. Had not the Russian Revolution emerged out of the First World War? Socialists' faith that great change was possible, even against great odds, fed the nascent anti-colonial movement forming in London.

Warburg had taken a chance in publishing James's *World Revolution* and Padmore's *Africa and World Peace*. Communists had worked themselves into positions as magazine editors and reviewers, and, Warburg feared, were certain to hand out rough treatment to books that were unsympathetic towards communism. Taking on ILP writers, he would be publishing 'authors the communists would smear with the label, Trotskyist or Trotskyite, words that in those days were made to sound like a bad smell ... [If their books] sold it would be without benefit of communist clergy'.[28] He would turn out to be right: the *Daily Worker* refused to run an advertisement for *World Revolution*[29] though an ad appeared in *Fight*, the smaller magazine published by James's own Marxist Group, along with a full-page approving review.[30] Sales for *World Revolution* were moderate 'if you apply low enough standards of sale', Warburg recalled. *Africa and World Peace* fared worse. Despite an introduction by Sir Stafford Cripps, an independent-minded Labour Member of Parliament marginalised in his own party, *Africa and World Peace* was, Warburg said frankly, a 'flop'.[31]

Any hope Padmore had that he would derive an income from this book was shattered. Necessarily, he did hope for income from his books. Padmore, James, Kenyatta, and just about everyone in their group of exiles lived on the margin. Kenyatta lived in serious poverty, selling stamps on letters from home so he could buy a penny bun, drying his single shirt on the radiator. His chief source of income was his work as linguistic informant for anthropologist Bronislaw Malinowski, with whom he began to work on a diploma in social anthropology.[32] James's and Padmore's financial need surfaced in a letter Padmore wrote to the Howard University professor Alain Locke soliciting Locke's help on James's behalf. James had written a play about the Haitian hero Toussaint L'Ouverture as a vehicle for the American actor Paul Robeson, but, although presented by the British Stage Society, the play 'was not a financial success', Padmore told Locke. 'For the British public is not too keen for such stuff as Black Revolutionaries when they have so many black colonies of their own to keep such ideas from.' Always looking for ways to promote his fellow writers, Padmore asked if Locke could get a journal to publish James's play or a theatre group to put it on. Or perhaps Locke could review James's novel and 'suggest how James can get a little money which he, like myself, is badly in need of'.[33] Padmore was earning something by teaching small groups of students from the colonies[34] and writing articles for newspapers in Britain and the United States, though all too often no compensation was forthcoming from the American editors who published his articles, he told his Harlem friend Cyril Ollivierre. 'What rogues the black bourgeoisie!' he commented.[35]

Padmore's economic position improved after he began a relationship with Dorothy Pizer, a working-class Jewish Englishwoman who had grown up in London's East End.[36] As Louise Cripps and other members of the Marxist group helped James produce *World Revolution*, Pizer – described once by St Clair Drake as 'very, very energetic'– helped Padmore gather material for *Africa and World Peace*, typed his manuscript, and, as he said in his acknowledgements, performed 'other thankless literary chores'.[37] Padmore had not made a clear break with his wife, Julia, left behind in the United States, and in fact, as late as the spring of 1938, referred in a letter to Ollivierre to the help she had given him 'morally & materially' and spoke of planning to return to the United States to see her if he could get a visa.[38] That trip did not materialise, and, although Padmore was never divorced from Julia, Pizer became known as his wife.[39] A bright and talented woman who was already a Marxist when she met Padmore, Pizer brought income from her secretarial job to their household and contributed so significantly to Padmore's writing that she would share billing with him as an author on a later book.[40] In addition, Padmore found financial support for the cause in Ras Makonnen, who turned out to be a resourceful businessman committed to launching publishing enterprises of their own. The vehicle for these ventures was a new organisation, the International African Service Bureau.

Although James gave Padmore credit for transforming the IAFE into the IASB, Makonnen would remember that the African Bureau, as it was often called, 'came together in an informal way'. He and Padmore had rented a basement where the coffee kept on the stove drew some thirty regular guests, the bureau's informal membership.[41] The Metropolitan Police had a narrower view of the bureau's origins, tracing them to the arrival in February 1937 of Sierra Leone's Isaac Theophilus Akunna Wallace Johnson, described by an American journalist some years later as a man 'possessed of a rare charm, wit and humour'.[42] Like Padmore, Wallace Johnson had demonstrated an early interest in journalism, editing a newsletter for the United Methodist Collegiate School he attended and, before the First World War began, contributing to a newspaper. Working on ships after the war, he edited a newsletter for sailors. He spent about a year as a clerk in the Gold Coast, then moved to Nigeria, where he organised the Nigerian Workers' Union, before travelling to Hamburg for a 1930 Negro workers' conference that Padmore helped to organise, then on to Moscow.[43] In the spring of 1931, he accompanied Padmore on the trip to Africa that led to Padmore's slim book *The Life and Struggles of Negro Toilers*. He served on the presidium of the International Trade Union Committee of Negro Workers, which Padmore ran, and contributed articles to the *Negro Worker*, which Padmore edited. In Moscow he roomed with Kenyatta while they studied at the People's University of the East (Kutvu University), where Padmore lectured. Returning to West Africa, Wallace Johnson had so stirred up the political air that he was run out of Nigeria, then arrested and fined in the Gold Coast for an article he published in the newspaper edited by Azikiwe.[44]

He arrived in London in early 1937 to appeal against that judgement, and his arrival apparently marked the start of regular British surveillance of Padmore, James, and others in the IASB. In a secret report to the Colonial Office on 21 June 1937, Colonel Sir Vernon Kell gave a rundown of Wallace Johnson's activities thus far. Wallace Johnson had succeeded in what he came to do – 'establish a central bureau for coloured people the object of which is to avoid interference from colonial governments'. Helped by 'George PADMORE's Pan-African Brotherhood', he had set up the International African Service Bureau at an office on Gray's Inn Road. The plan was to bring out a monthly journal; money for three issues had already been raised.[45] This report and the ones that followed document authorities' efforts to keep up to date on the IASB's activities.

On 6 July, in another report filed with the Colonial Office, the Metropolitan Police noted, first, that Wallace Johnson had spoken at a May Day rally staged by the Communist Party of Great Britain in Hyde Park. Then the report moved on to 'the Pan Afro Group', which had organised an International African Information Bureau at an 11 May meeting. The group meant to open an office at 53 Gray's Inn Road and had already brought out its first *Colonial Information Bulletin*. Contents included an article on Civil Liberties and Democratic Rights, 'and although it was unsigned it is recognised as from the pen of Wallace Johnson'. The author of this report speculated that Wallace Johnson might be considered the 'driving force' behind the bureau. He 'has stated that he is determined to place the Bureau on a firm footing before he leaves this country and he expects assistance in this direction from Miss Nancy Cunard who intends to visit London in the near future'.[46]

According to another Metropolitan Police report, it was Wallace Johnson who edited the IASB's publication, *Africa and the World*. This modest, typewritten affair, duplicated on inexpensive paper, apparently represented a threat to the colonial authorities in the Gold Coast. Warned by the Colonial Office to consider whether it might be seditious, Gold Coast officials took a close look at the second issue (27 July 1937), with its lead article, 'The Gold Coast Today'. The remarks that gave offence were comments by the Reverend Reginald Sorensen, Labour MP and IASB patron, and they were made in the House of Commons.[47] Despite their provenance, they provoked the Gold Coast Executive Council to ban the issue in the Gold Coast on 10 September, ruling that it violated the criminal code and that therefore 'all issues of this publication, past, present, and future, should be prohibited'.[48] An unsigned typescript accompanying the council's report to the Colonial Office in London did note dissent by the Attorney-General, who acknowledged that, while the publishers of *Africa and the World* did mean to 'promote feelings of ill-will between natives and Europeans', he doubted that the local courts would hold the issue to be seditious.[49] A later colonial official's account of the council meeting suggests the low bar for unacceptable speech in the Gold Coast: the issue's tone was 'objectionable in that it was calculated to promote feelings of hostility and ill-will between black and white and that the particular references in it to the Gold Coast were inaccurate, irresponsible and couched in such language as to render the circulation of the publication among a credulous and semi-educated people likely to give rise to discontent and disaffection'.[50]

The banning became a topic in the House of Commons, where the Under Secretary of State for the Colonies confessed on 24 November 1937 that he had not seen the issue in question. Wallace Johnson obligingly sent him a copy on 10 January 1938.[51] Then perhaps because of the dustup over *Africa and the World*, on 17 February 1938, Colonial Secretary William Ormsby Gore issued a confidential circular to the administering officers of the various colonial governments. In a document that opens a window on efforts to suppress speech in the colonies, he reviewed 'the whole question of the laws relating to sedition and to the importation of undesirable publications'. While laws varied from colony to colony, he asserted his own belief that governors had the power to keep out publications they deemed 'contrary to the public interest'.

Although this communication gave governors the green light to ban imported publications, it did not grant similar powers to ban local publications. Ormsby Gore weighed in on letting local courts take that action. A local publication could be guilty of sedition but would have to be properly charged under the criminal code and brought to court – not simply be found guilty by the governor alone. Seditious publications he defined broadly as material likely 'to raise discontent or disaffection amongst His Majesty's subjects or inhabitants of the Colony'. It would not be seditious, on the other hand, 'to point out, with a view to their removal, any matters which are producing or have a tendency to produce feelings of ill will and enmity between different classes of the population of the Colony'. This was slicing the distinction fine, leaving officials ample room to interpret any criticism as seditious or not, as they chose.

Penalties for importing, publishing, selling, distributing, or reproducing a publication already banned could be stiff: prison terms of up to three years and fines up to £100. Anyone found with a banned publication in his possession 'without lawful excuse' could be imprisoned for a year or fined up to £50. How would these 'undesirable' publications be detected? Any one of a variety of officials – postal, police, customs – could 'detain, open and examine any package or article' if he thought it may contain such a publication. Ormsby Gore appeared to be aiming for moderation. He thought penalties set forth in the laws of some dependencies were 'altogether too severe' – for instance, 'penal servitude for life for importing a forbidden book'. In fact, this whole document appears to be an attempt to rein in the governors, some of whom the Colonial Office regarded as prone to overreaction.[52]

While the new guidelines from London were meant to have a moderating effect, they reveal how firmly colonial authorities tried to keep the lid on dissent. For the IASB, banning became a cat-and-mouse game. When one publication was banned, the IASB simply came out with another. The *African Sentinel*, also edited by Wallace Johnson, made its appearance in October–November 1937. This higher-quality publication, printed on good paper, with photographs, devoted considerable space to the story of Wallace Johnson's own troubles with the Sedition Law, although the unnamed writer, presumably himself, did not mention him by name. The article included the information that after the victim's departure from the Gold Coast, another law was enacted allowing local officials to bar the entry of any 'non-native African' who might be undesirable. That would prevent Wallace Johnson from returning to the Gold Coast.[53]

He was, nevertheless, about to return to West Africa after a period of despondence when he considered moving to the United States and abandoning the African cause altogether, or even taking his own life. He was too penniless in London, at times, to afford food, bus fare, or rent; he wound up living at the African Bureau office. There have been allegations that he took money from the bureau, a possibility, given his difficult circumstances. He seemed a man at the end of his tether when he wrote to a colleague in the West African Youth League in Accra on 4 January 1938, 'I think so far, I have done my best and can hold on no longer. I have been made to suffer just because I love my race and people. But while I am prepared to sacrifice my very life in their interest, I am not prepared to suffer death and privation by cold in a strange country.'[54]

Finally, in April 1938, Wallace Johnson left London for Sierra Leone, taking with him two thousand copies of *African Sentinel* – which were promptly seized by customs agents at Freetown. The Governor explained to the Secretary of State, 'It is most undesirable that such nonsense should be circulated among the population of Sierra Leone'.[55]

Despite Wallace Johnson's departure and the roadblocks to distribution of publications in the colonies, the IASB pressed forward on multiple fronts. 'The prevailing feeling in these last few months before the war was that we should insist on seeing the colonial world as a whole', Makonnen recalled. A story on trade unions in Trinidad could become an occasion for a manifesto on black trade unionism on a broader front, from the West Indies to West Africa.[56] The IASB spoke out on issues across the colonial world. 'African Group Wants Natives' Rights Upheld' read the *Chicago Defender* headline on a 1 October 1938 story about the IASB's memorandum to a royal commission about to investigate conditions in West Indies.[57] Of the two IASB pamphlets that appeared in 1938, one was on the West Indies, the other on southern Africa. The author of *The West Indies Today* was W. Arthur Lewis, a St Lucian at the London School of Economics. Although Lewis had joined the IAFE, his chief sphere of political activity in the 1930s was the League of Coloured Peoples; he edited and wrote for the League's journal, *The Keys*, where he brought African issues to the attention of the League's largely West Indian leadership. Turned down for a reporting job at *The Economist* on the ground that he might be refused interviews because he was black, Lewis honed his writing skills in more political arenas. He followed his IASB pamphlet up with *Labour in the West Indies* (1939), written for the Fabians, and found Fabian socialism a better fit for him than the harder-edged politics of the circle around Padmore.[58] Yet he maintained ties with Padmore, and the day would come when both would work together in the independent government of Ghana.

The other IASB pamphlet, *Hands Off the Protectorates*, was by Padmore, who had emerged as the powerhouse behind the bureau. A man with enormous drive, Padmore maintained a 'tireless correspondence with Africans in all parts of the continent', James recalled, and, when they came to London on political missions, they conferred with Padmore about the best way to approach the Colonial Office.[59] He talked incessantly to Labour politicians and to visitors from all over the world. 'His encyclopaedic knowledge, his enthusiasm, his eagerness to explain, his hospitality, drew them like a magnet', James wrote in his memoir of Padmore. 'He initiated his colonial visitors into the intricacies of British politics. He taught and he learnt. He talked like a torrent, but always to an end, an article, a resolution, a manoeuvre with the Colonial Office, an approach to a Labour Member of Parliament, an avenue for some propaganda in the British press.'[60]

Padmore was by this time contributing regularly to not only the Independent Labour Party's *New Leader* but also its monthly journal, *Controversy*, a non-sectarian forum for socialist articles more argumentative than the *New Leader*'s news items. Leading European and American intellectuals contributed to *Controversy*, among them Simone Weil, Leon Trotsky, Ignazio Silone, and George Orwell. Padmore made an appearance in that distinguished lineup several times in 1938, twice with articles on Trinidad and twice with articles on South Africa (with a 'Pendant to Padmore' by Ras Makonnen attached to one of those).[61] *Controversy* reviewed James's *World Revolution* and published Pizer's review of his next book, *The Black Jacobins*.[62] After *Controversy* was renamed *Left*, Kenyatta appeared in the November 1939 issue as author of '"Democracy" in Kenya', which closed on this defiant note: 'The Africans are no longer contented with the "Commissions of Inquiry" and are taking action to improve their conditions. The police may shoot, the judges may send people to prison, but the struggle will continue until the victory is won.'[63] In addition to these articles – evidence of the IASB's close relationship with ILP socialists – *Controversy* also brought attention to IASB activities, publishing a letter from Makonnen about a forthcoming Trafalgar Square protest on South Africa and announcing the appearance of yet another IASB periodical, its new monthly, *International African Opinion*, to be sold at the Socialist Bookshop.[64]

In an editorial that led off the first issue of *International African*

Opinion, the IASB declared its newest journal's intent: to become 'the mouthpiece of the black workers and peasants, and those intellectuals who see the necessity of making the cause of the masses their own'. While the IASB could not liberate Africans and people of African descent by itself, what the IASB could do was act as an intermediary between Africans and Europeans. The IASB could

> help to stimulate the growing consciousness of blacks, to give them the benefit of our daily contact with the European movement, to learn from the black masses, the lessons of the profound experiences that they accumulate in their daily toil, to point out certain pitfalls that may be avoided, to co-ordinate information and organisation, to do an incessant propaganda in every quarter of Britain, exposing evils, pressing for such remedies as are possible, and mobilising whatever assistance there is to be found in Europe for the cause of African emancipation.[65]

The drawing that opened this and subsequent issues of the IASB's newest publication underlined its diasporic reach: a young woman, holding a torch high, stood before a map of the world, with shading to indicate areas populated by significant numbers of Blacks. Wearing a toga-style dress that left one breast bare, this female figure made a striking contrast to the icon used in anti-imperialist communist publications in the 1930s – a muscular male, hovering over a globe, breaking the chains that bound all Africans and people of African descent.

Although James served as the official editor of *International African Opinion*, Makonnen seems to have been the organising force for the new publication, at least by his own recollection.[66] 'James and Padmore would ask me what I wanted them to write up.' In this, as in all their enterprises, they seemed to operate in a relaxed collaborative mode, each bringing journalistic skills to the project. Padmore and James had the most experience as writers and editors, but Kenyatta had been editor of his Kikuyu publication and had written for several papers in England; he had also studied layout and newspaper production.[67] William Harrison, an Afro-American engaged in postgraduate studies at the London School of Economics, also helped with editing and writing.[68]

The *International African Opinion*, like the IASB's earlier publications, had a modest circulation. What, then, did Makonnen and the others accomplish by putting out their own small, short-lived papers on the fringes of the public sphere? As other political and social change movements have learned, if it accomplished nothing else, publishing accomplished this: it became a way of building solidarity among themselves. In addition, distributing their papers gave them a reason to show up at a variety of meetings held by a range of organisations.

Makonnen recalled that after the new issues came in, he would locate 'all the halls where leftist meetings or peace meetings were on that night, and sell this thing illegally at the door on the way out. I would make pounds and pounds this way, because many an old English lady would give me sh.10 just to get rid of me.' At Hyde Park, he would say, 'We, unlike those of you who are praying for peace, are asking for war; it's the only way we are going to get our rights'. After an hour of passionate speech, he would add, 'Now you know it is against the law to sell papers or to ask for aid, but all the things we have just been talking about, and much more, are right here in our paper *International African Opinion*'.[69]

Makonnen could collect more than £20 from a single session and have money left over after paying the printing bill. Using proceeds from the *International African Opinion* and unsolicited donations from its readers, Makonnen opened a bank account for the bureau. There was enough money to rent the upper floor of a building in south east London to provide a place for meetings and visitors needing a place to stay. Makonnen managed the place, doing the cooking and cleaning (including the toilet bowls). How he paid the bills was, James has said, 'beyond my comprehension'.[70] Funds trickled in from odd places. When some two thousand copies of Padmore's early book *Life and Struggles of Negro Toilers* showed up in the Communist Party's basement, Makonnen recalled, the IASB was able to sell them at protest meetings for 'sometimes ten shillings or more – especially if you were well dressed. George always was. Spic and span like a senator, and his shoes shone so you could see your face in them; his trouser creases could shave you.'[71]

The London circle was a stylish lot, each in a different way. Years later, white Kenyan Elspeth Huxley, who attended a class with Kenyatta in London, said that Kenyatta 'dressed flashily, in loud check trousers and a belted jacket, carried a walking-stick with an amber-coloured stone in its top, and wore the ring set with a semi-precious stone, perhaps a cornelian, that was to become, like his fly-whisk, a part of his insignia'.[72] James cut a more quietly elegant figure; his publisher Warburg recalled him as 'noticeably good-looking' and his memory as 'extraordinary. He could quote, not only passages from the Marxist classics but long extracts from Shakespeare, in a soft lilting English which was a delight to hear.'[73] James was also the most elegant writer of them all, and, although Warburg published only one book by Padmore, in 1938 he published two by James: a translation of Boris Souvarine's *Stalin: A Critical Survey of Bolshevism*, and *The Black Jacobins: Toussaint L'Ouverture and the San Domingo Revolution*.

Immersed in revolutionary thought by his own Trotskyist activities and his work on *World Revolution* and *Stalin*, in *The Black Jacobins* James told a story from the revolutionary past to inspire Africans and their descendants in the present. Toussaint L'Ouverture's revolt against the French at the time of the French Revolution had posed a research challenge for James. Most of the relevant documents and books were in French and in France. James made several research trips to Paris, including one in the spring of 1937 with Louise Cripps and a mutual friend. James and his companions strolled down the Left Bank, examining the books in the stalls along the way. They visited the Eiffel Tower, the Louvre, the Tuilleries, the palace at Versailles, unoccupied by a king since the revolution. Immersed in his research, James gave little lectures as they went along. His mind was encyclopaedic, and Cripps watched with amazement at the rapid improvement of his spoken French, although, for at least some of his research, he had the help of a translator.[74]

Written in the tradition of Oswald Spengler's *Decline of the West* (a book James admired), *The Black Jacobins* was history as argument – sweeping, impassioned, and powerful. In her review for *Controversy*, Pizer wrote of the 'extraordinary drama' with which James moved 'through the maze of revolution and counter-revolution'.[75] Pizer, of course, knew James and sympathised with his cause, but, after the book's publication by the Dial Press in the United States, even the *New York Times* offered up high praise: 'Mr James is not afraid to touch his pen with the flame of ardent personal feeling ... and his detailed, richly documented and dramatically written book holds a deep and lasting interest.'[76] *The Black Jacobins* would become one of the more studied works in James's canon after he became a literary figure of some renown, although later readers would not always be aware of the historical moment out of which the book emerged. 'Historical in form', James himself would write many years later, 'it drew its contemporaneousness, as all such books must, from the living struggle around us, and particularly from the daily activity that centred around Padmore and the African Bureau'. Just as Blacks of San Domingo had seemed backward to their French masters, so the African in the 1930s was considered 'backward, ignorant', he wrote at the end of *The Black Jacobins*. Who would have guessed that those eighteenth-century whipped slaves 'could shake off their chains and face extermination rather than put them on again'? African Blacks were 'nearer ready than were the slaves of San Domingo'. Looking back on *The Black Jacobins* from the 1970s, James wrote that he and others in the IASB believed that African independence could come only through armed revolt in both Europe and the colonies.[77] Or as Padmore wrote in *Controversy* in May 1928, because South Africa's future was tied to that of Europe, 'the native workers must close their ranks and prepare themselves, so that when the opportunity arrives they will be able to strike a decisive blow against the brutal system of Afrikander Imperialism.'[78]

Fiery though their rhetoric could be, the IASB writers were realistic about the limits of what they could say, as James suggested in a story he told about writing a little book called *A History of Negro Revolt* (1938) for Raymond Postgate's *Fact*, a monthly that featured one pamphlet-length article in each issue.[79] A former communist like Padmore, Postgate had invited Padmore to take on the assignment but Padmore had passed the job on to James. In the collaborative spirit that prevailed in this group, however, Padmore worked with James to produce the manuscript, and together they 'put in a number of provocative statements' they knew Postgate would take out. 'But by putting those and then agreeing to take them out, much really good stuff was sure to get in', James recalled.[80] Aware of the sensitivities of white British supporters, even in its own announcement of purpose the IASB tactfully asked for 'democratic rights, civil liberties', and – not independence – but 'self-determination'.[81] In truth, IASB members wanted more than constitutional rights within a colonial system. They regarded the colonial system itself as rotten to the core – meant not to civilise, as was so often claimed, but to exploit. They wanted self-government, and they wanted it on their own timetable, not whenever the British thought the colonies were ready to have it. They did not mean to wait until freedom was given. As James wrote later, they had 'complete confidence in the self-emancipation of the African people from imperialism'.[82]

This confidence was perhaps the African Bureau writers' greatest contribution at this point to African liberation. Their publications, like their speeches in Hyde Park, did not reach a wide audience in the 1930s. Their writing's impact on history lay elsewhere: in stiffening the backbone of their British sympathisers and shoring up their own self-assurance. Through writing and publishing together, James, Padmore, Kenyatta, Wallace Johnson, and their allies strengthened their common belief that they could bring into being a new, independent Africa. In the communal act of writing and publishing, they created an 'imagined community'[83] – an Africa free of imperial rule. They shared that vision with sympathetic audiences, reaching out through varied publications to multiple discursive communities, not only white British socialists and workers but also African Americans who read Padmore's articles in the *Crisis* as well as the *Pittsburgh Courier* and the *Chicago Defender* (where a tutor from his Howard days was an editor) – African-American newspapers to which he contributed almost weekly starting in 1938.[84]

They did not all imagine this new, independent Africa in the same way, as became clear when Secker and Warburg published Kenyatta's *Facing Mount Kenya*, which came out of the diploma thesis Kenyatta had written for the anthropologist Bronislaw Malinowski's seminars. Elspeth Huxley recalled Kenyatta as 'a favourite of Malinowski's, who gave him frequent opportunities to express his views. This he did with ease and virtuosity, never at a loss for the correct word. He had mastered the anthropological jargon perfectly.'[85] Still, according to Makonnen, Kenyatta needed assistance turning the work he had done for Malinowski into a publishable book. Kenyan Mbiyu (Peter) Koinange, who was studying at Cambridge after years of education in the United States, helped out, and Makonnen recalled thinking that one of the IASB members would arrange the essays in book form. In the end, though, it was Dinah Stock, a woman Kenyatta had met at a Trafalgar Square rally, who did that editorial work. Another of the series of English women who contributed to the bureau writers' publication efforts, Stock was secretary of the British Centre Against Imperialism and assistant editor of the *New Leader*; she had studied literature at Oxford. She finished the work in about three weeks.[86] There was some urgency about getting the manuscript into print. According to St Clair Drake, who later became closely acquainted with the Padmore circle, Kenyatta had heard that the white Kenyan L. S. B. Leakey meant to publish his own book, and Kenyatta hoped to pre-empt him. Thus Kenyatta's book was only partly completed when Warburg, at Fenner Brockway's suggestion, had a look at it. He saw its promise, and, encouraged by Malinowski's commitment to contribute an introduction (in which he attested to Kenyatta's competence as an anthropologist), Warburg offered Kenyatta more money for it than he had received for any other work he had done in Britain.[87]

Apparently a description of Kikuyu (Gikuyu) customs and beliefs, *Facing Mount Kenya*, published in 1938, the same year as *The Black Jacobins*, also struck overtly political notes. In his Preface, Kenyatta mentioned his activities on behalf of Kenya's land claims.[88] He devoted Chapter II to 'The Gikuyu System of Land Tenure' and presented land tenure 'as the most important factor in the social, political, religious, and economic life of the tribe'. Relying on Malinowski's understanding of indigenous culture as 'integrated', he implied that, in taking Kikuyu land, the British had undermined an entire way of life. He told the story of a Kikuyu medicine man who prophesied the coming of pale strangers who would bring sticks that could kill and an iron snake that arrows were defenceless against. The medicine man cautioned his fellow Kikuyu to mingle courtesy with suspicion since the strangers 'in the end would want to take everything from the Gikuyu'. When the Europeans arrived, however, the hospitable and innocent Kikuyu forgot the medicine man's cautions.[89]

Kenyatta then told another 'Gikuyu story' (of which he was the likely author) that illustrated the relations between Europeans and Africans. The story went like this. A man gave shelter to an elephant friend caught out in the rain, then the Elephant refused to leave. The man protested, but after intervention by the Lion and the appointment of a commission of enquiry, the man found himself dispossessed of his hut on the grounds that he had failed to put to use the 'undeveloped space' in his hut. In a parody of the rhetoric of colonisation, Kenyatta quoted the commission's conclusion: 'We consider that Mr Elephant has fulfilled his sacred duty of protecting your interests. As it is clearly for your good that the space should be put to its most economic use, and as you yourself have not reached the stage of expansion which would enable you to fill it, we consider it necessary to arrange a compromise to suit both parties.' The compromise: the man could find another site for his hut. He did that – several times, and Mr Rhinoceros, Mr Buffalo, Mr Leopard, and Mr Hyena took over one hut after another. As their huts fell into decay and the man built one final large hut, they rushed into it and began fighting among themselves for space. '[W]hile they were all embroiled together the man set the hut on fire and burnt it to the ground, jungle lords and all.'[90] Retelling the story many years later, Nigerian novelist Chinua Achebe saw in it 'a prophecy of the Kenya struggle for liberation, of the bitter armed rebellion the British called Mau Mau, the concessions they began to make thereafter, leading to independence under Jomo Kenyatta as Prime Minister in 1963'.[91]

Kenyatta ended the book with a reminder of the devastating blow the theft of land struck to the Kikuyu people.

> When the European comes to the Gikuyu country and robs the people of their land, he is taking away not only their livelihood, but the material symbol that holds family and tribe together. In doing this he gives one blow which cuts away the foundations from the whole of Gikuyu life, social, moral, and economic ... Along with his land they rob him of his government, condemn his religious ideas, and ignore his fundamental conceptions of justice and morals, all in the name of civilisation and progress.[92]

Reviewing *Facing Mount Kenya* for *International African Opinion*, James – demonstrating the ideological rifts within the IASB group – questioned Kenyatta's adherence to Kikuyu traditions. If the native peoples were to win their land back, they could not simply go back to living the way they had been living before the Europeans took their land away, adding here and there touches of European ways. 'When the land is won the African will have to modernise his method of production, and his religion will inevitably follow.'[93] Kenyatta and James had never seen politically eye to eye. Although Kenyatta had accepted education in Moscow and published articles in the British *Daily Worker*,[94] he was no Marxist, and in fact, after the Comintern's recent betrayal of the anti-imperial cause, Kenyatta was hostile towards Marxism altogether. James would lay out an argument for a policy in meticulous Trotskyist style, step by step, up to a conclusion, with Kenyatta apparently agreeing all the way, only to find Kenyatta in the end 'exactly where he was at the beginning' – unmoved.[95]

An 'ideological gulf' separated Kenyatta from James, St Clair Drake would say. 'Left-wing friends of Koinange and Kenyatta, whether black or white, found it difficult to understand why they so passionately defended the custom of female circumcision or clitoridectomy.' Pizer told Drake that neither Kenyatta's brush with Moscow nor Padmore's attempt to educate him turned him into a Marxist – 'He was always an unreconstructed Kikuyu tribalist.' Unlike Kenyatta, both James and Padmore – their own ties with African tradition attenuated by centuries in the New World – envisioned an Africa becoming more rather than less Western and leaving its tribal ways behind. Kenyatta had no such future in mind: he did not want to see Africa detribalised.[96] He dedicated the book to his son and daughter, named for his own parents: 'To Moigoi and Wamboi and all the dispossessed youth of Africa: for perpetuation of communion with ancestral spirits through the fight for African Freedom, and in the firm faith that the dead, the living, and the unborn will unite to rebuild the destroyed shrines.'

For his author's photo at the front of the book, Kenyatta wore a blue monkey cloak lent to him by Koinange and fingered the point of a spear – an implied threat. According to Koinange, the two of them experimented with syllables until they came up with a more African-sounding name than 'Johnstone' (although there is some evidence that Kenyatta used the name 'Jomo' earlier).[97] Despite the dashing photo, Malinowski's introduction, and the original material the book offered, the leading anthropology journals ignored the book, although it did receive attention in the political press. In the *New Leader*, Dinah Stock, who had helped produce it, said Kenyatta wrote 'like the spokesman of a people who have not yet been conquered'. In contrast, a reviewer who praised the book in the *New Statesman and Nation* described it as 'the protest of a deeply wronged people, whose traditional institutions are in decay'.[98] Sales were slight: just over five hundred copies, barely enough to cover Kenyatta's £30 advance, before a 1941 air raid destroyed the rest.[99] No American edition emerged until much later, during the Mau Mau rebellion, when Kenyatta had become a major political figure in Kenya.[100] The scholar Bruce Berman, examining the production and reception of *Facing Mount Kenya*, concluded that the book failed to achieve what Kenyatta had hoped: it had not established his right to speak as an authority for the Kikuyu.[101] However modest the impression *Facing Mount Kenya* made at the time, however, accounts by contemporaries suggest it did enlarge Kenyatta's presence on the London scene and inevitably enlarged his sense of himself as an iconic figure. Warburg would long remember the night Kenyatta came for dinner: 'There stood Kenyatta, tall, massively muscled, a high forehead over a bony face, curly black hair and beard close-cropped. Across his huge chest and over his right shoulder he wore a leopard skin; a long and dangerous spear was held in one hand. His appearance was magnificent.' Mrs Warburg invited him to set his spear in the corner and gave him a drink.[102]

In three years, IASB writers had explored a range of genres to build an enviable publication record. They had written and published six books – Padmore's *How Britain Rules Africa* and *Africa and World Peace*; James's *World Revolution, The Black Jacobins*, and *A History of Negro Revolt*, and Kenyatta's *Facing Mount Kenya* – and James had translated a seventh, Boris Souvarine's *Stalin*. They had published pamphlets and their own periodicals, along with articles in the publications of other organisations. They had sent letters to the editors of British papers. Padmore, the most experienced and prolific journalist among them and the one who both Makonnen and James considered the driving force behind the IASB, had taken their message to the world, supplying articles to magazines and newspapers in the United States, West Indies, and West Africa.

James later recalled the years before the Second World War as a time when '[m]any learned and important persons and institutions looked upon us and our plans and hopes for Africa as the fantasies of some politically illiterate West Indians'.[103] Makonnen recalled that the communists saw them as '"generals without an army, they have no base and must depend on their pens"'.[104] Their pens proved powerful: through their stream of publications they built a reputation as people to see in London if you were visiting from the colonies, or to confer with if you were a British politician with doubts about the colonial system. Their writing was important for another reason as well: diverse though their individual political views were, they were establishing both confidence and common ground for future action. Makonnen captured the elation they felt in the relatively free air of London. 'Despite the suffering of our people, there was never a gloomy moment, particularly when we realized how much we could do in

England: write any tract we wanted to; make terrible speeches; all this when you knew very well that back in the colonies even to say "God is love" might get the authorities after you!'[105] Speaking out in print, they had the support of Brockway, Warburg, and other sympathisers, and they drew on resources established by other organisations, but the creative energy and drive originated within the group itself. Its members were stimulated to act – and write – by the historic crossroads at which they found themselves: the dramatic failure of socialists and communists to hold the anti-imperialist line under the threat of war with Hitler, the left's failure to block Italy's takeover of Ethiopia, and the approaching war – an inevitable outcome, in their view, of capitalism and its twin, imperialism.

Padmore's former Howard University professor Ralph Bunche, who spent time with the IASB circle while he was studying under Malinowski in London in 1937, highlighted the opportunity afforded by the times when he observed in his diary, 'Greater bargaining power for Africans as result of war'.[106] He was right, and the IASB writers made the most of this opening in history. Relentlessly they pressed home the connection between imperialism and war. 'Whatever might have been the illusions of the British workers about Imperialism in the past', Padmore wrote in the *New Leader* of 25 February 1938, 'the mask is off to-day'. Japan, Italy, Germany were all 'Have-Not' powers seeking colonies from the 'Haves'. The consequence would be war, unending war unless capitalism was replaced with socialism. Thus, 'it is in the interest of the workers, who suffer most from war, to hasten the downfall of Imperialism by helping the colonial peoples in their struggle for national freedom'.[107]

In London, as war neared, the IASB was subjected to continued surveillance. Reporting on a Trafalgar Square rally in early May 1938, the Metropolitan Police noted Padmore's, Kenyatta's, and James's equation of British imperialism with German and Italian fascism in South Africa, Kenya – in fact, throughout the Empire.[108] While the Prime Minister Neville Chamberlain went back and forth to Germany in a last-ditch effort to keep Hitler's demand for Czechoslovakia from escalating into war, the IASB issued 'A Manifesto Against War' addressed to colonial peoples everywhere and deposited in Metropolitan Police files. 'You, the most oppressed and exploited, will soon be called upon to take part in a war which threatens the slaughter millions of men, women and children and bring ruin, misery and devastation on a scale undreamt of before.' This war would not be fought for democracy – 'Black brothers, what do we know of democracy?' Denouncing Europeans on both sides as 'imperialist exploiters', the IASB's executive committee called on 'our brothers everywhere' to prepare themselves to seize the opportunity war provided and press towards their only goal: 'INDEPENDENCE'.[109]

As war seemed ever more certain, Padmore wrote to Alain Locke on 3 October 1938 that 'every obstacle was put in our way for normal functioning'.[110] Friends in high places warned that, when war broke out, IASB leaders would be interned and their organisation suppressed.[111] Remembering the police sweep of his ITUC-NW office in Hamburg, Padmore sent IASB documents out of the country to locations where he thought they would be safe. He was working on another book on Africa – an urgent matter, he felt, since, as he told Locke, he expected Hitler to bring the colonial question 'very sharply onto the international scene'. Among his other demands, Hitler wanted the colonies Germany had lost during the First World War.[112] Padmore sent one copy of that manuscript to Locke at Howard, and another to the West Indies, both places, he thought, that would be neutral at least at the start of conflict.

Makonnen, ever resourceful, proposed that they move to Norway,[113] where Padmore had travelled in February 1938 to solicit Scandinavian support for the anti-colonial cause.[114] That idea did not materialise, but Padmore did set to work trying to get out of the country himself. His colleagues urged him to leave, he told Locke, 'so that I could continue to be of some service to our people in precisely the circumstances when they most need aid and advice'. The United States, where he had spent several years and still maintained ties, was a likely destination, but possibly out of the question. Back in the spring, wanting to lecture there and see his wife, Julia, he had actually applied for a visa and learned that the name on his passport, 'Malcolm Nurse', appeared on a blacklist of people who could not enter the country. There was a loophole: if he could find an American citizen to put up a bond on his behalf. He thought then of asking Locke 'or some of your friends' to sign a bond for him but had not done that yet.[115]

Now, in this hour of crisis, the best alternative he could think of was Haiti. The Haitian consul in London admired the bureau's work and was happy to give him a visa. But he needed money for the trip – he was virtually broke. As Londoners dug trenches in the parks and were fitted for gas masks,[116] Padmore was anxious to leave England before the borders were closed. He cabled Locke, asking for a loan; Locke sent him $100. By the time the money arrived Chamberlain had returned from Munich, and Britain no longer stood on the brink of war. 'For we are living in a period in which history moves faster even than communication through the earth, at least communications involving banking transactions', Padmore wrote to Locke on 3 October. 'And so here I am, sitting by my fire, writing you this letter in an atmosphere of relative calm, but still carrying on my shoulders the responsibilities of a great cause.'[117] The IASB, he wrote, was 'the most formidable anti-imperialist organisation co-ordinating the national liberation struggles among the Negroid peoples within the British, French and other European systems', and he was its chairman. Locke could see from the reviews the reception the British press had given his work. '[A]ll things considered, it has been good, for it requires a courageous man to indict the colonial system in this citadel of British Imperialism.' He was not bragging, really; he wanted Locke – a literary man and far away in the United States – to understand that he was not simply doing Padmore a personal favour when he sent him that $100. Now, given time he had thought he did not have, Padmore had decided to hold off on going to Haiti. Instead, he would try to get someone in the United States to take out a bond allowing him entry there. The same day that he wrote to Locke, he asked his Harlem friend Cyril Ollivierre to write him along these lines: 'Dear M. Glad to hear of your proposed trip. While here I shall be glad to entertain you as my guest.'[118]

As things turned out, Padmore stayed in London, but James sailed for the United States on 8 October 1938. According to *International African Opinion*, he went 'to recuperate from a serious illness and to undertake certain literary work'. The reasons for his trip to the US were more complex than that and have been variously stated by different narrators. Like Padmore, James wanted to get out of the country before the start of war might lead to his imprisonment as a subversive. He had had a standing invitation for some time to join the efforts of the American Socialist Workers Party. Trotsky encouraged him in that direction, in part, apparently, to remove him from the British scene, where James had too often deviated from the International Secretariat's party line. The break-up of James's relationship with Louise Cripps after her second abortion may have made him more willing to leave England.[119]

Remaining with Pizer in London, Padmore repeated his views on the war in the *New Leader* and, for the moment, published *International African Opinion* with Makonnen, Harrison, and another IASB member, Chris Jones, organiser of the Colonial Seamen's Union. The February–March 1939 issue carried an urgent appeal for financial help. Despite the fact that none of the IASB's officers received any compensation, the bureau's expenses had mounted up – £20 a month to publish the magazine, £48 to print five thousand copies of *West Indies Today* (much of that still unpaid), £31 for *Hands off the Protectorates*. 'Due to occasional confiscation of our literature by colonial governments ... many of the copies addressed to our branches and agencies in the colonies never reach their destination. Such suppression places additional financial burdens on our shoulders.' Readers could help by ordering the pamphlets, buying a subscription to *International African Opinion*, or sending donations to the Africa Service Bureau, 12A, Westbourne Grove, London, W.2. 'Your donation to keep INTERNATIONAL AFRICAN OPINION alive will be appreciated.'[120] The May–June issue would be the journal's last.

In the meantime, Padmore did still have a periodical outlet in Britain: the *New Leader*, where, despite the jeopardy in which he placed himself, he proclaimed, even after Germany seized Czechoslovakia, 'I am uncompromisingly opposed to Imperialist war'. Capitalists were simply, once again, squabbling among themselves over the spoils of imperialism. The only way to prevent a second world war was 'by getting rid of the capitalist war-mongers in the Fascist, as well as the so-called democratic, countries'.[121] Doing his part, in that summer of 1939 Padmore travelled to Paris for a European socialists' conference, spending the first night in what one observer called 'a dirty, down-and-out sixpenny dosshouse' until his ILP friend John McNair asked him to share his hotel room. Padmore spoke on the third day of the conference, with McNair translating. '[H]is English hearers were spellbound', McNair told Padmore's early biographer James R. Hooker. 'When I translated his speech fully into French it brought the house down ... [H]e had vision and imagination and his was the voice of the oppressed.'[122] With war nearing, however, on 14 August 1939 Parliament approved a law that would silence voices of the oppressed across the Empire: an Emergency Powers (Defence) Act imposed controls across a wide spectrum of British and colonial life.[123] One of its earliest victims was Wallace Johnson.

As in London and before that the Gold Coast and Nigeria, Wallace Johnson had injected new force into the Sierra Leone political scene. He founded a newspaper, the *African Standard*, and angered colonial authorities so much that they cast around for ways to rid themselves of him. They had just arrested him on a charge of criminal libel when Britain's declaration of war with Germany on 3 September 1939 gave them a pretext for stronger retaliation: they detained and interned him under the new emergency defence regulations.[124] Padmore publicised the arrest in the *New Leader*,[125] and Wallace Johnson's name appeared on a manifesto the IASB released in late November and published in the *New Leader*: a warning that, if the British expected the colonies to support this war, they needed to grant their colonies self-government. The manifesto delivered a dramatic call for action: 'Let Mr Chamberlain get up at Westminster and M. Daladier in the French Chamber of Deputies and issue a declaration to the world granting their colonies full democratic rights and self-government – Now!'[126] Padmore repeated the words of the manifesto as if they were his own (they likely were) in a *Crisis* article that same month and further said, 'As long as Britain and France reserve the right to rule over 500 million colored peoples and exploit their labour in the interests of plutocracy, they cannot expect Germany to be satisfied'.[127] Writing to American readers at a time when the British government was hoping for American support, Padmore in effect discouraged American participation in the war.

Without the promise of self-government of the colonies, the leading members of the IASB refused to enlist in a war effort on behalf of the Empire and feared arrest as a consequence. '[W]e expected all the time that they would come and put us away,' Makonnen recalled. 'They didn't, however, so we dispersed.' Kenyatta retreated with Dinah Stock to Storrington, a village in West Sussex, where he avoided military service by working on a farm. Makonnen moved to Manchester where he enrolled at Manchester University to study history – 'the Anglo-Saxon period, because I noticed that there were certain defects in my knowledge about the growth of the realm'. James sat out the war in the United States. Koinange, his studies finished, had returned to Kenya in 1938. Padmore remained in London, partly perhaps because he was suffering from a throat condition and relied on a trusted physician there.[128] He tried to publish the manuscript he had sent off earlier for safekeeping, but the very crisis that made it timely dimmed the likelihood it would see print. A reader for the publisher George Allen and Unwin observed of *The Black Man's Burden in Africa*, 'Whether it is wise or even practicable to publish what is in effect anti-British propaganda at the present time seems to me more than doubtful; Mr Padmore should have spoken earlier – or hereafter; there would have been a time for such a word. But now?'[129] The stream of publications that had given the IASB its coherence and public presence had all but ceased. The IASB community was breaking up under the force of war.

Notes

1. C. L. R. James, 'Notes on the Life of George Padmore', carbon copy, typescript with author's corrections, microform (Chicago, IL: Center for Research Libraries, 1959), pp. 30–1a.
2. James, 'Notes', pp. 3–4.
3. James R. Hooker, *Black Revolutionary: George Padmore's Path from Communism to Pan-Africanism* (New York, Washington and London: Praeger, 1970; first published 1967), p. 2.
4. Kelvin Singh, *Race and Class: Struggles in a Colonial State, Trinidad 1916–1945* (Calgary: University of Calgary Press, and Kingston: The Press-University of West Indies, 1994), pp. 35–6.
5. *Ibid.*, pp. 45, 53.

6   Hooker, *Black Revolutionary*, pp. 3–4.
7   James, 'Notes', p. 5.
8   C. L. R. James, 'Appendix: From Toussaint L'Ouverture to Fidel Castro', in *The Black Jacobins: Toussaint L'Ouverture and the San Domingo Revolution* (London: Allison and Busby, 1994), p. 402.
9   C. L. R. James, *Beyond a Boundary* (Durham: Duke University Press, 1993), p. 110.
10 *Ibid.*, pp. 115–21.
11 Louise Cripps, *C. L. R. James: Memories and Commentaries* (New York and London: Cornwall Books, 1997), pp. 11–13.
12 *Ibid.*, pp. 32–3.
13 Jeremy Murray-Brown, *Kenyatta*, Second edition (London: George Allen and Unwin, 1979), p. 197.
14 James, 'Appendix', *Black Jacobins*, p. 402; italics James's.
15 James, 'Notes', p. 31a.
16 Ras Makonnen, *Pan-Africanism from Within*, recorded and edited by Kenneth King (Nairobi, London, New York: Oxford University Press, 1973), pp. 102, 105–12, 118.
17 D., 'Abyssinia-1935 and 1940', *New Leader* (1 February 1941), 8.
18 Makonnen, *Pan-Africanism*, p. 118.
19 Moorland-Spingarn Research Center, Howard University, Nkrumah Papers, Box 154–7, Folder 52 (Dorothy Padmore), letter, Ivar Holm to Dorothy Padmore [Pizer], 4 April 1962.
20 George Padmore, *Africa and World Peace*, Second edition (London: Frank Cass, 1972, first published 1937), p.155.
21 Stephen Howe, *Anticolonialism in British Politics: The Left and the End of Empire, 1918–1964* (Oxford: Clarendon Press, 1993), p. 86; 'The Abyssinian Debate', *New Leader* (17 April 1936), 4.
22 Robert Wuthnow describes nineteenth-century socialists tapping the resources of 'more established institutions' in *Communities of Discourse: Ideology and Social Structure in the Reformation, the Enlightenment, and European Socialism* (Cambridge, MA and London: Harvard University Press, 1989), p. 364. Paul Anderson gives the membership numbers in 'Introduction' in Anderson (ed.), *Orwell in Tribune* (London: Politico's, 2006), p. 8.
23 Fredric Warburg, *An Occupation for Gentlemen* (Boston: Houghton Mifflin Company; Cambridge: The Riverside Press, 1960), pp. 182, 206.
24 Kent Worcester, *C. L. R. James: A Political Biography* (New York: State University of New York Press, 1996), p. 43.
25 Cripps, *C. L. R. James*, p. 47.
26 C. L. R. James, *World Revolution, 1916–1936* (Westport, CT: Hyperion Press, 1973; reprint of London: Martin Secker and Warburg, 1937), p. 421.
27 Padmore, *Africa and World Peace*, p. 271.
28 Warburg, *Occupation*, p. 206.
29 'Correspondence', *Fight* (June 1937), 11. See *Fight: Facsimile Edition of British Trotskyist Journals of the 1930s* (Gothenburg: S.L. Publications, 1999).
30 The review, 'World Revolution', appeared in May 1937, p. 16; the advertisement appeared in April 1937, p. 13, with a further promotional note, 'A Book to Read', on p. 14.
31 For Warburg's comments on James's and Padmore's book sales see *Occupation*, pp. 215–16. For a description of Stafford Cripps's political views and activity at this time see Anderson, 'Introduction', *Orwell in* Tribune, pp. 7–11.
32 Jeremy Murray-Brown, *Kenyatta*, p. 183; Bruce Berman, 'Ethnography as Politics, Politics as Ethnography: Kenyatta, Malinowski, and the Making of *Facing Mount Kenya*', *Canadian Journal of African Studies*, 30: 3 (1996), 326.
33 Locke Papers, Box 164–76, Folder 16, Padmore to Locke, 17 December 1936.
34 Hooker, *Black Revolutionary*, p. 43.
35 Padmore Papers, Padmore to Ollivierre, 30 March 1938.
36 Cunard Papers, Box 17, Folder 10, D. Padmore [Pizer] to N. Cunard, 28 April 1961.

St Clair Drake identified Pizer as Jewish and energetic in George Shepperson and St Clair Drake, 'Fifth Pan-African Conference, 1945 and the All African People's Congress, 1958', *Contributions in Black Studies*, 8 (1986–87), 46.

37 Padmore, *Africa and World Peace*, p. 9.
38 Padmore Papers, Padmore to Ollivierre, 3 March 1938.
39 Blyden Cowart, Padmore's daughter, told me on 29 March 2008 that Padmore and Julia had not got a divorce.
40 For a description of her financial support and other contributions to Padmore's writing see James, 'Notes', pp. 54–5.
41 Makonnen, *Pan-Africanism*, p. 118. For information on the Africa Bureau, a different organisation, see Howe, *Anticolonialism*, p. 198.
42 A biographical report on Kenyatta prepared by the British Criminal Investigative Department calls Wallace Johnson the organiser of the IASB; see Donald C. Savage, 'Jomo Kenyatta, Malcolm MacDonald and the Colonial Office 1938–39: Some Documents from the P.R.O.', *Canadian Journal of African Studies*, 3: 3 (Autumn 1969), 628. Henry Lee Moon described Wallace Johnson as charming in 'British Imperial Rule Defied by African Unionist at World Parley', *Chicago Defender* (14 April 1945), 4.
43 Leo Spitzer and LaRay Denzer, 'I. T. A. Wallace Johnson and the West African Youth League', *International Journal of African Historical Studies*, 6: 3 (1973), 418; Hooker, *Black Revolutionary*, p. 17; Edward Thomas Wilson, *Russia and Black Africa before World War II* (New York and London: Holmes and Meier, 1974), p. 217.
44 Stanley Shaloff, 'Press Controls and Sedition Proceedings in the Gold Coast, 1933–39', *African Affairs*, 71: 284 (July 1972), 244–5; Spitzer and Denzer, 'I. T. A. Wallace Johnson', 419–22; 440–2.
45 United Kingdom / The National Archives (UK/TNA), CO 323/1517/2, Colonel Sir Vernon Kell to F. J. Howard, 21 June 1937.
46 UK/TNA, MEPO38/91/99495, Metropolitan Police, 'Special Report: Wallace Johnson', 6 July 1937. Material in the National Archives in the copyright of the Metropolitan Police is reproduced by permission of the Metropolitan Police Authority.
47 Copy in UK/TNA CO847/11/16. Hooker identifies Sorenson as a Bureau patron in *Black Revolutionary*, p. 49.
48 UK/TNA, CO847/11/16, 'Extract from Minutes of the Meeting of the Executive Council held at Government House, Christiansborg, Accra, on Friday, 10 September, 1937 at 10 a.m.'
49 UK/TNA, CO847/11/16, untitled statement, unsigned.
50 UK/TNA, CO847/11/16, letter from Government House, Accra; indecipherable signature, to W. Ormsby-Gore, 26 February 1938.
51 UK/TNA, CO847/11/16, Wallace Johnson to Under Secretary of State for the Colonies, 10 January 1938.
52 UK/TNA, CO847/11/16, W. Ormsby Gore to The Officer Administering the Government of [left blank in original document], 17 February 1938.
53 'Gold Coast Youth Reviews Working-Class Conditions in Colonial Empire', *African Sentinel* (October–November 1937), 8–9.
54 Spitzer and Denzer, 'I. T. A. Wallace Johnson', 450–1.
55 *Ibid.*, 566.
56 Makonnen, *Pan-Africanism*, pp. 160–1.
57 'African Group Wants Native Rights Upheld', *Chicago Defender* (1 October 1938), 24; see also Padmore, 'Labour Unrest in Jamaica', *International African Opinion*, 1: 1 (July 1938), posted in the Marxist Internet Archive, www.marxists.org/archive/padmore/1938/unrest-jamaica.htm, accessed 10 May 2008. Other periodical articles and pamphlets by Padmore and James during this period are available in the Marxist Internet Archive, www.marxists.org.
58 Robert L. Tignor, *W. Arthur Lewis and the Birth of Development Economics* (Princeton and Oxford: Princeton University Press, 2006), pp. 19, 34–5, 53.

59 C. L. R. James, *Nkrumah and the Ghana Revolution* (Westport, CT: Lawrence Hill and Company, 1977), p. 65.
60 James, 'Notes', p. 37.
61 Padmore, 'Fascism in the Colonies', *Controversy*, 2: 17 (February 1938), 94–7; 'An Outrageous Report', *Controversy*, 2: 18 (March 1938), 103–4; 'White Workers and Black', *Controversy*, 2: 20 (May 1938), 152–3; 'The Government's Betrayal of the Protectorates', *Controversy*, 2: 21 (June 1938), 166–8; Makonnen, 'Pendant to Padmore, II: 20 (May 1938), unnumbered last page.
62 J. R. Campbell and H. Wicks, 'Lunacy or Logic? Two Views of One Book', *Controversy*, 1: 8 (May 1938), 36–7; Dorothy Pizer, 'A Lesson in Revolution', *Controversy*, 38 (January 1939), 318–20.
63 Jomo Kenyatta, 'Democracy in Kenya', *Left*, 38 (November 1939), 296–9.
64 Inside back covers, *Controversy*, May and August 1938.
65 'Editorial', *International African Opinion* (July 1938), 3.
66 Makonnen, *Pan-Africanism*, p. 119.
67 Murray-Brown, *Kenyatta*, p. 107; UK/TNA, CO533/513/13, Neil Stewart, Superintendent Criminal Investigation Department, 'Secret. Jomo @Johnstone Kenyatta'. The document is also reprinted in Savage, 'Jomo Kenyatta, Malcolm MacDonald and the Colonial Office 1938–39: Some Documents', pp. 627–9.
68 Padmore, *Pan Africanism or Communism?*, p. 150.
69 Makonnen, *Pan-Africanism*, p. 119.
70 James, 'Notes', p. 35.
71 Makonnen, *Pan-Africanism*, p. 120.
72 Elspeth Huxley, *Out in the Midday Sun: My Kenya* (London: Pimlico, 2000), p. 196.
73 Warburg, *Occupation*, p. 214.
74 Cripps, *C. L. R. James*, pp. 48–50.
75 Pizer, 'A Lesson in Revolution', *Controversy* (January 1939), 318.
76 'The Black Jacobins of San Domingo's Revolution', *New York Times* (11 December 1938), 111.
77 C. L. R. James, *Nkrumah*, pp. 68–9; *The Black Jacobins*, p. 376. See also Robert A. Hill's discussion of *The Black Jacobins*, 'In England, 1932–1938', in Paul Buhle (ed.), *C. L. R. James: His Life and Work* (London and New York: Allison and Busby, 1986), pp. 61–80.
78 Padmore, 'White Workers and Black', *Controversy*, 2: 20 (May 1938), Marxist Internet Archive, www.marxists.org/archive/padmore/1938/white-workers-black.htm, accessed 10 May 2008.
79 John and Mary Postgate describe the magazine in *A Stomach for Dissent: The Life of Raymond Postgate: 1896–1971* (Keele: Keele University Press, 1994), pp. 198–200; see also Paul Anderson, 'Introduction', *Orwell in* Tribune, p. 19. *A History of Negro Revolt* was published by *Fact* in the September 1938 issue and was also published in the US by Haskell House Publishers (1938).
80 James, 'Notes', p. 37.
81 UK/TNA, MEPO 38/91/99495, printed mission statement, 'The International African Service Bureau'.
82 James, 'Notes', p. 37; James, *Nkrumah*, p. 68.
83 The phrase comes from Benedict Anderson, *Imagined Communities: Reflections on the Origin and Spread of Nationalism* (London and New York: Verso, 1983). For analysis of how publishing activities strengthen political communities' sense of purpose, see Susan Herbst, *Politics at the Margin: Historical Studies in Public Expression Outside the Mainstream* (Cambridge: Cambridge University Press, 1994), especially Chapter 1, 'Politics, Expression, and Marginality'.
84 Penny M. Von Eschen, *Race Against Empire: Black Americans and Anticolonialism, 1936–1957* (Ithaca, NY and London: Cornell University Press, 1997), p. 13. Hooker mentions the Howard tutor Metz Lochard in 'Africa for Afro-Americans: Padmore and the Black Press', *Radical America*, 2: 4 (July–August 1968), 5.
85 Huxley, *Out in the Midday Sun*, p. 196.

'GENERALS WITHOUT AN ARMY'

86 Makonnen, *Pan-Africanism*, p. 162. In his Preface, Kenyatta also thanks Dr Raymond Firth for his advice on the manuscript and his brother Moigai for checking information and providing photographs; Jomo Kenyatta, *Facing Mount Kenya: The Tribal Life of the Gikuyu* (London: Secker and Warburg, 1959; first published 1938), xvii.
87 Malinowski, 'Introduction', *Facing Mount Kenya*, p. viii; St Clair Drake, 'Mbiyu Koinange and the Pan-African Movement', in Robert A. Hill (ed.), *Pan-African Biography* (Los Angeles: African Studies Center, University of California / Crossroads Press, 1987), p. 174; Makonnen, *Pan-Africanism*, p. 162; Warburg, *Occupation*, p. 251.
88 Kenyatta, *Facing Mount Kenya*, pp. xx–xxi.
89 *Ibid.*, pp. 21, 43–4.
90 *Ibid.*, pp. 46–52.
91 Chinua Achebe, *Home and Exile* (Oxford and New York: Oxford University Press, 2000), p. 67.
92 Kenyatta, *Facing Mount Kenya*, pp. 317–18.
93 C. L. R. James, 'The Voice of Africa', *International African Opinion* (August 1938), 3.
94 Murray-Brown, *Kenyatta*, p. 120.
95 James, 'Notes', p. 31.
96 Drake, 'Mbiyu Koinange', pp. 175–7.
97 Berman, 'Ethnography as Politics', 342, n. 27.
98 Warburg, *Occupation*, p. 252; Dinah Stock, 'An African Describes His Own People', *New Leader* (1 July 1938), 7; H. N. Brailsford, 'An African on African Life', *New Statesman and Nation* 16: 395 (17 September 1938), 420.
99 Berman, 'Ethnography as Politics', 338–9; also source for failure of anthropology journals to review the book.
100 Warburg, *Occupation*, p. 252.
101 Berman, 'Ethnography as Politics', 338.
102 Warburg, *Occupation*, pp. 253–4.
103 James, 'Appendix', *Black Jacobins*, p. 399.
104 Makonnen, *Pan-Africanism*, p. 159.
105 *Ibid.*, p. 123.
106 Brian Urquhart, *Ralph Bunche: An American Life* (New York, London: W. W. Norton, 1993), p. 69.
107 Padmore, 'Hands off the Colonies', *New Leader* (25 February 1938), 2.
108 UK/TNA, MEPO 38/91/99495, Metropolitan Police, 'Special Report,' 8 May 1938.
109 UK/TNA, MEPO 38/91/99495.'INTERNATIONAL AFRICAN SERVICE BUREAU MANIFESTO AGAINST WAR', undated but accompanied by a letter from the Chief Constable, Metropolitan Police, 28 September 1938 (MEPO 38/91/99495). A similar manifesto titled 'A Warning to the Colonial Peoples' was issued by the IASB and the British Centre Against Imperialism on 29 August 1939 (MEPO 38/91/99495).
110 Locke Papers, Box 164–76, Folder 16, Padmore to Locke, 3 October 1938.
111 Murray-Brown, *Kenyatta*, p. 209.
112 A book that captures the urgency of the colonial question at this time is S. Fowler Wright's *Should We Surrender Colonies?* (London: Readers Library, n.d.)
113 Murray-Brown, *Kenyatta*, p. 209.
114 ANP, 'Tells Scandinavians of US Color Status,' *Atlanta Daily World* (7 February 1938), 1.
115 Locke Papers, Box 164–76, Folder 16, Padmore to Locke, 3 October 1938; also, Murray-Brown, *Kenyatta*, p. 209, says that Makonnen 'made arrangements for four of them, including Kenyatta, to move to Norway'.
116 Philip Ziegler, *London at War, 1939–1945* (London: Pimlico, 2002), pp. 16–17.
117 Locke Papers, Box 164–76, Folder 16, Padmore to Locke, 3 October 1938.
118 Padmore Papers, Padmore to Ollivierre, 3 October 1938.
119 Cripps, *C. L. R. James*, pp. 76–9; Al Richardson, Preface, *Fight: Facsimile edition*, unnumbered page; Worcester, *James*, p. 50.

120 'Appeal to Our Readers', *International African Opinion* (February–March 1939), 3.
121 Padmore, 'Why I Oppose Conscription', *New Leader* (2 June 1939), 4.
122 Hooker, *Black Revolutionary*, pp. 56–7.
123 Ziegler, *London at War*, p. 33.
124 Leo Spitzer and LaRay Denzer, 'I. T. A. Wallace Johnson and the West African Youth League. Part II: The Sierra Leone Period, 1938–1945', *International Journal of African Historical Studies*, 6: 4 (1973), 596.
125 Padmore, 'Police Swoop on Workers' Leaders in Colonies', *New Leader* (20 October 1939), 2.
126 African Workers Ask "What Can the Blacks Know of Democracy?"', *New Leader* (24 November 1939), 3.
127 Padmore, 'The Second World War and the Darker Races', *Crisis*, 36: 11 (November 1939), 328.
128 Makonnen, *Pan-Africanism*, p. 133; Murray-Brown, *Kenyatta*, pp. 206–11; James describes Padmore's refusal to serve in the British army, 'Notes', p. 48.
129 Reading University Library, Records of George Allen and Unwin Ltd, AVRR 10/1/97, reader's report signed B.M.

CHAPTER THREE

Writing while the bombs fall

Night after night in September 1940, German bombers pounded London, shattering buildings and setting off fires. St Bride Street, where the *New Leader* had its offices, was hard hit: a high-explosive bomb struck the *Evening Standard* building, not five hundred yards from the *New Leader*'s offices. The *New Leader* kept publishing but against heavy odds. The paper's prewar printer had refused to go on printing the anti-war *New Leader* after war began; now it was printed up in Leicester, and just getting the copy and layouts to St Pancras station could mean dashing through air raids in the dark only to find the station clerks had gone off to a shelter. One such mid-September Monday, it took half an hour at the dark station to locate a porter who took charge of the *New Leader* packet. Bundles from one printing were lost in a jumble of packages sprawled across three platforms at St Pancras. 'We know our readers will understand our difficulties', *New Leader* editor Fenner Brockway wrote in the issue for 19 September 1940. 'Even this short article has twice been interrupted by raids, partly written above ground, partly in a cellar. We stay above until the 'planes and gun-fire are close; then go below.'[1]

Despite the sixteen weeks of intensive bombing during the Battle of Britain, the *New Leader* did not waver from the anti-war stance it had maintained while German troops moved into Norway, Denmark, the Netherlands, Belgium, and France. The way to peace, in the Independent Labour Party's view, passed through revolution. If British workers were to take control of their government, workers on the continent would be inspired to take control of theirs. In preparation for that day, the ILP collected equipment to broadcast news of the revolution to the continent.[2]

In that summer when revolution seemed possible, George Padmore called for self-government of the colonies as an essential step towards it. '[T]he liberation of the colonial peoples ... from the fetters of Imperialism is an essential prerequisite for the victory of the Social Revolution, which ALONE can defeat Fascism', he wrote in the *New Leader*.[3] With the leadership of the IASB dispersed, Padmore relied increasingly on publications associated with the Independent Labour Party as forums for his views. For a while he both wrote for *Left* and served as its co-editor, and throughout the war scarcely a month of the *New Leader* went by without a Padmore contribution, his identity sometimes underscored with a drawing or a photograph paired with a descriptive phrase: 'the best known of African spokesmen' or 'Socialist Leader of Colonial Peoples'.[4] A diligent reader of the colonial press, he became a conduit for views expressed there (including those by Azikiwe's *West African Pilot*) in a *New Leader* roundup of colonial opinion on the war.[5]

He also passed along news from the colonies to American newspapers. The *New York Amsterdam Star-News* identified him in May 1940 as its London correspondent, and he wrote regularly as well for other African-American newspapers throughout the war. Historian Patrick S. Washburn has counted 575 Padmore bylines in the *Pittsburgh Courier* and *Chicago Defender* – newspapers with a combined weekly circulation of half a million – from December 1941 to May 1945. Some articles were about African-American troops, especially in Britain, but a majority threw the spotlight elsewhere, for instance on Ethiopia, the West Indies, South Africa, India, French Equatorial Africa, the Gold Coast, and Nigeria. In addition to running his bylined articles, African-American newspapers quoted articles he had written for the *New Leader* and the *Crisis*, the NAACP's magazine, where he had settled in as a long-term contributor.[6] During his communist days Padmore had regarded the NAACP with scorn as a bourgeois reformist organisation; now, he took his American audience where he found it with the hope of strengthening the ties that joined peoples of colour everywhere. After President Franklin D. Roosevelt agreed in 1941 to give Britain used destroyers in exchange for long-term air and naval bases on British territory from British Guiana to Newfoundland, Padmore disapproved of the deal but wrote to his former Howard professor Alain Locke that he hoped America's alliance with Britain would lead to a closer relationship between Afro-Americans and Afro-West Indians. He suggested founding a joint society modelled on the Anglo-Saxon English Speaking Union. The society would provide scholarships in the States for West Indians and sponsor lectures, studies, and a journal to popularise the project. He wished he could donate $100 to get it started, 'But as you know, men of ideas seldom have the next meal guaranteed, so I'll have to leave it to some fairy godfather to finance. In the meanwhile I console myself with the satisfaction of having lived to see historic events throwing our peoples together.'[7]

Satisfactions were few enough that April of 1941. More than a thousand people died in an attack 16 April 1941. 'It was hell', Padmore wrote on 18 April to his New York friend Cyril Ollivierre. 'I never expected to see daylight. And when it broke – God be praised!' A night later, the bombers returned for another devastating attack. Again, more than a thousand died, and thousands were left homeless. Minimal coverage of both nights of bombing appeared in *The Times*. Wartime censorship rules prohibited the press from publishing anything that might help enemy forces, and periodicals that violated that prohibition could be shut down. Although the government rarely even threatened to invoke a wartime rule against fomenting opposition, it did close the communist *Daily Worker* in January 1941 for a year and a half.[8] Nearly a thousand delegates from 640 organisations gathered in London in June 1941 for a conference on freedom of the press. They condemned defence regulations giving the home secretary authority to ban newspapers without trial. They also criticised censorship in the colonies and in India and indirect censorship in England by wholesalers who, Fenner Brockway told the delegates, were boycotting the *New Leader*.[9] The *New Leader* took another blow when a bomb destroyed the office on St Bride Street. Relocating on Regent's Park Road, editors put out calls to readers to provide more than £1,000 needed to set up in the new location.[10]

The war made journalists' jobs harder than ever just at a time when readers had more reason than ever to want to know what was happening in the world. An article Padmore sent to the *New York Amsterdam News* was censored,[11] and, after black and white American troops arrived in Britain, Americans posted at the Ministry of Information blocked his long cable to the *Pittsburgh Courier* and *Chicago Defender* describing how American southerners' racial prejudice was affecting Britain. Only after a talk with the censor and cuts in the cable was he able to get it through.[12] In June 1943, the US National Censorship Office intercepted Padmore correspondence with the *Crisis*.[13] News from the colonies was also disrupted. Kenyatta, who had moved with Dinah Stock to the Sussex village Storrington, was not even getting news from the Kikuyu Central Association, which he represented in England. Its leaders had been arrested when the association was banned in May 1939, and a little more than two years later Kenyatta wrote to Arthur Creech Jones, a Labour Party Member of Parliament who specialised in colonial affairs, 'I have had no news from Kenya for over a year'.[14]

Some news, however, did trickle through. Padmore wrote in the *New Leader* on 5 July 1941, 'Despite the most rigid censorship of news from the Colonies, from time to time reports about what is going on in the Colonial Empire reach the outside world'. He would not endanger his sources by revealing them but vouched for the authenticity of the news he was about to share – labour upheaval in Sierra Leone, socialists in the West Indies imprisoned, two Irish women locked away in a military camp in Trinidad for expressing 'views detrimental to the war effort'. One of them escaped but was 'found drowned in the harbour'.[15]

Padmore's old friend and colleague Nancy Cunard was in Trinidad at that point and possibly provided that information. She had gone to Trinidad from Mexico in the hopes that she could catch a ship back to England. Ship travel was not only hazardous but also hard to book at a time when ships were needed to transport troops and supplies. She could have shipped out on a tanker if she had been a man, she reflected, but she wasn't, and so she spent several months waiting for passage. Travelling through the West Indies, she met people who would bring out from hiding their copies of her anthology, *Negro*, which had been banned. 'Whenever the name of Padmore came up, it was spoken with the greatest admiration, and not only by his friends, but by all kinds of people who had never seen him, but knew about his writing and other work', she recalled later. She thought the authorities worried about his influence, and she believed that her friendship with him, along with her own record, helped account for their interest in her own activities.[16]

She finally arrived in England in August 1941, travelling in a convoy of ships that crossed Prime Minister Winston Churchill's path. Churchill was returning from Argentia Bay, off Newfoundland, where he had held a secret meeting with President Roosevelt to formulate their common war aims. Out of that meeting came the Atlantic Charter, a banner of hope to colonial people. Affirming American and British respect for 'the right of all peoples to choose the form of Government under which they live', the charter maintained that, where those rights had been taken away, they should be restored. Could this not be read as a promise for self-determination in the colonies? Churchill set the record straight in an address to the House of Commons: 'At the Atlantic meeting we had in mind, primarily, the restoration of the sovereignty, self-government and national life of the states and nations of Europe now under the Nazi yoke.' The issue of self-government for the Empire's subjects was a different matter altogether. In Nigeria, Azikiwe's *West African Pilot* expressed astonishment that the prime minister could say such a thing 'during an unparalleled destructive war which has cost Colonial peoples their material resources and manpower ... What, now, must we expect to be our fate after the war?'[17] Despite Churchill's effort to take them back, the words of the Atlantic Charter had been spoken, and they became a strong arguing point for Padmore and other opponents of the colonial system, including African Americans who read Padmore's articles on the Charter in the African-American press.[18]

Soon after Cunard arrived in London and blacked out the windows of her flat with Padmore's help, she, Pizer, and Padmore set to work to press the point home in a pamphlet: *The White Man's Duty: An Analysis of the Colonial Question in the Light of the Atlantic Charter*. Cunard would remember Padmore arriving at a pub on Tottenham Court Road 'with stacks of paper under his arm, exhausted but valiant'.[19] During their conversations on this little book, Cunard posed questions to Padmore and he responded, while Pizer took notes and offered suggestions. Pizer and Padmore seemed to Cunard 'a superb team', and (as she told Pizer later) 'often did I think how good it was that you had found each other, for you seemed to complete each other and there was harmony between [you], and, when at work, such admirable competence'.[20]

While the three of them worked together, events underlined the pamphlet's central message: that if Britain wanted to win this war, it had better grant at least the promise of self-government to its colonial subjects. In December, launching attacks on the United States at Pearl Harbour and the Philippines, Japan opened a strong offensive across south-east Asia and the Pacific.[21] One by one, British colonies fell to the Japanese. Hong Kong surrendered on Christmas Day 1941. Japan occupied Malaya except for Singapore Island by the end of January; Singapore acknowledged defeat on 15 February 1942. Writing in *The Times*, Margery Perham, the colonial British scholar who had reviewed Padmore's *How Britain Rules Africa*, described the seismic shift these defeats brought about. In the wake of the Asian defeats, she said the time had come for Britain to build 'a new and more intimate and generous relationship' with the Empire's peoples. She did not yet suggest, however, that Britain give up its Empire.[22]

Such stopping short of the obvious conclusion was all too typical, to Padmore's way of thinking. Reviewing two new books on the colonial system, the Christian socialist Norman Leys's *Colour Bar in East Africa* and Rita Hinden's *Plan for Africa* (which set out the Fabian Society's colonial policy), he remarked on the failure of even left-wing critics of the Empire to take the next logical step: support for self-government.[23] Padmore took that step, repeatedly. Writing in the *Crisis* in July 1942, he asked how the British could expect the people of Singapore to rise up in defence of a regime in which they played no part. By this time the Japanese had occupied Burma, with the help of Burmese nationalists.[24] The loss of Burma opened Japan's path to India, whose people, resources, and industries were essential to the British war effort. The Japanese assault had precipitated a 'Crisis in the British Empire', as the title of the *Crisis* article and a Padmore series in the *New Leader* proclaimed.[25]

Indian nationalists had hoped the crisis would force Britain to give them self-government, and their hopes rose higher when the government sent Nehru's friend Sir Stafford Cripps to India in March with a proposal. Cripps was a socialist who had written a preface to Padmore's *Africa and World Peace* and helped Padmore out financially, but when Cripps made the government's offer – a promise of dominion status after the war – he lost Padmore's good opinion of him.[26] Gandhi dismissed Cripps's offer as 'a post-dated cheque on a bank that was failing', and responded with a 'Quit India' campaign that resulted in his arrest and that of all top leaders of the Indian National Congress. Within months, at least sixty thousand Indians had been imprisoned, and British planes bombed Indian towns where resistance surfaced. Here, to Padmore, was evidence that 'Imperialism's final resort is to force'. The imprisonment of Gandhi was folly, he and Cunard said in *White Man's Duty* (which bore both their names as co-authors). 'Gandhi was the one person who could have kept the masses in leash; without him there is danger of the people rushing ahead ... [A]ny time the Japanese decide to attack they will meet a population not merely apathetic but actively hostile to the British.' Liberty is a powerful motivator. 'If the people of India and the Colonies are to be asked to throw their full weight into this conflict they must be given that incentive.' The British government ought to declare the right of the Empire's people to self-determination, a policy 'in itself just, and consistent also with the Atlantic Charter'.[27] Padmore and Cunard called for a promise that, when the war was over, the colonies would be free. Yet they implied the former colonies would still be partners with Britain – equal partners in a 'new Commonwealth of Nations'. What they meant by that Padmore made clear in a September 1941 article in *Left*: the transformation of the empire into 'federated commonwealths based upon Socialist principles'.[28]

Completing their manuscript near the end of 1942, Padmore and Cunard set about finding a publisher, a challenge that wartime paper shortages made daunting even while demand for books soared – partly, Padmore thought, because books were among the few items people could buy without coupons.[29] While tens of thousands of books were destroyed by bombing, fewer books could be published, not only because paper was rationed but also because labour was scarce. Even small publishers like the Woolfs' Hogarth Press, which had published C. L. R. James, were suffering. Woolf recalled the war years as 'a publishing nightmare'. Hogarth relied financially on books that sold steadily, if modestly; keeping those books in print used most of the press's paper allotment, with little left over for new books. As the war went on, readers became increasingly desperate for books. Publishers found they could sell anything they already had on hand.[30] This was not much solace for writers who had new books they wanted published, especially lesser known writers like Padmore and Cunard – or a young writer of European and black African ancestry, Peter Abrahams, who joined Padmore in London during the war.

Abrahams had shipped out of South Africa as a seaman in the hopes, like Padmore and James, of finding freedom to be a writer in England. He would recall how a teacher had laughed when he said one day in class that he wanted to be a writer so he could have 'cakes and ginger beer for breakfast, and fish and chips for lunch, and whole fowl at night'. That afternoon he fainted and spent the next several weeks in the hospital, treated for starvation.[31] He had eventually gone to college, given speeches, demonstrated, written articles for newspapers, and consorted with Trotskyists, Stalinists, and unionists. He had published a book of poetry and begun to write novels, although he had not yet published any. He had worked his way to England on a ship dodging submarines up the African coast from the Cape of Good Hope. A slight, lean twenty-one-year-old, his muscles taut from stoking the ship's furnace, he was glad to be in London, even with the bombs falling. The day he arrived (in either 1940 or 1941 – he gives both dates in different memoirs) was foggy and cold. When he found no one at the flat where he hoped to stay the night, he climbed a slope at Hampstead Heath and felt so at home that he stretched out under a big tree with his head on his suitcase and fell asleep. He awoke as the sun was setting. Though he saw people on the heath, they did not seem to mind his presence or the fact that he slept there at twilight.[32]

He went off again to the flat where a woman he had known in South Africa lived with three friends. They gave him tea and he studied the titles of the Left Book Club editions on their bookshelf, among them George Orwell's *Down and Out in Paris and London*. They found him a job at a communist book distribution centre and a room in a comrade's flat. Settling into London, Abrahams soon met Padmore, who was carrying on business as usual, pounding out despatches on a worn office typewriter that could make multiple copies. Working at a big table buried in papers and books, Padmore or Pizer would type an article through twice on thin paper, yielding a dozen or more copies, which Padmore would mail out to little magazines and newspapers around the world with the request: 'Please pass on to other periodicals'. To Abrahams, looking back, 'that small, one-man operation was a major early version of a new, Third-World way of looking at the news'. Abrahams had been on the receiving end of these despatches when he lived in Durban and edited a little newsletter there for an Indian political group. Now, here was their author himself: George Padmore, seeming 'taller than he was because he held himself so ramrod straight. He was thin, austere, always neatly dressed, with crease-lines in his usually dark trousers and spotless white shirt under jacket and tie. His shoes always shone.' Meticulous in other ways, Padmore carefully recorded receipts of the nominal fee he charged for the news service. Those who had not paid up would get reminder slips, clipped to the despatches. Pizer helped with typing at night and on weekends. Padmore, supplementing his own reading of colonial newspapers at the Ministry of Information, also enlisted the help of friends to clip newspaper articles he could rewrite for colonial and African-American papers. By noon, Abrahams recalled, he would have fifteen to twenty envelopes of stories ready to send out by airmail. Abrahams would see the articles Padmore sent out returned to him printed up in periodicals. Writing about the whole operation later, Abrahams said it reminded him of Marcus Garvey's *Negro World*, carried from seaport to seaport by black seamen.[33]

Garvey had died in London by the time Abrahams arrived, but Amy Ashwood Garvey was still there, running the Florence Mill Club where, Ras Makonnen recalled, 'you could go ... after you'd been slugging it out for two or three hours at Hyde Park or some other meeting, and get a lovely meal, dance and enjoy yourself'.[34] Abrahams was more attracted to the West Indians with their nightclubs and restaurants than to the West Africans, cold and withdrawn in the English winter. Although both groups had their organisations and communities, they did get to know one another: here, Abrahams would reflect later, 'was the seedbed of the later unity of African, American and Caribbean black folk'. While Kenyatta was 'something of a lion' on the London left and his *Facing Mount Kenya* was still talked about, 'Padmore was the man to whom the politically-inclined among the blacks in Britain gravitated'. When Abrahams met him, Padmore had undergone a tonsillectomy, and after the operation, performed by a Jamaican surgeon, Belfield Clarke, Padmore spoke with an impediment, but he got right back up on public platforms and went on speaking. He seemed to Abrahams 'a totally political animal' and still a Marxist who did not appear unsympathetic to the British communists. For Padmore the fault lay not in the party and its principles but in the men who ran it. If they had been as honest, as hardworking, as committed as the women communists, things would be different. Sometimes when Padmore came for lunch he would chat with Abrahams's English wife, Dorothy, a communist, as if Abrahams were not in the room.[35] Nor did Padmore seem to have any objection to Abrahams's taking jobs with the communists, first at Central Books and later at the *Daily Worker*.

These jobs were less important to Abrahams himself than his work as a creative writer. Abrahams had brought with him to England most of the pieces that made up the manuscript of *Dark Testament*, which he submitted to the respected firm of Allen and Unwin.[36] The manuscript evoked a mixed response from an Allen and Unwin reader, the translator Bernard Miall. Whether or not the book was publishable appeared to depend on the author's identity. 'Ostensibly the work of an educated Cape Negro', the book had social significance if its author were Negro that it could not claim if he were merely a Jew 'with a dash of African blood' or simply a Jew writing out of sympathy with his 'fellow-outcasts'. Despite the sentimentality of some of the stories, if the author were Negro the book would have 'a sort of curiosity value and a social significance independently of its literary merits'. Therefore, if these were ordinary times, Miall would recommend its publication, but these were not ordinary times. The war had put the South African and American markets out of reach. 'I doubt if you could sell a thousand copies.'[37] Despite these discouraging notes, Allen and Unwin published *Dark Testament*. Criticism came from an unexpected quarter – the communists at the *Daily Worker*, which gave it an unkind review. Abrahams believed he had angered the communists by not submitting the book to them for approval before publishing it.[38] Writing to his publisher on 9 December 1942, he said, 'My friends are apparently still not done with their debating on the political merits or otherwise of *Dark Testament*'. Unhappy with the communists' response to the book, Abrahams seemed equally unhappy with his publisher, from whom he detected a whiff of condescension. '[E]ven if you do think my colour is selling you the book I should think it hardly polite to say it to the person concerned.'[39]

Abrahams was more fortunate in finding a good publisher at this time than he may have recognised. Padmore never found a publisher for the African manuscript he was working on just before the war began, although he may have recycled some of the material in articles and a later book.[40] Nancy Cunard did, however, find a publisher for the book they had written together, *The White Man's Duty*. W. H. Allen brought it out in early 1943 (though it bore a copyright date of 1942).[41] 'My dearest, What excellent news!' Padmore responded. 'The firm of Cunard & Padmore launches forth in the New Year with a bouncing half-caste. How tongues will wag!'[42] Close to twenty thousand copies sold at 9d apiece.[43] A few months later, when Azikiwe arrived in England with a group of newspaper editors invited to tour British papers, he and several of the others took up the book's call for self-rule in a memorandum, 'The Atlantic Charter and British West Africa', although, cautiously, they laid out a fifteen-year timeline leading to full independence.[44]

Meanwhile, Padmore was trying to find a publisher for another, bigger book lent urgency by the war: *How Russia Transformed Her Colonial Empire*. The argument that the Soviet Union provided a model for an egalitarian multinational state had been bouncing around socialist circles since the Russian revolution; in 1919, the Harlem socialist W. A. Domingo wrote of Soviet Russia as 'a country in which dozens of racial and lingual types have settled their many differences and found a common meeting ground'.[45] Britain's wartime alliance with the Soviet Union against Germany created a choice moment for making that argument again. By summer 1942, as German troops pushed their way towards the oil-rich Caucasus, the Soviet Union had lost four million troops to death, injury, or capture, yet refused to give in. While Soviet soldiers defended Stalingrad street by street, the publisher Allen and Unwin considered Padmore's argument that the British might have seen a defence of Asia as fiercely fought if Britain had only granted its colonies there the self-determination granted to the Soviet republics. Because the communists had acknowledged the right of all ethnic groups in the Soviet Union to secede and had poured resources into development across the federation, Russia's diverse peoples had rallied to the defence of the larger nation. When Japan attacked Britain's Asian colonies, in contrast, Britain's call for support met with indifference.

While Padmore's argument for self-determination gained urgency from the war, in the Soviet book he also made his contribution to wartime thinking about postwar life. He differed with those who thought Britain should chiefly do more to develop the colonies economically and socially, preparing them for eventual self-rule, a position put forth, for example, in *The Case for African Freedom* (1941) by the novelist Joyce Cary, a former colonial administrator in West Africa. The evidence thus far, Padmore thought, suggested that development, under the British, could be a long time coming. Like the czarist regime, the British had kept colonial people uneducated, untrained, unindustrialised – a shortsighted policy. Appealing to British self-interest (and thinking as a writer), he pointed out 'what an extension of the British publishing market there would be if there were literate populations in the colonies'.[46] Just as the Soviet Union had rapidly brought its rural populations into the industrial world, so could African states if they followed the Soviet model. Thus, to Padmore, there was no reason to wait for development to grant self-rule. Self-rule should come first, immediately; development would follow. He condemned as patronising and paternalistic the idea, accepted even by some on the left, that the British should decide which colonies were advanced enough for self-governing. The Soviet Union had succeeded in educating Asian peoples more backward, to his mind, than Africans and had brought them rapidly into the industrial, modern world. Africa could do the same if Africans ruled themselves and if African states were socialist. Socialism was essential because the ethnically diverse African states would necessarily be multinational. In a capitalist economy, divisions might be expressed as racial conflict, but the true cause would be economic. Without planned economies, multinational states would break apart.

As he moved through his argument, describing the social and economic changes communists had brought to the former Tsarist Empire, Padmore did not pause to reflect on the costs of these changes: the famine and social disruption wrought by collectivisation of agriculture, the political force used to reshape the economy – the executions, imprisonments, exiles. He did not reflect on the irony of granting self-determination to the Asian peoples, then attempting to transform their culture – educating them in Western ways, removing their women's veils, turning them from peasants into industrial workers. What they retained, it appears, were their languages, in which they could now publish newspapers, magazines, books: this, in his eyes, was 'cultural emancipation'.[47] Indifferent to his own blind spots, Padmore wrote to Nancy Cunard that this book was 'one of the best pieces of sociological work I have yet done'.[48]

That was not the assessment of Allen and Unwin's manuscript reader, W. E. Simnet. Padmore had quoted Simnet critically in the manuscript and identified him as 'editor of Crown Colonist, official organ of the Crown Agents for the Colonies'. In his reader's report Stinnet nevertheless claimed to render an impartial assessment of Padmore's manuscript. 'Knowing George Padmore's record in the Colonial sphere very well, I have not allowed our completely opposite views on Colonial questions to influence my judgment in any way.' Then he unleashed a tirade:

> The Foreword is typical of Mr Padmore's point of view and is a keynote to the book. Every reference to the British Empire is an all too familiar travesty of the true facts, a hotch-potch of half-truths, false premises and misleading deductions. This kind of 'argument' (save the mark) is characteristic of many coloured people like Mr Padmore who have perhaps been embittered by unfortunate experience of race prejudice, who have fixed ideas about a defunct 'imperialism' and have acquired a sort of vested interest in an attitude which goes down too well with

> equally embittered and uninstructed compatriots and in certain other quarters which welcome it for interested reasons or prejudices. Though they may be sincere, they are flogging a dead horse.

What Padmore had produced here was propaganda, he argued, and although there was justification for publishing propaganda, it ought to be published by a publisher sympathetic with its point of view.[49] He therefore recommended against its publication by Allen and Unwin, which followed his advice.

Failing in his own efforts to publish the book, Padmore turned the manuscript over to Cunard to see what she could do. He wrote on 8 January 1943 to say that Pizer was typing a copy for her and enclosed an article in which the novelist and social commentator H. G. Wells mentioned the way the Soviet Union dealt with the national question. 'And here I have a book going begging. Such is life! If my name was Wells what a difference it would make.'[50] He was encouraged when an article he wrote on the book's topic was published in *Tribune*, a socialist weekly launched by Sir Stafford Cripps, and drew so much attention that the issue sold out. 'I think that your publisher could find a ready market for such a book, especially on the present wave of pro-Russian sentiment', he wrote to Cunard. 'I am prepared to offer him every concession of a financial character if he is interested in publishing it at an early date.'[51] He gave her freedom to make whatever arrangements for publication she could. 'I am prepared to make any changes as long as I am not expected to distort the truth. I will never do this consciously. But I am otherwise open to suggestions.'[52]

Confiding to Alain Locke his inability to find a publisher for the book, Padmore explained, 'Due to the paper famine (everything is rationed) young authors are having a hard time finding publishers. Only established writers have a chance.' Apparently, though he had published three books, he did not yet include himself in that category. He did not, however, sound downcast in his letter to Locke on 31 December 1942. He had spent Old Year's Eve with Cunard and a US embassy official who had just returned to London from Washington. They had talked about 'the Poll Tax, the South, Wendell Willkie, and foreign policy'. Padmore asked Locke to send him a copy of *Survey Graphic*'s November issue on 'Color: Unfinished Business of Democracy', which Locke had edited.[53] Padmore wanted his 'coterie' to read it.

> As I am a sort of 'Elder Statesman' and 'Father Adviser' to the Leftward elements among the West African Students Union over here, I am able to draw their attention to your efforts on their behalf on your side of the Atlantic. As to be expected all the Colonial Students here are taking a keener interest than ever before in world affairs & the application of the

Atlantic Charter & 4 Freedoms to other countries. They are anxious to establish links with your friends in the USA.[54]

Two years later Padmore still had not found a publisher for his Soviet book although Leonard Barnes, a Liverpool University lecturer, had managed to publish a book somewhat like his own; Padmore would mail Locke a copy. 'The war has been a great blow to all the young coloured colonial writers here. Quite a number have MSS which I fear will have to wait until after the war to find publication.'[55]

Finally, early in 1944, Padmore met Dennis Dobson, a young teacher in Cambridge who wanted to start a publishing company. Padmore was by this time anxious that the political situation which had been favourable to the book's reception was about to alter radically: once Hitler was defeated, the British alliance with the Soviet Union would break apart and Britain would turn on Russia. 'Do let me hear from you', he wrote to Dobson on 22 April 1944, 'as I think the whole question of Empire and socialism is to be one of the big issues brought home to the British people in the near future'. Dobson asked Walter Kolarz, author of *Stalin and Eternal Russia*, to read the manuscript and give him an opinion. Kolarz had criticisms of the book (he doubted Padmore really knew his Russian history) but sympathised with Padmore's cause. The book's value lay in the connection Padmore had made between Soviet policy and 'the problem of the coloured peoples in general'. Kolarz suggested that a subtitle be added to bring attention to this theme and, when Dobson eventually published the book, it was; the book would appear as *How Russia Transformed Her Colonial Empire: A Challenge to the Imperialist Powers*. Although Kolarz's report was largely favourable, Padmore was stung by his critique. 'Rubbish, how these people hate Lenin!' he wrote on Dobson's copy.[56]

Padmore's manuscript was moving slowly towards publication in the midst of a fierce assault on London. Just a few months earlier, after his district had been heavily hit, Padmore had written Locke, 'Oh, what suffering! War is really hell.'[57] In the wake of D-Day, the massive allied invasion of the continent on 6 June 1944, Germany had begun targeting London with unpiloted aircraft full of explosives.[58] In late July, Padmore wrote to Dobson, 'I am so tired that I have very little energy to do more than is absolutely necessary these days ... I am anxious to see the proof sheets before Hitler starts sending over his V-3.' A couple of days later he wrote again, mentioning the destruction of Arthur Ballard's Socialist Book Shop, where Padmore had met the ILP writer F. A. Ridley and through him other ILP leaders. 'Poor fellow! One lives from day to day and must prepare for the worst.' In case anything happened to Padmore, Dobson should get in touch with

Joseph de Silva of 8 Belsize Lane, Padmore's friend and executor. 'The MS must be published as it stands. There must be no changes.'[59]

Although Padmore had put much of his energy during the war into his books, he also kept up his work for periodicals. His labour was not always rewarded. He tracked down photographs for Claude Barnett's Associated Negro Press service, for which – along with Nancy Cunard – he served as correspondent,[60] but after the war he told the American anthropologist St Clair Drake that Barnett had not paid him for them. Padmore was stuck with a bill for £50. 'All he's after is getting what he can out of you without paying', he said. When Drake told Padmore that the Negro papers had made money in the war years, Padmore asked, 'What did they do with it? Divide it up among the owners?' When Drake said he thought the ANP itself had not made money, Padmore said, 'I know Barnett's racket. I send a story over there and he takes the story and sends it around to the papers, and then they get all the cuttings and go to the advertisers and collect on it.' Of the *Crisis*, he once told Alain Locke that the books he got from the Crisis Book Shop were 'the only way' he could 'get anything out of the Crisis'. Padmore found British papers more generous.[61] 'They'd like to buy us off', he told St Clair Drake, 'but I don't fall for that'.[62]

In addition to writing for *Left* and the *New Leader*, he was writing and editing pamphlets to be published as an IASB series under the imprint of Panaf Service, Manchester, where the entrepreneurial Makonnen had established himself as a restaurateur. As Padmore recalled the story, the pamphlets' publication was linked to a new umbrella organisation, the Pan-African Federation, for which he served as secretary. Formed in 1944 and based in Manchester, the Federation included the West African Students Union, the Kikuyu Central Association, and other colonial and exile groups, but the IASB led the way.[63] Makonnen was the engine pulling the publishing effort, which he financed with profits from his restaurants. In his own recollection of the Pan-African Publishing Company's origin, he set the company up himself, with Padmore, Kenyatta, and the British Guianan physician Peter Milliard – chairman of the Pan-African Federation – serving as directors.[64] From the start of his work in England, Makonnen had demonstrated a commitment to developing autonomous publishing institutions, controlled not by whites but by Africans and descendants of Africans, like himself; this new publishing company was his most ambitious venture.

The several pamphlets that came out under the Panaf Service imprint drew attention, with reviews in the *Times Literary Supplement*, *International Affairs*, the journal of the Royal Institute of

International Affairs, and *Empire*, published by the Fabian Colonial Bureau.[65] The first pamphlet, *Kenya: The Land of Conflict*, appeared under Kenyatta's name but owed some of its contents to Padmore. The result of their joint effort was, as the Kenyatta biographer Jeremy Murray-Brown described it, 'an odd mixture of straightforward IASB political argument with Kenyatta's theme of an African Eden before the appearance of the European serpent'.[66] Other pamphlets included a new edition of *The White Man's Duty* and proceedings of a 1945 labour conference. The one that produced the most controversy was the Trinidadian Eric Williams's *The Negro in the Caribbean*.

A longtime friend of Padmore's and former student of James, Williams had never been a core member of the IASB group, but as a student at Oxford University he had often visited Padmore and the others in London. Padmore passed on to him Alain Locke's expression of interest in young scholars,[67] and after Williams received his degree he was offered a teaching post at Howard University. Locke published Williams's *The Negro in the Caribbean* in the United States as part of his Bronze Booklet series on the Negro in America. As Williams himself described it in a later autobiography, the slender book – product of a 1940 visit to the West Indies – was 'an out-and-out attack on colonialism in the Caribbean'. The US State Department purchased copies and Williams received congratulatory notes from several Caribbean officials.[68] Padmore told Locke he thought it 'a brilliant short survey', and on 29 April 1944 Padmore wrote to Williams to say that he had explored possibilities for the book's British publication. Because of the paper shortage, however, 'no commercial publisher would under-take printing as priority is given to their regular authors'. As an alternative, Padmore said the African Bureau could publish the book using money donated by Makonnen. Williams accepted the terms Padmore offered (10 per cent royalties); publication could proceed. He reminded Padmore to advertise in the West Indies. 'They are anxious to get it.' And in his introductory note to the volume, would Padmore mention the forthcoming publication of Williams's new book *Capitalism and Slavery*, which the University of North Carolina Press was bringing out in the autumn of 1944? Williams hoped Padmore might locate an English publisher for that book, too. 'Let it, however, be a neutral firm. I do not want the subject & its treatment compromised by bringing it out under the auspices of a firm with a political affiliation. You understand, I know.'[69]

More than a concern for his scholarly identity motivated Williams to avoid identification with a political organisation. A couple of months earlier he had joined the research staff of the Anglo-American Caribbean Commission, an organisation created after the United States' exchange of destroyers for bases. When Williams took the part-time position, he had volunteered to show the commission anything he intended to publish or say in a lecture in order to protect himself from inaccurate reports of what he said. The offer caused him no end of trouble, he later wrote, as his American and British superiors tried to get him to tweak lectures and essays this way and that. Worried about his precarious position as a member of the commission, he eventually had second thoughts about Padmore's publication of *The Negro in the Caribbean*. As he explained to the commission, 'The African Bureau is well-known in London as an anti-imperialist organisation. I have never been identified with the group though I know many of its members personally, and they once asked me to read over a publication on theirs on the West Indies. I feel that, in view of my present position with the Commission, the publication of my book under such auspices might give rise to embarrassment.' At the commission's suggestion, Williams asked Padmore to add a prefatory note to the book saying that Williams was not and had never been an African Bureau member, nor did he 'subscribe to its views and policies'.[70] Padmore did as he asked, but Williams's opinions alone were enough to get him into trouble. Although *The Negro in the Caribbean* received favourable reviews in England, the *Antigua Star* attacked it, and in its attack mentioned his connection with the Anglo-American Caribbean Commission, which in turn let Williams know that the controversy was embarrassing the commission. Williams eventually resigned his commission post, concluding that his talents would 'bear more fruitful results in scholastic work'.[71] In the long run that resolution would prove temporary; Eric Williams would rise to political power in the postwar anti-colonial movement that would bring independence to Trinidad and Tobago, as well as to the African nations on which Padmore had fixed his sights.

In that last winter of the war, snow fell heavily in London, and coal was scarce. Food was still rationed and queues stretched out of shop doors. Much of London lay in ruins, thousands were homeless, hotels packed. Yet peace was in sight, and the world had been changed. In a sign of the times, I. T. A. Wallace Johnson was flown to a World Trade Union conference in London by the same British government that had imprisoned him in wartime. Speaking to representatives gathered from all over the world, Wallace Johnson asked the conference to oppose the colour bar, forced labour, and flogging, and to support freedom of speech, assembly, press and movement. 'To guarantee the implementation of these demands', he said, 'we delegates from the colonies – I am speaking for every delegate here, ask that this Conference endorse the principle of self-determination for the colonial peoples as enunciated in Clause 3 of the Atlantic Charter'. Moreover, the conference should ask colonial powers who signed the charter 'to declare a time limit when the principle shall be translated into practice'. Although the conference rejected that proposal, it did pass a resolution favouring 'a world order in which non-self-governing communities and nations can attain the status of free nations'.[72] After the meeting, some of the delegates adjourned to Manchester, where the organisations that made up the Pan-African Federation planned a conference that would launch the postwar movement to end European rule in Africa.[73]

In the United States, the august W. E. B. Du Bois – initiator of Pan-African Congresses one to four – was taken aback when he spotted Padmore's *Chicago Defender* story about this upcoming Pan-African conference in Europe. 'You know, of course, that I am interested in such a meeting and have been connected with attempts along this line since 1918', he wrote Padmore on 22 March 1945, just a few days after the story appeared. Du Bois took issue with several parts of the plan – holding the conference in Europe instead of Africa, meeting so soon, and issuing a manifesto before the conference was held. Attempting to seize the reins of what appeared to be a runaway horse, Du Bois delicately put Padmore in his place by expressing his interest in having Padmore's advice, along with 'the names of persons and organisations who have similar ideas'.[74] To Du Bois, accustomed to his status as leading intellectual, writer, and political fighter on the African-American scene, Padmore must have seemed relatively small fry.

Padmore soon set him straight. The conference organisers had not meant to undermine any effort Du Bois was making to plan a Pan-African Conference; they had used the term 'Pan-African' simply because it captured the idea they had in mind for the conference. In this and the several letters that followed, Padmore's responses to Du Bois were respectful, detailed, and measured. He spoke of 'our trans-Atlantic collaboration', he answered Du Bois' questions and explained the decisions of the British group, but he gave no ground; he retained the reins of the conference firmly in his own hands, though he did ask Du Bois to recruit delegates from American organisations.[75] Other NAACP leaders had reservations about sponsoring the congress, however, and, as subsequent letters passed between Padmore and Du Bois, Du Bois dropped his hauteur.[76] What started out as a duel turned into a wary waltz. On 16 June, the New York bureau of the *Chicago Defender*, reporting on a press conference on Du Bois' newest book (*Color and Democracy: Colonies and Peace*), proclaimed, 'Pan-African Parley in Paris Set for September, Du Bois Announces'.[77]

By the time that article appeared, Padmore was hard at work publicising the conference from his kitchen in 22 Cranleigh House, turning out letters as fast as if his typewriter were a printing press.[78] 'Padmore, the master planner, was in his element', Peter Abrahams recalled. 'We were each assigned specific tasks and had to make written reports at our regular weekly meetings ... Padmore's network of contacts throughout the Commonwealth and empire was alerted, fact sheets, newsletters, bulletins went out in a steady stream.'[79]

Although Abrahams did his part, a new recruit, Francis (Kwame) Nkrumah, was Padmore's right-hand man. As a young teacher in a Catholic seminary at the old Gold Coast slave town of Elmina, Nkrumah had been inspired by Azikiwe's nationalist writings in the *African Morning Post* and, following Azikiwe's example, had studied in the United States.[80] During his ten years there, Nkrumah had involved himself fully in American life, preaching often and strengthening the African Students Association in the United States and Canada. He and another Gold Coast student, S. Ako-Adjei, had used the association's newspaper to promote West African unity in the face of opposition by Nigerian students who argued that each colonial territory should fight for independence for itself. Furthering his political education, Nkrumah read a range of political thinkers; he found Marx, Lenin, and Marcus Garvey the most inspiring. He also tried to get to know as many American political organisations as he could. 'These included the Republicans, the Democrats, the Communists and the Trotsky- ites', he wrote in his 1957 autobiography. 'It was in connection with the latter movement that I met one of its leading members, Mr C. L. R. James, and through him I learned how an underground movement worked.'[81] James, who had made a place for himself in American Trotskyist circles, found Nkrumah 'quite a striking personality but quite ignorant about Marxism'.[82] However, Nkrumah's unpublished manuscript 'Towards Colonial Freedom' did impress him; he wrote to Ras Makonnen that the pamphlet was 'just perfect'.[83] He put Nkrumah in touch with Padmore, whose articles Nkrumah had read.

When Nkrumah arrived in London in May 1945 with a plan of studying law, Padmore met him at Euston station. With Padmore at the station was Nkrumah's countryman Joe Appiah, who had come to London the year before to study law. The three of them went directly to a railway union meeting where Appiah was to speak. As Appiah told the story, he had launched a fiery speech when he felt a tug at his coat, 'Joe, abrofo ye wonkyi wo a?' Nkrumah said to him ('Won't these whites have you arrested?'). Appiah went right on and finished to loud applause. Later, as he and Padmore took Nkrumah to the West African Students Hostel, Nkrumah said, 'Joe, in America, you and all of us would have been lynched or deported halfway through that speech'.[84]

Not only in America: in early July, word of suppressed speech came from Nigeria. After the civil servants' union had launched a strike for a cost-of-living rise, the acting governor accused Azikiwe's *Daily Comet* and *West African Pilot* of instigating the strike and publishing false news. The newspapers (both of which ran Padmore's columns) were banned on 8 July under the Nigerian Defence Regulations. Ever resourceful, Azikiwe promptly relocated a paper he had started in Warri to Lagos and, 'hey presto', as he wrote later, 'we were back in the streets of Lagos selling our newspapers'.[85] Azikiwe himself went into hiding after he received information that suggested colonial authorities might be planning his assassination.[86] By 19 August, however, Padmore was writing to his Harlem friend Cyril Ollivierre that the strike appeared to be over; the workers had triumphed. '[W]hen Zik, who was taken to some place of safety after his life was threatened, emerges from his retreat, he should be a kind of national hero.'[87] Azikiwe did reemerge; the ban on his papers was lifted thirty-six days after it was imposed. Making the most of the moment, Azikiwe chronicled the events in a pamphlet, *Suppression of the Press in British West Africa*, a defiant coda to this war fought for democracy. Energised by the prospect of a postwar world, the anti-colonial movement was about to surge forward.

Notes

1 Fenner Brockway, '"*New Leader*" Carries On!', *New Leader* (19 September 1940), 3. Brockway mentions the prewar printer's refusal to go on printing in *Inside the Left* (London: George Allen and Unwin, 1942), p. 348.
2 Fenner Brockway, *Towards Tomorrow* (London: Hart-Davis, MacGibbon, 1977), p. 137.
3 Padmore, 'To Defeat Nazism We Must Free Colonials', *New Leader* (25 July 1940), 5.
4 Padmore, 'This Is the French Empire', *New Leader* (21 November 1942), 3. 'The I.L.P. in the Past and Now', *New Leader* (12 December 1942), 7.
5 Padmore, "Colonials Demand Britain's War Aims", *New Leader* (15 February 1941), 2.
6 Padmore was identified as the *New York Amsterdam News* correspondent in 'Garvey Is Still Alive!' (25 May 1940), 1, and 'Little Equality Found in France', *Atlanta Daily World* (5 March 1940), 6. Patrick S. Washburn reports his findings in a chapter in a book on war correspondents in Europe, 1914–1945, forthcoming from Cambridge University Press. 'Hitler Makes Britons Forget Old Color Bar', *Atlanta Daily World* (18 March 1941), 1, drew on a March article in the *Crisis*. A. M. Wendell Malliett, 'World Fronts', *New York Amsterdam Star-News* (13 June 1942), 7, quotes a Padmore article in the *New Leader*.
7 Locke Papers, Box 164–76, Folder 16, Padmore to Locke, 11 April 1941; see also Padmore, 'West Indies Reply to Churchill and Roosevelt', *New Leader* (19 September 1940), 3.

8   Padmore Papers, Padmore to Ollivierre, 16 April 1941; '"Daily Worker" Suppressed', *The Times* (22 January 1941), 1; '"Daily Worker" Ban Lifted', *The Times* (27 August 1942), 4.
9   'Millions Demand Free Press', *New Leader* (14 June 1941), 5.
10 Advertisement, 'Have We Yours Yet?', *New Leader* (21 June 1941), 3.
11 'African Warrior Tribe Joins Enemies of Axis', *New York Amsterdam Star-News* (23 May 1942), 3
12 Schomburg Center for Research in Black Culture, St Clair Drake Papers, Box 64, Folder 4, G[eorge] P[admore] to Dr Harold Moody, 4/10/42 [sic]; with the letter is a typescript of the cable.
13 US/TNA. This item is listed in the name index for the Central Decimal File, General Records, Department of State (Padmore, George), 811.711, 'Intercepts – The Crisis; Mail communications intercepted by United States National Censorship office', 18 June 1943, but I was unable to locate it in Department of State files.
14 Jeremy Murray-Brown, *Kenyatta*, Second edition (London: George Allen and Unwin, 1979), pp. 209–10.
15 Padmore, 'George Padmore Lifts the Veil of the Censorship Over the Colonies', *New Leader* (5 July 1941), 7.
16 Cunard Collection, 'For Dorothy', November 1959.
17 Padmore, 'No Atlantic Charter for Colonies', *New Leader* (24 January 1942), 3.
18 Penny M. Von Eschen, *Race Against Empire: Black Americans and Anticolonialism, 1937–1957* (Ithaca, NY and London: Cornell University Press, 1997), p. 26.
19 James R. Hooker, *Black Revolutionary: George Padmore's Path from Communism to Pan-Africanism* (New York: Praeger Publishers, 1967), p. 65.
20 Cunard Collection, 'For Dorothy'.
21 James MacGregor Burns, *Crosswinds of Freedom* (New York: Vintage Books, 1990), p. 176.
22 Margery Perham, 'The Colonial Empire - II. Capital, Labour, and the Colour-Bar, the Spirit of Reform', *The Times* (14 March 1942), 5.
23 Padmore, 'No Solution within Empires', *New Leader* (9 May 1942), 4.
24 Padmore, 'Crisis in the British Empire', *Crisis*, 49: 7 (July 1942), 218; Roy Douglas, *Liquidation of Empire: The Decline of the British Empire* (New York: Palgrave / Macmillan, 2002), p. 39.
25 Padmore, 'Crisis in the British Empire', *New Leader* (13 June 1942), 3, and *New Leader* (27 June 1942), 4; 'Socialists Can't Bargain for India's Freedom', *New Leader* (4 July 1942), 3; 'Imperialists Can't Solve African Question', *New Leader* (11 July 1942), 3.
26 Padmore with Dorothy Pizer, *How Russia Transformed Her Colonial Empire: A Challenge to the Imperialist Powers* (London: Dennis Dobson, 1946), pp. 149–50.
27 Padmore and Cunard, *White Man's Duty* (London: W. H. Allen, 1942), p. 47.
28 Padmore, 'The Socialist Attitude to the Invasion of the U.S.S.R.', *Left* (September 1941), 196.
29 Locke Papers, Box 164–76, Folder 16, Padmore to Locke, 31 December 1942.
30 Leonard Woolf, *The Journey Not the Arrival Matters* (New York: Harcourt, Brace and World, 1970), pp. 106–7.
31 Peter Abrahams, *Dark Testament* (London: George Allen and Unwin, 1942), p. 10.
32 Abrahams describes his journey to London and what happened on his arrival in *The Black Experience in the 20th Century* (Bloomington and Indianapolis: Indiana University Press, 2000), pp. 20–30.
33 Abrahams, *Black Experience*, pp. 36–8; see also Rukudzo Murapa, 'Padmore's Role in the African Liberation Movement' (Ph.D. dissertation, Northern Illinois University, 1974), pp. 79–80.
34 Ras Makonnen, *Pan-Africanism from Within*, recorded and edited by Kenneth King (Nairobi, London and New York: Oxford University Press, 1973), p. 130.
35 Abrahams, *Black Experience*, pp. 38–42.
36 Kolawole Ogungbesan, *The Writing of Peter Abrahams* (New York: Africana Publishing Company, 1979), p. 10.

37 University of Reading Library, Records of Allen and Unwin Ltd, AURR 10/2/08, B.M., 'Dark Testament', n.d.
38 Peter Abrahams, *Return to Goli* (London: Faber and Faber, 1953), p. 16.
39 Allen and Unwin – AUC 129/3, Abrahams to Unwin, 9 December 1942.
40 Padmore refers to this manuscript in a letter to Locke, 3 October 1938 (Locke Papers, Box 164–76, Folder 16), where he says he was trying to finish it up 'just at the time when Mr Chamberlain was flying to see his colleague at Berchtesgaden'. That would have been in 1938, the year after he published *Africa and World Peace*.
41 Anne Chisholm, *Nancy Cunard* (New York: Alfred A. Knopf, 1979), p. 265 .
42 Cunard Collection, Box 17, Folder 10, Padmore to Cunard, n.d.
43 Chisholm, *Cunard*, p. 265.
44 Nnamdi Azikiwe, *My Odyssey* (London: C. Hurst and Company, 1970), 358–9; George Padmore, *Pan-Africanism or Communism?* (London: Dennis Dobson, 1956), pp. 152–3.
45 Joyce Moore Turner, 'Richard B. Moore and His Works', in W. Burghardt Turner and J. M. Turner (eds), *Richard B. Moore, Caribbean Militant in Harlem* (Bloomington: Indiana University Press; London: Pluto Press, 1992), p. 27.
46 Padmore with Pizer, *How Russia Transformed*, p. 111.
47 Ibid., p. 109.
48 Cunard Collection, Box 17, Folder 10, Padmore to Cunard, Wed., n.d.
49 Allen and Unwin - AURR 10/1/95, W. E. Simnett, reader's report on *How Russia Solved Her Colonial and Race Problem*.
50 Cunard Collection, Box 17, Folder 10, Padmore to Cunard, 8 January 1943.
51 Ibid., Friday, n.d.
52 Ibid., Wed., n.d.
53 *Survey Graphic*, 31: 11 (November 1942).
54 Locke Papers, Box 164–76, Folder 16, Padmore to Locke, 31 December 1942.
55 Ibid., 28 February 1944.
56 Hooker, *Black Revolutionary*, pp. 74–5.
57 Locke Papers, Box 164–76, Folder 16, Padmore to Locke, 28 February 1944.
58 Ziegler, *London at War* (London: Pimlico, 2002), pp. 282–6.
59 Hooker, *Black Revolutionary*, pp. 76–7.
60 James W. Johnson mentions Padmore's wartime reporting for the ANP in 'The Associated Negro Press: A Medium of International News and Information, 1919–1967' (Ph.D. dissertation, University of Missouri-Columbia, 1976), p. 99; Lawrence D. Hogan mentions Cunard's contributions to the ANP in *A Black National News Service: The Associated Negro Press and Claude Barnett, 1919–1945* (Rutherford, Madison, Teaneck: Fairleigh Dickinson University Press; London, Toronto: Associated University Presses, 1984), pp. 121–2.
61 Drake Papers, Box 64, Folder 10, handwritten notes, 'An African on American Negro Press: Geo Padmore', 27 January 1948; Locke Papers, Box 164–76, Folder16, Padmore to Locke, 28 February 1944.
62 Drake Papers, Drake notes, 'An African on American Negro Press'.
63 Padmore, *Pan-Africanism or Communism*, pp. 149–50; Padmore erroneously mentions the prewar *International African Opinion* as a publication of the Pan-African Federation; P. Olisanwuche Esedebe, *Pan-Africanism: The Idea and Movement, 1776–1991*, Second edition (Washington, DC: Howard University Press, 1994), pp. 126–7.
64 Makonnen, *Pan-Africanism*, p. 145.
65 Esedebe, *Pan-Africanism: The Idea and Movement*, p. 130.
66 Murray-Brown, *Kenyatta*, p. 221.
67 Locke Papers, Box 164–76, Folder 16, Padmore to Locke, 20 May 1936.
68 Eric Williams, *Inward Hunger: The Education of a Prime Minister* (London: André Deutsch, 1969), pp. 68–9.
69 Locke Papers, Box 164–76, Folder 16, Padmore to Locke, 31 December 1942; University of the West Indies, St Augustine, Trinidad, Eric Williams Memorial Collection,

Folder 96, Padmore to Williams, 29 April 1944; carbon copy, Williams to Padmore, May (date unclear), 1944.
70 Williams, *Inward Hunger*, pp. 82–5; Padmore's statement appeared on p. 5 of *The Negro in the Caribbean*, International African Service Bureau Publications, No. 5 (Manchester: Panaf Service Ltd, n.d.).
71 Williams, *Inward Hunger*, pp. 69, 85–7, 91.
72 Padmore (ed.), *The Voice of Coloured Labour: Speeches and Reports of Colonial Delegates to the World Trade Union Conference – 1945* (Manchester: PanAf Service, 1945), pp. 18–19, 39.
73 Padmore, 'Call for African Parley in Paris Drafted by British Colonial Leaders', *Chicago Defender* (17 March 1945), 18.
74 W. E. B. Du Bois to Padmore, 22 March 1945, in Herbert Aptheker (ed.), *The Correspondence of W. E. B. Du Bois, III, Selections, 1944–1963* (Amherst: University of Massachusetts Press, 1978), pp. 56–7.
75 *Ibid.*, pp. 62–5, 66–8, 75–81, 86–8.
76 David Levering Lewis describes the reservations in *W. E. B. Du Bois: The Fight for Equality and the American Century, 1919–1963* (New York: Henry Holt and Company, 2000), p. 512.
77 Earl Conrad, 'Pan-African Parley in Paris Set for September, DuBois Announces', *Chicago Defender* (16 June 1945), 4.
78 Kwame Nkrumah, *Ghana: The Autobiography of Kwame Nkrumah* (New York: Thomas Nelson and Sons, 1957), p. 53.
79 Abrahams, *Black Experience*, pp. 45–6.
80 Nkrumah, *Ghana*, pp. 22, 24, 33–5.
81 *Ibid.* pp. 42–5; also Marika Sherwood, *Kwame Nkrumah: The Years Abroad, 1935–1947* (Legon, Ghana: Freedom Publications, 1996), pp. 89–103.
82 University of West Indies at St Augustine, James Collection, Folder 243, James to [no name], 31 October 1982.
83 Makonnen, *Pan-Africanism*, p. 154.
84 Joseph Appiah, *Joe Appiah: The Autobiography of an African Patriot* (New York: Praeger, 1990), p. 163.
85 Azikiwe, *My Odyssey*, p. 371.
86 Azikiwe describes these developments in *My Odyssey*, pp. 368–83, and in a pamphlet, *Suppression of the Press in British West Africa* (Onitsha, Nigeria: African Book Company, 1946).
87 Padmore Papers, Padmore to Ollivierre, 19 August 1945.

CHAPTER FOUR

'A constant stream'

The war came to an official end on 2 September 1945. '[E]urope lies stricken and bleeding from the sounds of war', the *New Leader* reported.[1] It was a challenging time to hold the international conference that Padmore and the others had been planning throughout the summer. They abandoned their earlier idea of meeting in Paris where delegates to the trade union conference would already be gathered, but conditions in London were dire, too, and a colour bar there would make accommodation and dining difficult for those attending. At the last minute, the Fifth Pan-African Congress was relocated in the industrial city of Manchester, where Ras Makonnen could provide food at his restaurants and accommodation in the homes of his friends.[2]

Considering the challenges of the hour, the political talent gathered in Manchester that third week of October was formidable. Padmore was there with his inner circle – Kwame Nkrumah, Jomo Kenyatta, Peter Abrahams, Joe Appiah, Ras Makonnen, and I. T. A. Wallace Johnson. Other delegates included an array of men and a few women who had already played leading roles in African and West Indian political life and some who would go on to head the first independent governments of their countries. The Gold Coast's Bankole Awooner-Renner was there – Wallace Johnson's ally in the West African Union League. Nigeria's Obafemi Awolowo was there – later a leading Nigerian politician and opponent of Azikiwe. Hastings Kamuzu Banda of Nayasaland was there – future leader of Malawi's powerful Congress Party.[3] And there too was W. E. B. Du Bois, who had failed in his assigned task of assembling an American delegation but did get to the conference himself to preside over the gathering. '[I]t was lively for a week', Ras Makonnen said later; 'we discussed the imponderables, our plight and the role of the few African intellectuals that existed. We talked about how independence is never given: that it has to be taken.' True, they were few in numbers, but that did not worry them; 'there was plenty of evidence from Russia and elsewhere that a small committed group could soon win support from the people'.[4]

Committed they were – the delegates pronounced themselves 'determined to be free'. They asserted political independence as their first goal, with economic independence to follow. They resolved to 'fight in every way we can for freedom, democracy and social betterment'. They urged colonial peoples to organise strikes and boycotts. Without specifically mentioning socialism, they set their demands for freedom squarely in a frame of anti-capitalism; they called for economic democracy. They exhorted intellectuals and professionals to fight for 'trade union rights, the right to form co-operatives, freedom of the press, assembly, demonstration and strike, freedom to print and read'. They saw ahead 'only one road to effective action – the organisation of the masses'.[5] Here was a turning point: the end of one stage in the anti-colonial movement and the beginning of another. 'The colonial struggle has entered a new phase', Peter Abrahams wrote in his report for the *New Leader*. His article bore the prophetic headline, 'Big Struggle Begins for African Freedom'.[6] Years later, Makonnen would caution against making too much of the congress as a single event. It was important, yes, he said, but it had to be seen as one of a series of conferences that began in the 1930s – all part of a 'ferment of pan-African activity'. Still, he said, the conference was significant because of the agreement that came out of it: that the struggle was not in Europe but in the colonies.[7]

Important as the congress was for those present, it stirred little public attention in Britain. Years later, in a letter to the *Manchester Guardian*, the Labour Party's Arthur Creech Jones, a former patron of the International African Service Bureau and a high-ranking official in the Colonial Office at the time of the conference, downplayed its significance as a turning point. 'We hardly noticed, in shaping policy, the Manchester Congress, and though the individual members of the congress were soon to matter in their own respective countries, it was our liberal thought and constructive ideas which shaped Labour's activity in the Colonial Office.'[8] Officialdom was not entirely indifferent to the Manchester Congress, however. The London Metropolitan Police took note of it, observing that, because the congress had drawn so little press notice, its organisers planned further events in London.[9] On an icy cold day in early December, Padmore, Makonnen, Wallace Johnson and several other speakers gathered at Trafalgar Square. No doubt the weather kept attendance down, Inspector Arthur Cain surmised, though the number did grow from fifty at the start of the meeting at 1.15 to almost five hundred, mostly sightseers. He estimated only seventy-five of the average 250 present most of the time were 'coloured people'. Padmore led off with the provocative claim that African colonial subjects lived lives no better than Jews' lives in Hitler's Germany. Wallace Johnson described his own incarceration in a 'British concentration camp'. Makonnen said that the British Empire had been built by pirates, not saints, and that, since coloured people had fought for freedom during the war, they should now have it.[10]

While this little band of agitators for a new postwar world order shivered in the cold at Trafalgar Square, a new forum for discussing the fate of the colonies was taking shape: the United Nations – and one of Padmore's former Howard University professors was at the heart of the action. Leaving his academic post during the war, Ralph Bunche had climbed rapidly up the policy-making ranks of the American government, first at the Office of Strategic Services, later in the Department of State. As a member of the US delegation to the San Francisco conference that founded the United Nations, Bunche had helped to see that the UN charter contained a commitment to developing self-government for territories without it. Yet he was also a practitioner of the art of the possible, and he believed that British co-operation was necessary if self-government was to be achieved with minimal violence. Therefore he favoured an intermediate measure: establishing a Trusteeship Council that would hold nations accountable for their administration of trustee territories[11] – the former mandate territories set up under the League of Nations, the colonies of Italy and Japan, and any other colonies voluntarily converted to trusteeship status by their European rulers. The trusteeship system would allow African Americans like himself to speak for Africans, who had almost no representatives at all in the United Nations. As director of the Trusteeship Division of the UN Secretariat, a position he took in 1946, Bunche could hope to keep the colonial question alive as an international issue.[12]

The trusteeship plan was not welcomed by Padmore and others in London's African circles.[13] After the General Assembly met at the start of 1946, Padmore attacked the trusteeship proposal in a four-part series in the *New Leader* (compressed into one article in the *Crisis*).[14] To Padmore, trusteeship was an 'Old Firm with a New Name', as the title of one of his *New Leader* articles proclaimed.[15] The difference between the ways Padmore and Bunche saw trusteeships was sharp. Bunche regarded trusteeship as a practical step towards independence, providing the support colonies needed to govern themselves and build their economies and at the same time encouraging colonial powers to release their hold on colonial rule. Padmore saw 'trusteeship' as a concept invoked as far back as the late nineteenth-century conferences that divided up Africa. Imperialist powers had long masked their rule with benign assurances of acting in colonial subjects' best interests.

'Imperialism, open or however disguised, is imperialism', he wrote. Instead of wresting their independence from one particular power, nationalists would face an array of world power against them. Padmore was not at all surprised that Americans supported the plan, nor did he see their support as evidence of Americans' love of freedom; international trusteeship would open the trustee territories to American capitalism.[16]

Aside from published protests like Padmore's, colonial subjects themselves had little opportunity to have a say in the postwar fate of empires. Unrepresented in the early meetings establishing the United Nations, they were unrepresented, too, at the Paris peace conference in the summer of 1946, as Peter Abrahams pointed out to readers of the *Socialist Leader* (formerly the *New Leader*). Paris was just beginning to emerge from the sadness of war when Abrahams, Padmore, and Pizer arrived for the peace conference. New clothes had begun to appear in shop windows, although even modest meals at restaurants were still expensive.[17] Padmore had barely shown up in time for the opening session, so busy had he been writing and meeting with visitors passing through London from all over the colonial world.[18] He covered the conference for the *Free Press Journal* of Bombay, filed stories for other colonial papers and the African-American press, and interviewed the Vietnamese leader Ho Chi Minh for American Dwight Macdonald's magazine *politics*. Then, even before the conference was over he left Paris with Pizer and spent nearly three weeks relaxing at the Mediterranean seashore in a villa owned by an English artist they knew.[19]

'It is my first holiday since the war', he wrote a new correspondent, American writer Richard Wright, 'and basking on the beach I feel as carefree as a happy school-boy'.[20] Wright, the leading American Black novelist, was like Padmore a former communist and deeply disillusioned by his experience with communism. Wright had known C. L. R. James in New York, and, when Padmore had learned just before he left Paris that Wright was living there, he told Peter Abrahams that he ought to try to get in touch with him. Abrahams did, and the meeting would bear fruit for Abrahams; over the next few years, Wright would mentor the younger writer, giving him feedback on his manuscripts and introducing him to his own publisher. For Wright himself, however, the relationship he began with Padmore that summer would prove more significant and enduring. Wright was thinking about going to Africa, and Padmore promised to give him African contacts. 'The intellectuals in West Africa will gladly welcome the author of "Native Son"', Padmore wrote. Padmore hoped that when he and Dorothy returned to Paris around 1 October that he would himself meet Wright. The two men did meet, and Padmore was impressed, as Abrahams told Wright in a letter of 23 October from London. 'Now for a bit of chatter on George', Abrahams wrote. Padmore was 'a Marxist to the core', with objectives identical to those of the Communist Party. '[T]he pattern of life for him, at all stages, in all aspects, culturally, socially, is a political pattern. I know George pretty well and yet if I were to try, mentally, to take George out of his political setting and see him as a person divorced from all political interests, I honestly don't know what kind of person he would be.'[21]

Indeed, when the Wrights stopped in London for three weeks on their way back to the United States, Wright observed of Padmore and Pizer in his journal, 'All political talk. Nothing to lift the mind or the emotions'.[22] Still, just before the Wrights sailed for America in January 1947, Wright gave his own political talk to the Coloured Writers' Association meeting at a Soho restaurant. Cedric Dover, a Eurasian West Indian born in India, author of *Half-Caste*, and proofreader at Oxford University Press, presided.[23] Padmore was present, and so was Abrahams. Others included West Indian writer Peter Blackman, British author Jack Lindsay, and several political figures, including someone from the Burmese Anti-Fascist League and a representative of a delegation from Sudan. *Pan-Africa*, a monthly periodical Makonnen put out, reported that Wright urged his listeners to form an international network of 'cultured progressives'.[24]

Such a network in fact already existed, and in these early years after the war, as the movement for independence gathered energy, it stretched this way and that, enlivened by the possibility of imagined change and held together, in part, by George Padmore. The delegation from the Sudan, for instance, had a link to Padmore through his friendship with one of its members, Yagoub Osman, a Sudanese newspaper editor Padmore had known in London before the war. Padmore's interest in the Sudan was longstanding – he contributed to the *Sudan Star*[25] – and now he went to work publicising the Sudanese delegation's demand for independence and opposition to union with Egypt, which had some involvement in British rule of Sudan. Padmore interviewed Osman for the *Socialist Leader* and the *Crisis*[26] and sent an article to his friend Ivar Holmes in Norway with the hope that it could be published there.[27] In *Africa: Britain's Third Empire*, probably already underway at this point, he wrote at length about the Sudanese situation, offering an analysis more complex than his journalistic reports.

> Subtly exploiting the differences in Egypt–Sudan relationships, the British Foreign Office is playing a skilful game behind the scenes. With

all the cunning and experience of centuries of diplomacy, the British are trying to give the Sudanese the illusion that they are protecting them from the rapacity of the Egyptians. In actuality, they have contrived to maintain the status quo by delicate manipulation of the contending parties.[28]

While the Sudanese were in Britain, they visited Makonnen, who took them to the sympathetic *Manchester Guardian* and coached them on political strategy. Makonnen pointed out the need for good relations with Ethiopia and warned of the threat northern Nigeria might pose to Sudanese sovereignty. 'I warned them against the designs of these reactionary Fulani boys from Nigeria who already had a presence in Sudan ... [T]o these and to later delegations we would stress the primacy of Sudan being free, independent and unfettered with Egyptian influence.'[29] With visitors like the Sudanese coming and going, Padmore wrote to Du Bois on 12 December 1946, 'I am, if anything, more busy than ever. There is a constant stream of people passing through here, and there is always some question being brought which takes time and attention ... I am using my influence to assist the growth of movements and a forward-looking vanguard wherever the opportunity seems to be ripe.'[30]

Du Bois and Padmore had kept in touch sporadically since the Manchester Congress, corresponding both about political strategies each was pursuing and about their work as writers. Once after Du Bois explained that he had not written sooner in part because his publisher wanted a new book from him, *The World and Africa*, Padmore assured Du Bois that he was right to push on with the book. 'The points of view which we seek to present in a hostile white world have to be put forward at psychological moments, so when one can get a publisher receptive to the idea of presenting our manuscripts, one has to put all other matters aside and seize the opportunity.' If Du Bois would send him a copy of the manuscript, Padmore would see if Victor Gollancz – an early patron of the IASB and a publisher 'usually receptive to minority points of view' – would publish it.[31]

In this characteristic exchange with each other, Padmore and Du Bois demonstrated their shared commitment to independent lives as writers. While both were associated with political organisations, they also wrote as free agents. Their work appeared in a variety of forums, from the pages of the weekly *Chicago Defender*, where Du Bois had a column and Padmore's news stories appeared in nearly every issue, to the books they published through commercial presses. As writers, they could reach out to people not associated with their organisations. They could say things without clearing them through a central committee.

They could act spontaneously, nimbly; they could, as Padmore said, 'seize the opportunity' that presented itself. They could take advantage of opportunities when they saw them, making associations with useful others. Their own relationship was one such association. Thus, after Du Bois publicised a petition to the United Nations General Assembly requesting representatives for Africa's colonial peoples in matters that concerned them,[32] Padmore spotted news items on it in the colonial newspapers that he monitored in London and reported back to Du Bois that publicity seemed 'pretty wide'. He promised to include the petition in the report of the Manchester Congress which he was getting ready for publication.[33]

He also asked Du Bois for reciprocal aid, expressing the hope that the National Association for the Advancement of Colored People could help cover publishing costs for that pamphlet,[34] which included reports and resolutions along with historical essays by Abrahams and Du Bois. Before the Manchester Congress, Du Bois had held out the NAACP's financial resources as inducement for giving the NAACP a leadership role in planning the congress, but now Du Bois saw no point in even asking the NAACP to chip in. He told Padmore that he had attended the Pan-African Congress against the wishes of the NAACP secretary and several NAACP board members whose commitment to 'the African program' was still not clear. A request for funds to publish the congress's report would, Du Bois said, 'be quite in vain'.[35] In the end, Padmore collected £5 donations from friends to get out the congress pamphlet. When he sent small sets to the colonies, he got letters back saying the copies had 'sold out within an hour', as Pizer told Wright. Although Padmore had priced them below cost for Africans, 1s was still high, yet there were requests for more copies.[36]

Padmore had had to get the pamphlet ready for press himself, he wrote to Du Bois, 'as no one else seemed to have got on with the job'.[37] Nkrumah might reasonably have been expected to help Padmore out since he had helped Padmore organise the congress, but Nkrumah was otherwise occupied. With the entrepreneurial spirit the times encouraged, Nkrumah and Wallace Johnson and other West Africans who attended the Manchester Congress had started a new organisation, the West African National Secretariat (WANS) to press for regional independence. The anthropologist St Clair Drake, who had known C. L. R. James in New York and was at this point doing his dissertation research at Cardiff, would recall the irritation that Padmore, Makonnen, and others in the Pan-African Federation felt over Nkrumah's decision to start a West African organisation instead of helping Makonnen edit *Pan-Africa* and run the Pan-African Federation.[38] Although part of the Pan-African Federation, WANS had its origins in a desire to move beyond what its organisers saw as the moderate declarations of the Pan-African Congress and actually seize power in Africa.[39] Territories in close geographical proximity with one another appeared to have the best shot at helping each other achieve that goal. A free, united West Africa might then be used as a platform for supporting liberation movements throughout Africa. Although WANS's members were all English-speaking, Nkrumah reached out to African members of the French National Assembly in Paris, and a joint conference with the West African Students Union featured speakers from Dahomey and Senegal. WANS's monthly paper, the *New African*, published French articles on Belgian and French colonies.[40]

The Metropolitan Police were still paying attention to the activities of these London agitators – they took note when Padmore began putting out a little newsletter through his new African Press Agency – the *Colonial Parliamentary Bulletin*, which provided excerpts from Hansard on colonial affairs around the world.[41] Not long after WANS started publishing the *New African* in March 1946, its office files and drawers were rifled, and the indifference of the police station across the way convinced Joe Appiah that the police themselves had done the deed.[42] Certainly, WANS was worth watching. Shortlived as it was, it made itself heard. Its views were published in the *Manchester Guardian* and the journal *West Africa* and, as the researcher Marika Sherwood has shown in detail, WANS spread its message in West African newspapers.[43]

Sherwood has also brought together evidence of a chill in the relationship between Nkrumah and Padmore, who disapproved of not only WANS's regional emphasis but also its involvement with communists.[44] St Clair Drake has described Padmore's concern that identification with the British Communist Party would hurt the Pan-African cause.[45] Makonnen has recalled visiting the WANS office and finding there a Moscow publication but no copies of *Pan-Africa* or other publications he had been bringing out in Manchester. He confronted Nkrumah in the presence of Kenyatta, Padmore, and others on the Pan-African Federation's Central Committee, warning him that association with communism could 'damn the movement towards freedom from colonialism'. Nkrumah did not argue the point; 'he may have calculated that even if I couldn't harm him, George had access to the whole West Africa press through Zik [Azikiwe], and could finish his reputation in a single dispatch'.[46]

Whatever the precise relationship between Nkrumah and Padmore at this point, clearly Nkrumah was busy handling his own wing of the movement. Padmore's closest co-workers as he moved the Manchester Congress proceedings towards publication were Abrahams and Pizer,[47] but they also had other demands on their time. Pizer had a secretarial job and Abrahams was busy trying to earn a freelance living after his break with the Communist *Daily Worker* over his publication of *Dark Testament* (as he told the story in a 1953 book) or (as he told the story in a later autobiography) the party's discovery that he was not a card-carrying member.[48] For a time, Abrahams thought he might be editing *Pan-Africa*, and he did help Makonnen with the first issue, inviting Richard Wright to contribute an article or story. But Abrahams needed an income; before he could see what his role in the journal would be, he would have to 'see how the business side of it shapes'.[49] He had a potential source of income in his fiction – a London publisher, Dorothy Crisp, had recently published two novels, *Song of the City* in 1945 and *Mine Boy* in 1946. Of *Mine Boy* Abrahams told Wright, 'So far the press over here has been kind, uniformly kinder than they've been to any other writing of mine'. One exception was an article about Abrahams that the West Indian Cedric Dover had written for a new monthly *Meridian* and showed Abrahams before its publication. Abrahams reported to Wright that Dover had produced 'a study in supercilious, pontifical, dean-of-colored letters, patronizing condescension'. What Abrahams disliked most was 'the veiled sneering, the assailing of my politics because they don't follow the "line"'.[50] Abrahams was experiencing the tension between writerly independence and a movement's demands for unity and conformity.

Abrahams had the satisfaction of seeing *Mine Boy* become the book that established his international reputation – as the Nigerian scholar Kolawole Ogungbesan has pointed out, 'the first South African novel written in English to attract international attention'.[51] It found success even on Abrahams's home ground. 'Wonder of wonders the South African press and radio has chosen *Mine Boy* as one of the three books of the year for 1946! You could have knocked me down with a feather', Abrahams wrote Wright. Encouraged by his success, Abrahams was hoping that Wright's publisher Harper would bring out his newest novel, then called *Quiet Valley* but retitled *The Path of Thunder* when Harper did publish it in 1948. He was also already at work on a memoir he was calling *A Song for Our Time*, published in 1954 as *Tell Freedom*.[52] Hard as he worked at it, however, authorship was not enough to make a living for Abrahams.[53] He brought in what he could in other ways: by giving paid lectures for the Workers Education Association, a job he got through Padmore's help,[54] and, like Padmore and Wallace Johnson (until his return to Sierra Leone), contributing to the *Socialist Leader*.

With Abrahams occupied with his own affairs, Padmore's closest working ally was Pizer. She typed his manuscripts, helped him with research, and wrote letters on his behalf. Trained as a stenographer, she 'spoke French with a good accent', according to James (who also admired her taste in fashion).[55] She wrote and thought well. She told Richard Wright early in their friendship that she had authorial ambitions. Describing to him an idea she and a friend had come up with – a series of children's books 'about Africa and African people and those of African descent' – she wrote,

> For a good many years, in fact, since before I left school, I have always thought that I would write and get published. So I might have done if I didn't have a solid streak of laziness which I have always tried to excuse by assuring myself that I was always too busy doing other things – earning my own living, or helping other people with their writing. But murder will out, and a strong inclination cannot be stifled forever – maybe![56]

Not long after this letter she published a piece on Liberia ('Centenary of a Black Republic') in the *Socialist Leader*.[57]

Viewing the Pizer–Padmore relationship from the vantage point of a later day, it would be tempting to see Padmore as exploiting Pizer's talent and interest in writing for his own purposes. Yet it is also possible to see Padmore as opening a door to her that would have otherwise remained closed: the opportunity to create books, albeit as a junior partner. After his death, she wrote to Nancy Cunard about her childhood in the East End where she had lived 'amid poverty and sickness and racial animosities'. There was not one book in her parents' house. 'How could I ever have dreamed in my young days, when I knew no-one and never met anyone who was important, that I should find myself ... so involved in one of the most important struggles of our time?'[58] When she met Padmore, he was already a published writer, already well versed in the habits and discipline of authorship. Living with him, she participated in the writing life. On the other hand, working at her secretarial job, she brought in income that sustained them; and the work she did on his behalf – writing, researching, typing – must have drained whatever energy and time she had left. Could she have been a writer in her own right if she had not poured her energies into working with Padmore? In her many long letters to Richard and Ellen Wright – letters that display her skill as a writer – she never expressed any such regrets. She left the impression that she and Padmore were partners in a joint enterprise. She shared Padmore's political views in general but had distinct views of her own. It is clear that they shared a common lively intellectual life, reading the same books, meeting the same political people, talking about events and ideas. Padmore's correspondents were sometimes hers, and she sometimes wrote to them on his behalf. If Padmore played a central role in a political publishing network advancing a vision of a postcolonial world, then her own place was not far off centre. She contributed so much to Padmore's newest book, *How Russia Transformed Her Colonial Empire*, that her name appeared on the title page: 'by George Padmore, in collaboration with Dorothy Pizer'.

'Our book is finally out', Pizer wrote to Ivar Holmes on 18 December 1946. Padmore had found someone to translate it for Norwegian publication but, if Holmes did find a Norwegian publisher, Pizer and Padmore hoped Holmes would read the final draft. 'You see, we took a very great deal of trouble over the political formulations, and there is much in the last chapter itself which anyone might alter slightly in sense without our knowing in view of our ignorance of the foreign language', Pizer wrote.[59] She was right to be concerned about how the book would be read. The Soviet Union's relationship to Britain had shifted dramatically since Padmore wrote the book during the war. Then, the Soviet Union had been an ally and had gained British sympathy through its fierce and sacrificial defence against German attack. Now the Cold War had already begun, and in the months before *How Russia Transformed Her Colonial Empire* came out, English newspapers and magazines had reported political and cultural suppression in various Soviet republics – some of it quite dramatic, involving relocations of large populations. The reviews reflected the shift of attitude towards the Soviet Union.

In the *Common Wealth Review* Walter Padley, a Labour Member of Parliament who had urged Padmore himself to run for Parliament during the war, pointed out that the republics making up the Soviet Union did not in fact have the autonomy Padmore claimed for them. Thus, 'Padmore's main thesis is completely inconsistent with the facts'. Padley had considered himself a friend and admirer of Padmore, he said, but 'simple honesty compels me to say that I regret his latest book'.[60] Not satisfied with his having his say in his own review, Padley responded to the *Socialist Leader*'s positive review with a letter to the editor pointing out further failings of *How Russia Transformed Her Colonial Empire*.[61] Padmore responded to that attack at some length, noting sharply that Padley had abandoned the Independent Labour Party for 'the party which is now running the empire'.[62] Padmore also complained to C. A. Smith, who had assigned the book to Padley (while publishing an article by Padmore on Vietnam in the very same issue). Smith's and Padmore's relationship went back to the years before the war; Smith had published Padmore in *Controversy*, and, after *Controversy* was renamed *Left*, he had turned the editorship over to Padmore and a co-editor in June 1942. But after Smith ran Padley's review in

February 1947, Padmore and Smith did not meet again. Padmore's biographer James R. Hooker marked this moment as a possible 'start of Padmore's estrangement from the ILP and the world of the British left' – an overstatement, since Padmore went on writing for the *Socialist Leader*, although his articles there did become more sporadic; after three in 1949, there were none 1950, before he returned with three in 1951. If he was not as close to the ILP as he had been, that probably had other explanations as well. One of his key links to the ILP, Fenner Brockway, had abandoned the ILP in January to join the governing Labour Party and would be elected to the House of Commons as a Labour candidate in the 1950 election.[63]

Reviewers other than Padley criticised Padmore's Soviet history as oversimplified. The reviewer for the *New Statesman and Nation* granted that the Soviet Union's Asian peoples had made 'astounding progress' since the revolution but maintained that they had not been 'as primitive' as Britain's African colonies to start out with. Nor had Padmore explained how this progress in the Soviet Union had been achieved. 'For one thing there is scarcely a word about the role of the Communist Party, whose ruthless, if well-intentioned dictatorship has played the chief part in the transformation of Russia in Asia.' Nor did Padmore seem aware that some of the Soviet Union's Asiatic peoples had helped the Germans in the war and been punished for it.[64] A reviewer for the *Times Literary Supplement* questioned whether Padmore 'appreciates the methods by which Moscow has sought to promote the "fraternal solidarity" of the peoples of a "Unique multi-national and multi-racial State"'.[65] The moderately socialist Fabian Society's magazine *Empire* asked, 'But does he know that since June, 1945 (when this book was written) every non-Russian region in the path of the German invader has had its separate identity removed?'[66] Farther left on the spectrum, the Communist *Daily Worker* refused an advertisement for the book, Pizer told a correspondent, 'on account of its being George's, I suppose'.[67] Three American publishers found the book too pro-Soviet to publish.[68] Padmore had had a stiff lesson in the minefield of Cold War politics.

Predictably, a favourable review appeared in the *Socialist Leader*, where the ILP stalwart F. A. Ridley praised the publisher for 'his courage in issuing so iconoclastic a book'. In fact, Ridley pronounced himself astonished 'that this factual hard-hitting contrast between the policy of Russian Bolshevism and British Labour in relation to Imperialism can find a publisher in Britain'. Both publishers and politicians on the left, he said, 'usually recoil in horror when sacrilegious hands are laid upon the Ark of the Covenant itself; upon the Holy of Holies of British Imperialism'.[69] Another favourable review appeared in *Pan-Africa*, this one apparently written by Dinah Stock ('D. S.'), the Englishwoman who had helped Kenyatta with *Facing Mount Kenya*.[70]

Dinah Stock briefly became a central player in Makonnen's publishing enterprise. In the first issue of *Pan Africa*, which appeared in January 1947, she was listed as secretary, with Makonnen as managing editor. By the time the journal's second issue appeared, it was Stock who had risen on the masthead to the title of editor, and when she left the magazine for India a few months later an editor's note regretted the loss. 'We think of her not as a European, but as a person with all the characteristics of true greatness.'[71] Stock was yet another of several white English women who contributed their talents and energy to the movement's publishing activities. 'Our contacts with white girls were invaluable in all this literary and promotional activity', Makonnen later wrote.

> They would hear us addressing meetings at Trafalgar Square or in some of the London halls, and they'd come round and ask if there was anything to be done. Dinah in particular was invaluable because of her contact with Reg Reynolds who was involved with the Peace Group ...
>
> We recognized naturally that the dedication of some of these girls to our cause was an expression of equal rights for women. One way of rejecting the oppression of men was to associate with blacks.[72]

Contributions by British women led Joe Appiah to pay them this special tribute in his memoir: 'To the women of Britain, in particular, we owe a special debt of gratitude for their clerical help, their comforting words of hope in times of frustration and despair and, above all, their love and human affection so freely given, often in the face of opposition from families, friends and workmates.' So valuable was their assistance, he wrote, that the West African Students Union passed a resolution that when their countries became independent a gold monument be raised to 'the white women of Europe, for making our stay in Europe possible'.[73] This general appreciation did not always translate into acknowledgement of individual effort: in his acknowledgements for *Facing Mount Kenya*, Kenyatta thanked his brother for taking pictures for the book and the anthropologist Raymond Firth for advising him on the manuscript but made no mention of Dinah Stock.[74]

In contrast, her work on *Pan-Africa* was visible, and she appears to have been more involved in the running of *Pan-Africa* than Padmore himself; his name disappeared from the list of associate and contributing editors in May 1947. *Pan-Africa* was, however, above all Makonnen's project. It was Makonnen, as publisher and managing editor, who sent letters out from Manchester to current subscribers. He tailored a letter specifically for African-American subscribers, speaking as a representative of 'Continental Africa' and acknowledging African Americans' 'manifold achievements' as 'a spur and an inspiration to us'. As he described the publication, it was not to be narrowly political: it was to be 'a living expression, a reflection of the everyday life and deeds of the African people'. He hoped it would challenge scholars 'to engage in those fields of study which will bring spiritual and material benefit to their peoples'.[75]

Makonnen worked hard in these postwar years to establish conduits for the ideas and knowledge of an African nationalist intellectual vanguard. He set up a mail order service, the Pan-African Bookshop, which he advertised in *Pan-Africa*, and an actual bookshop, the Economist, where he sold the books he was publishing, other books on Africans and the diaspora, and also books required for courses at Manchester University. He had ambitious plans for the store. University students needed the updated texts available to American students, and he would have liked to import them, but currency controls prevented him from sending payment to American publishers; nor did he have an import licence. Without an import licence, he could not have books mailed from American publishers. He tried to get around the obstacles by writing to an American not long after the bookstore opened near the university and asking him to order books and mail them in small lots to Makonnen. Once Makonnen had the textbooks, the West Indian Arthur Lewis, then teaching economics at Manchester University, could recommend them to students.[76] Whether or not Makonnen was able to put this plan into place, it demonstrates his ingenuity and determination.

Makonnen did not think of his bookstore as 'a race bookshop', but he did give special promotion to race books – Kenneth Little's *Negroes in Britain*, Padmore's *How Britain Rules Africa*, Eric Williams's *Capitalism and Slavery* (which he also offered, along with Padmore's book on Russia, as a bonus for subscribers to *Pan-Africa*).[77] With the bookstore in place, Makonnen wrote, 'you could say that Oxford Road was my main street'. Ticking off his establishments there, he said 'you could go from the Ethiopia, to the Cosmopolitan, to the Forum, to the Orient, and finally to the Economist, then down to the university'. Padmore would tease him – 'You damn businessman; you'll become an octopus and we'll have to restrain you'. Makonnen thought there was an element of seriousness in Padmore's playfulness, maybe because he was thinking of Garvey's enterprise or even of Azikiwe's newspaper group,[78] which by the war's end included five newspapers scattered across Nigeria's western and eastern regions, with plans to move one to the north.[79] Makonnen could understand Padmore's concern that his own publishing operation, begun for political purposes, might turn into simply a commercial venture. Makonnen himself had no illusions of making money from *Pan-Africa*; in fact, he subsidised the journal with money from his other enterprises.[80]

In the first issue of 1948, Makonnen laid out his problems for the readers: over the past year the journal had lost some £400, partly because he had sent thousands of free copies to prospective readers, partly because of the long time it took to get payments from readers and agents scattered across Africa, the West Indies, the United States, and Latin America. Furthermore, there was another problem: newsagents and bookshops were refusing to carry *Pan-Africa*. 'Their refusals are not due so much to a belief that the journal would not sell, as to a feeling that they should not encourage a publication of its kind.' Makonnen asked readers to recruit subscribers and make financial contributions; he suggested that discussion groups might share a subscription.[81] Makonnen's appeal failed to keep the journal alive; *Pan-Africa* disappeared after the next issue. In a later book, Padmore would say that it closed because it had been banned in East Africa and subscribers caught with it could be jailed, but, not long after it shut down, he wrote to Drake that it had been 'suspended due to lack of funds'. He blamed colonial agents for not paying their bills.[82]

Other doors to the world closed as well. Padmore's work for the Associated Negro Press ended in 1947, possibly because he was tired of not being paid by that financially strapped institution, or possibly, as the historian Penny Von Eschen suggests, because African-American editors lured by Truman's promise of fairer treatment in the United States preferred a less combative stance towards American policy abroad. Whatever the reason for Padmore's break with the ANP, it had a 'devastating impact on [ANP] news coverage of Africa', Von Eschen concluded, and contributed to 'the collapse of a transnational black press' that had 'helped create and disseminate the politics of the black diaspora'.[83] Still, when the *Pittsburgh Courier* conservative columnist George Schuyler visited Padmore in 1950 on his way to a Congress for Cultural Freedom conference in Berlin, he considered Padmore the *Courier*'s London correspondent,[84] and when African American Roi Ottley featured Padmore in a 1951 book, he referred to the 'profound if distant influence' Padmore's newspaper articles in the United States, Africa, and the West Indies had 'on the Negro world'.[85] A check of the *Crisis* shows his publication at first holding steady there with four articles in 1948, before a decline between 1949 and 1955 to only an article a year and in a couple of years none at all. Toward the end of 1954, Padmore would write to Du Bois, 'It is a great pity that the Afroamerican newspapers are not giving the struggle the publicity it deserves. Even the *Courier* and *Defender* that at one time carried my despatches are no longer interested.'[86]

In Britain, Padmore continued his relationship with the *Socialist Leader*, a fact that Makonnen found irritating as he struggled to keep *Pan-Africa* afloat. While Makonnen recognised there was a time when they needed the ILP's resources, things had changed, now that they had mounted their own conference and brought 'brothers from far and wide to it'.[87] For Padmore, the *Socialist Leader* had a significant advantage over *Pan-Africa*: it could publish what he wrote without delay. Timeliness was important; events in East and West Africa had been moving rapidly. In Kenya, more than three thousand people meeting in Nairobi passed a series of resolutions very much in the spirit of the Manchester Congress, calling for self-government, improvement of schools and agriculture, free speech, press, and assembly, equal pay for equal work. Kenyatta was among the speakers addressing the crowd. The *Socialist Leader* reported the meeting on an inside page while Padmore concentrated a front-page article on one target of the Nairobi meeting: Colonial Paper 210 and the federation it proposed: a single legislative body for the colonies of Kenya, Tanganyika, and Uganda combined. The Colonial Paper assured white Europeans of a dominant position on the council. Padmore reported that funds were being raised to send delegates from Kenya to London to protest against this ' betrayal' by the Colonial Office.[88]

Hard on the heels of this news from Kenya, Azikiwe arrived in London with a delegation from Nigeria protesting the constitution proposed by Nigeria's Governor, Sir Arthur Richards. During the Nigerians' visit, Padmore acted as their press secretary. In St Clair Drake's view, Padmore and Makonnen were both so caught up with helping Azikiwe and Nkrumah that they had little time for Peter Mbiyu Koinange when he arrived from Kenya to present the opposition to the proposed East African federation. It seemed to Drake that Koinange was getting more help in London from Brockway and the broad-based Movement for Colonial Freedom. During Drake's visits to London off and on for three months, he roomed with Koinange, whom he had known at Hampton Institute in Virginia in the late 1920s when Drake was in college and Koinange in high school there. Drake thought Padmore did not take Koinange as seriously as he should have done, unfairly comparing him to Kenyatta.

One of the best educated Africans in Kenya, Koinange had started a teacher training college after his return to Kenya in 1938; it was a much-needed institution, providing teachers for the independent village schools that had sprung up to meet educational needs left unmet by the government. After Kenyatta returned to Kenya in September

1946, Koinange had given him the post of vice-principal, and turned the school over to him when he left for England. Kenyatta had also married into the Koinange family. Kenyatta and Koinange were thus in the thick of things together, and, although Kenyatta was the more charismatic figure, Koinange, as his presence in London indicated, had an important political role to play. '[B]oth Padmore and Makonnen had a tendency to underrate Koinange's native intelligence and to distrust what they considered his devious behaviour, which was, in fact, a reaction to Padmore's cocksure directness', Drake later wrote. 'Padmore also had a tendency to lecture Koinange about his contact with certain communists in London, black and white. Koinange was quite aware that they were trying to woo him but was willing to take some types of aid without obligating himself to them.'[89]

Although Drake had a closer relationship with Koinange than he did with Padmore, Drake did talk several times with Padmore and Makonnen about the Pan-African Congress. Drake thought of his conversations with Makonnen and Padmore as interviews and thus he became the congress's first historian. The son of a Barbadian immigrant active in Marcus Garvey's Universal Negro Improvement Association, Drake was both a sympathetic and a reliable witness, trained as an ethnographer to listen carefully and take notes on what he heard. He was, moreover, hearing about the congress less than two years after it was held, while participants' memories were still fresh.

> When the conference ended [he later wrote] there was a sort of an agreement, as I understand it ... They had an agreement that what they ought to do, now that the conference was over, was to get home as soon as possible and put themselves at the head of the mass movements that were already brewing. Movements were breaking out here and there around the African continent asking for a greater degree of self-government and more humane programs under colonialism. These young people, certainly the young intellectuals, took the position that we've got to go out and convince our people that if you want to get what you want you've got to hit for complete sovereign independence and not just start asking Britain and France to make some reforms. So the idea was that they get home as soon as possible, put themselves at the head of movements that were already there, and give some direction to them.[90]

Their strategy would be to use the strike and boycott to win independence. As Drake understood the story, 'The Pan-Africans of London and Manchester made a policy decision, namely to try every means short of violence to use what they called Non-Violent Positive Action'.[91]

That policy was about to be put into effect in the Gold Coast. Nkrumah's former American associate S. Ako-Adjei, president of the West African Students Union and a delegate at the Manchester

Congress, had returned to the Gold Coast in late April. Three weeks later he sent a twelve-page letter back to London describing his meetings with the leading Gold Coast political figure Dr J. B. Danquah and others. 'What thrilled us most,' Appiah recalled, 'was the news about a contemplated formation of a united front political movement for independence'. This organisation of merchants and lawyers came into being as the United Gold Coast Convention in August 1947, the month India became independent of British rule.[92] Just at this delicate political moment two hundred copies of Padmore's book on the Soviet Union arrived in the Gold Coast and were promptly seized at customs. Ako-Adjei, who had ordered the copies, protested in a letter to the Gold Coast governor, pointing out that the Fabian Colonial Bureau was selling the book in nearby Nigeria. In England, the League of Coloured Peoples reported the seizure in its newsletter, noting that the Secretary of State for the Colonies, Arthur Creech Jones, had gone on record approving of Africans' freedom to read. The *Socialist Leader* reprinted the item.[93]

Then the London circle had other news from the Gold Coast: at Ako-Adjei's suggestion, Kwame Nkrumah had been chosen secretary-general of the United Gold Coast Convention (UGCC).[94] Padmore joined Joe Appiah in seeing Nkrumah off from Euston station. There, Appiah recalled, Nkrumah 'poured out his fears and doubts about the great task ahead that he was to execute without us – his trusted friends and comrades in the struggle'. They reassured him that 'from London – the enemy's headquarters – we would continue to watch over and protect him from all the attacks of the minions at home; that from London would come to him ammunition and support needed for the battles ahead'.[95]

Not long after Nkrumah left, in an internal document the Colonial Office expressed some concern about this London hub of the independence movement. '[M]ost of the Colonials in this country receive their information about affairs in the Colonies from practically no wider source than their own politically-minded minority, who themselves get their information chiefly through such bodies as the Pan-African Bureau, led by George Padmore and other able, trained Communists.'[96] Yet when revolt erupted in the Gold Coast after Nkrumah's return and an officer at the American Embassy in Paris asked the Colonial Office for information on Padmore, he was told that the Colonial Office had no information about organisational links between Padmore and either the West African National Secretariat in London or the Gold Coast Convention. The Colonial Office knew him, rather, 'as a contributor of provocative material to the West African (native) press'.[97] He was that, but he was considerably more. As book author and contributor to periodicals in Africa, Asia, Britain, and the American hemisphere, Padmore was poised to fulfil the promise made to Nkrumah on his departure: to speak for the Gold Coast movement to the rest of the world.

Notes

1 Walter Padley, 'Ruin Hangs over Europe', *New Leader* (8 September 1945), 3.
2 Ras Makonnen, *Pan-Africanism from Within*, recorded and edited by Kenneth King (Nairobi, London and New York: Oxford University Press, 1973), p. 163.
3 Marika Sherwood provides biographies of delegates in Hakim Adi and M. Sherwood, *The 1945 Manchester Pan-African Congress Revisited* (London, Port of Spain: New Beacon Books, 1995), pp. 125–49.
4 Makonnen, *Pan-Africanism*, p. 165.
5 Adi and Sherwood, *Pan-African Congress*, pp. 55–6.
6 Abrahams, 'Big Struggle Begins for African Freedom', *New Leader* (20 October 1945), 6. Although Abrahams wrote the article, the *New Leader* featured a photograph of Padmore, 'Negro Socialist Leader'.
7 Makonnen, *Pan-Africanism*, pp. 163, 168.
8 'The Prophets of Independence', *Guardian* (3 September 1963), 8; James R. Hooker identifies Creech-Jones as an IASB patron in *Black Revolutionary: George Padmore's Path from Communism to Pan-Africanism* (New York: Praeger Publishers, 1967), p. 49.
9 UK/TNA, MEPO 38/91/99495, Metropolitan Police report on Fifth Pan-African Congress, 8 November 1945.
10 UK/TNA, MEPO 38/91/99495, surveillance report by Metropolitan Police, 9 December 1945.
11 Brian Urquhart, *Ralph Bunche: An American Life* (New York and London: W. W. Norton, 1993), pp. 119, 126.
12 Padmore, 'Big Three Compromise on Colonial Question', *New Leader* (9 February 1946), 4.
13 See Marika Sherwood, *Kwame Nkrumah: The Years Abroad, 1935–1937* (Legon, Accra, Ghana: Freedom Publications, 1996), p. 129, for the West African National Secretariat's opposition.
14 Padmore, 'Trusteeship: The New Imperialism', *Crisis*, 53: 10 (October 1946), 302–5, 318.
15 Padmore, 'The Old Firm Under a New Name', *New Leader* (23 February 1946), 4.
16 Padmore, 'Big Three Compromise on Colonial Question', p. 4.
17 Abrahams, 'Imperialists Cannot Make Peace', *Socialist Leader* (7 September 1946), 3; Janet Flanner, *Paris Journal: 1944–1965* (New York: Atheneum, 1965), pp. 56–7.
18 Nkrumah Papers, Box 154–7, Folder 52, Padmore to Ivar Holmes, 23 July 1946.
19 Bibliothèque de documentation internationale contemporaine, Université Paris – X Nanterre, Daniel Guérin papers, Mémoires, 1904–1988 / F Res 688–19 / Folder 2, Pizer to Daniel Guérin, 18 December 1946.
20 Beinecke Rare Book and Manuscript Library, Yale Collection of American Literature, Richard Wright Papers, Series II, Correspondence / Personal Correspondence / George Padmore – 103/1522, George Padmore to R. Wright, 19 September 1946. Pizer's and Padmore's letters to Wright were microfilmed by my request.
21 Wright Papers, Peter Abrahams – Box 93, Folder 1161, Abrahams to Wright, 23 October 1946.
22 Hazel Rowley, *Richard Wright: The Life and Times* (New York: Henry Holt, 2001), p. 347.
23 Makonnen describes Dover in *Pan-Africanism*, p. 58.
24 Rowley, *Richard Wright*, p. 347; 'Richard Wright and the Coloured Writers', *Pan-Africa* (August 1947), 35–6. An interview with Wright followed this report.

25 Hooker, *Black Revolutionary*, pp. 103–4; Padmore, *Africa: Britain's Third Empire* (London: Dennis Dobson, 1949), p. 250; Makonnen, *Pan-Africanism*, p. 186.
26 Padmore, 'Sudanese Fears Sacrifice to Egyptian Pashas,' *Socialist Leader* (18 January 1947), 1–2; and 'The Sudanese Want Independence', *Crisis*, 54: 6 (June 1947), 178–80.
27 Nkrumah Papers, Box 154–7, Folder 52, Pizer and Padmore to Holmes, 18 December 1946.
28 Padmore, *Africa: Britain's Third Empire*, p. 250.
29 Makonnen, *Pan-Africanism*, pp. 186–7.
30 Du Bois, *Correspondence, III*, p. 158.
31 Du Bois to Padmore 12 July 1946, in *Correspondence, III*, p. 142; Padmore to Du Bois, 9 August 1946, p. 147. Hooker identifies Golancz as an IASB patron in *Black Revolutionary*, p. 49.
32 Du Bois, *Correspondence, III*, p. 154.
33 *Ibid.*, Padmore to Du Bois, 12 December 1946, in *Correspondence, III*, p. 157.
34 *Ibid.*
35 *Ibid.*, Du Bois to Padmore, 30 December 1946, p. 159.
36 Wright Papers, Dorothy Padmore – Box 103, Folder 1522, Pizer to R. Wright, 29 May 1948.
37 Padmore to Du Bois, 12 December 1946, in *Correspondence, III*, p. 157.
38 Rukudzo Murapa, 'Padmore's Role in the African Liberation Movement' (Ph.D. dissertation, Northern Illinois University, 1974), p. 221.
39 Sherwood, *Kwame Nkrumah*, p. 127.
40 Hakim Adi, *West Africans in Britain, 1900–1960: Nationalism, Pan-Africanism and Communism* (London: Lawrence and Wishart, 1998), pp. 130–1.
41 UK/TNA, MEPO 38/91/99495, indecipherable signature, Deputy Commander, report, 3 May 1946.
42 Joseph Appiah, *Joe Appiah:The Autobiography of an African Patriot* (New York: Praeger, 1990), p. 167.
43 Sherwood, *Kwame Nkrumah*, pp. 129, 131,144–6. See also Sherwood's account of WANS activities and Nkrumah's relationship to Padmore in 'Kwame Nkrumah', in David Killingray (ed.), *Africans in Britain* (Ilford: Frank Cass and Company, 1994), pp. 164–94.
44 Sherwood, *Kwame Nkrumah.*, p. 161.
45 Murapa, 'Padmore's Role', pp. 176, 272.
46 Makonnen, *Pan-Africanism*, p. 263.
47 Padmore to Du Bois, 9 August 1946, in *Correspondence, III*, p. 146.
48 Peter Abrahams, *Return to Goli* (London: Faber and Faber, 1953), p. 16; *The Black Experience in the 20th Century: An Autobiography and Meditation* (Bloomington: Indiana University Press, 2000), p. 59.
49 Wright Papers (Abrahams), Box 93, Folder 1161, Abrahams to Wright, n.d.
50 *Ibid.*, Abrahams to Wright, 18 February 1947.
51 Kolawole Ogungbesan, *The Writing of Peter Abrahams* (New York: Africana Publishing Company, 1979), p. 38.
52 Wright Papers (Abrahams), Box 93, Folder 1161, Abrahams to Wright, 23 October 1946.
53 He discusses his finances in Wright Papers (Abrahams), Box 93, Folder 1161, Abrahams to Wright, 18 February 1947.
54 Abrahams, *Black Experience*, pp. 66–8.
55 C. L. R. James, 'Notes on the Life of George Padmore', carbon copy, typescript with author's corrections, microform (Chicago, IL: Center for Research Libraries, 1959), p. 54.
56 Wright Papers (Dorothy Padmore), Pizer to R. Wright, 9 July1947.
57 Pizer, 'Centenary of a Black Republic', *Socialist Leader* (16 August 1947), 3.
58 Cunard papers, D. Padmore [Pizer] to Cunard, 28 April 1961.
59 Nkrumah Papers, Box 154–7, Folder 52, Pizer to Ivar Holmes, 18 December 1946.
60 Padley, 'A Mirage over the Russian Steppes', *Common Wealth Review*, 3: 16 (February 1947), 9–10.

'A CONSTANT STREAM'

61 Walter Padley, 'Padmore, Stalin and P.O.U.M.', *Socialist Leader* (11 January 1947), 9.
62 Padmore, 'Russia & the Colonial Question/Letter from George Padmore', *Socialist Leader* (25 January 1947), 9.
63 Fenner Brockway, *Outside the Right* (London: George Allen and Unwin, 1963), pp. 36, 45.
64 John Lawrence, 'Soviet Thought and Action', *New Statesman and Nation*, 32: 827 (28 December 1946), 486.
65 'Russia's Empire Making', *Times Literary Supplement* (11 January 1947), 19.
66 H.S. in 'Guide to Books', *Empire*, 9: 7 (January 1947), 10.
67 Nkrumah Papers, Box 154–7, Folder 52, Pizer to I. Holmes, 18 December 1946.
68 Hooker, *Black Revolutionary*, p. 79.
69 F. A. Ridley, 'Searchlight on Imperialism', *Socialist Leader* (14 December 1946), 7.
70 D. S., 'Socialism and the Colour Bar', *Pan-Africa* (May 1947), 36–8.
71 'Miss Dinah Stock', *Pan-Africa* (August 1947), 3.
72 Makonnen, *Pan-Africanism*, pp. 146–7.
73 Appiah, *Joe Appiah*, p. 155.
74 Jomo Kenyatta, *Facing Mount Kenya: The Tribal Life of the Gikuyu* (London: Secker and Warburg, 1959; first published 1938), p. xvii.
75 Drake Papers, Box 60, Folder 3, letter on Pan-Africa letterhead, n.d.
76 *Ibid.*, Makonnen to George F. McCray, 23 June 1948.
77 Shepperson in George Shepperson and St Clare Drake, 'The Fifth Pan-African Conference, 1945 and the All African People's Congress, 1958', *Contributions in Black Studies*, 8 (1986–87), 53.
78 Makonnen, *Pan-Africanism*, p. 146.
79 Nnamdi Azikiwe, *My Odyssey* (London: C. Hurst and Company, 1970), pp. 301–2.
80 Makonnen, *Pan-Africanism*, p. 146.
81 'A Word from the Editor', *Pan-Africa* (January–February 1948), 4–6.
82 George Padmore, *Pan-Africanism or Communism?* (London: Dennis Dobson, 1956) p. 174; Drake Papers, Box 8, Folder 5, Padmore to Drake, 28 October 1949.
83 Penny M. Von Eschen, *Race Against Empire: Black Americans and Anticolonialism, 1937–1957* (Ithaca, NY; London: Cornell University Press, 1997), pp. 107, 118, 147, 159, 120.
84 George S. Schuyler, *Black and Conservative* (New Rochelle, NY: Arlington House, 1966), p. 326.
85 Roi Ottley, *No Green Pastures* (London: John Murray, 1952, first published in the US by Charles Scribner's Sons in 1951), p. 69.
86 Padmore to Du Bois, 3 December 1954, in Du Bois, *Correspondence, III*, pp. 373–4.
87 Makonnen, *Pan-Africanism*, p. 180.
88 Anonymous, 'Kenya Africans Present Demands', *Socialist Leader* (7 June 1947), 3; Padmore, 'Unrest Spreading Throughout Africa', *Socialist Leader* (24 May 1947), 1, 8.
89 Drake, 'Mbiyu Koinange and the Pan-African Movement' in Robert A. Hill (ed.), *Pan-African Biography* (Los Angeles: African Studies Center, University of California Los Angeles, and Crossroads Press / African Studies Association, 1987), p. 181.
90 Drake in Shepperson and Drake, 'Fifth Pan-African Conference', p. 42. For Drake's description of his father's influence, see George Clement Bond's interview with him in 'A Social Portrait of John Gibbs St Clare Drake: An American Anthropologist', *American Ethnologist*, 15: 4 (November 1988), 763.
91 Drake Papers, Box 23, Folder 33, manuscript, 'Pan-Africanism: Myth or Reality?' p. 4.
92 Appiah, *Joe Appiah*, p. 169.
93 'Books banned in Gold Coast', *Socialist Leader* (20 September 1947), 3.
94 Appiah, *Joe Appiah*, p. 169.
95 *Ibid.*, p. 171.
96 UK/TNA, CO 537/2574, 'Note on conclusions to be drawn from the Fabian Colonial Bureau Conference at Pasture Wood', 17–18 January 1948.
97 US/NA, Department of State, 111.20A/8–1248 American Embassy, London, 'Biographic Notes concerning Malcolm NURSE, Alias George PADMORE', 12 August 1948.

CHAPTER FIVE

Strategist, publicist

On a cold day in March 1948, St Clair Drake was warming himself by the stove in the League of Coloured Peoples' London office when Padmore dashed in with news: Nkrumah, Ako-Adjei, and four others in the United Gold Coast Convention had been arrested in connection with a riot for which they were not responsible but for which they were blamed. Padmore organised a demonstration at Trafalgar Square, where dockworkers and students joined in protest under the statue of Lord Nelson while Drake took pictures from the platform.[1] Padmore also wrote a front-page article in the *Socialist Leader* and, in his first paragraph, mentioned British newspapers' 'self-imposed censorship' of news about what he called 'Murder on the Gold Coast'.[2] Thus, as Rukudzo Murapa has put it in his study of 'Padmore's Role in the African Liberation Movement', Padmore became 'Nkrumah's public relations man in London'.[3] When authorities blamed the UGCC for demonstrations in towns outside Accra and saw communist influence at work, Padmore told the American readers of the *Crisis* that the very idea that those involved were communist dupes was 'wicked, to say the least'. Padmore chronicled the events in detail and concluded (accurately, according to a report by the official Watson Commission, which investigated them) that the allegation by the Under Secretary of State for Colonies was 'completely without foundation. It is merely an attempt to discredit the popular progressive movements in Africa which are agitating for self-government.'[4]

Nkrumah was freed, but his relations with other UGCC leaders had frayed and he was removed as general secretary of the UGCC. He immediately launched the *Accra Evening News*, which would become both his own political voice and the voice of George Padmore. Even before he returned to the Gold Coast, Nkrumah had stressed the Gold Coast's need for 'a politically fearless and militant newspaper'.[5] Once he returned, he wrote later, he had done his best to convince the others of the need to set up a newspaper to give voice to the movement. 'They would not hear of it, their excuse being that we would probably get ourselves embroiled in sedition cases. Personally I failed to see how any liberation movement could possibly succeed without an effective means of broadcasting its policy to the rank and file.' Strapped for funds, he initially put out just a single sheet that was passed from hand to hand, increasing in value until sometimes it brought 6d a copy. It did so well that, like Azikiwe in Nigeria, he started another newspaper, this one in Sekondi, and then a third, in the Cape Coast.[6] After he formed the Convention People's Party (CPP) in June 1949, his newspapers became the voice of the party.[7] He used them to publicise a Positive Action campaign to protest against a proposed constitution and call instead for an elected constituent assembly to consider the constitutional question. He kept the paper's printing machine going through the night to print up five thousand copies of a pamphlet explaining what he meant by Positive Action – using non-violent protest and noncooperation and press campaigns. 'The Era of Positive Action Draws Nigh', the *Accra Evening News* proclaimed in a front-page story in mid-December. The Gold Coast government arrested the editors of Nkrumah's newspapers and Nkrumah himself, although supporters paid his fine so he could stay out of prison. Then followed a battle of the media, as the government used radio to try to convince the public that the Positive Action campaign had been called off while Nkrumah used public speeches and his newspapers to build energy for the campaign.[8]

In response, the government declared an emergency throughout the Gold Coast and imposed a curfew. Stores shut down, trains stopped running, workers stayed home and, Nkrumah wrote in his autobiography, his newspapers 'fanned the flame' until all three papers were banned and their editors arrested again, as were CPP leaders, in numbers that increased after two African policemen were killed in a conflict with demonstrating ex-servicemen. Nkrumah himself was also arrested again, tried, and sentenced to two years for encouraging the illegal strike. Next he was taken off to the Cape Coast for another trial on a sedition charge for an article that had appeared in his paper there, the *Daily Mail* (its editor was already in prison). In Cape Coast, a third year was added to Nkrumah's prison term.[9] Nkrumah's early model Nnamdi Azikiwe would say in his own autobiography that when he was thinking of becoming a journalist on his return from the United States, his West African friends had warned him that 'in West Africa an editor had only one foot in his office; his other foot was always in prison'.[10] Azikiwe had already suffered that fate; now it was Nkrumah's turn. While Nkrumah was not arrested solely for being an editor, his calls for Positive Action through the megaphones of his newspapers had given the government the excuse it needed to arrest him.

In light of this suppression of opinion and information in the Gold Coast, Padmore's newest book, *Africa: Britain's Third Empire*, appearing in early 1950 (though it bore a 1949 publication date), could not have been better timed. Speaking as an African expressing the Fifth Pan-African Congress's will, Padmore chronicled the ongoing struggle for self-government throughout British Africa, the third empire that remained after Britain lost India and what became the United States.[11] Drawing on his own experience and connections, he moved across the map, country by country, following his usual strategy, once described by James as 'a remorseless compilation of the facts of tyranny and oppression'.[12] First he described the sorry state of affairs under colonial rule and then, in a later section, the strikes, delegations, memoranda, and demonstrations by Africans contesting that rule. Throughout the book he chronicled African resistance, not only in these recent years but stretching into the past. He challenged the reigning idea that the British had brought democracy to Africa. On the contrary, in a line of thought articulated in *How Britain Rules Africa* and again at the Manchester Congress,[13] he argued that the British had destroyed the democracy that was already there by making chiefs accountable to the British rather than to their own people. The British had unravelled local economies, forcing farmers to produce crops for export instead of meeting their own needs. Through taxes they had pushed Africans into a labour force where they were low-paid and torn loose from their own homes and communities. They had set tribe against tribe in a policy of 'divide and rule'. '[T]o claim, as British Imperialists do, that they have introduced "political democracy" into the Gold Coast, is sheer humbug. What the British Imperialists have done is to put a brake on the development of an indigenous system of government that was fundamentally democratic and which would certainly have evolved to meet the social and economic needs of the twentieth century.'[14]

He took particular aim at the governing Labour Party's program of colonial economic development. Brought to power at the end of the war, the Labour Party had proved a disappointment to Padmore and his associates. Just as Padmore's new book came out, Joe Appiah published a bitter cry of reproach in *Left*, 'Et Tu Labour?' – rebuking Labour for, among other things, 'encouraging private enterprise, in all its ruthlessness, to get on in the colonies'.[15] Now, in *Africa: Britain's Third Empire*, Padmore wrote that Labour's development plan was a sham if the true goal was to let Africans stand on their own feet; not nearly enough money was being pumped back into Africa to meet development needs. Nor were Africans themselves participating in the plans. The corporations controlling imports, exports, and manufacturing were still foreign – European or Indian. Economic development was simply economic imperialism in new dress. Debunking the whole notion of the 'white man's mission' – the idea that the British were civilising Africa – Padmore put forth the contrary view that Africa would have been much farther along if the British had never intervened. As Jawaharlal Nehru had argued in *The Discovery of India* (1946),[16] Padmore believed the colonisers had retarded the development of the colonised. Britain had used Africa for its own economic purposes, and, now, in the aftermath of the war, Britain planned to go on using Africa. Losing control of its Asian empire, Britain was turning to Africa to shore up an economy battered by war. It was hard not to conclude, from Padmore's presentation, that the best way for the British to civilise Africa was to return to Africa the wealth they had taken and get out of the way.

At the same time, Padmore was aware of the grave problems that would face Africans if the British withdrew. In the south and east, white-governed South Africa and Southern Rhodesia were eager to spread their control over the regions around them, instituting the colour bar and pass laws and defining self-government as government by whites. In West Africa, tribal conflicts exacerbated by British rule could result in disaster. Padmore worried particularly about conflict in Nigeria, where some Yoruba intellectuals resented the leadership of Azikiwe, an Ibo from the east. Of the All-Yoruba Movement he wrote, 'However charming and amiable some of the traditional Yoruba rulers might be as individuals, a movement which sets out to bolster up these patriarchal tribal chiefs, who are already subordinated to, and dependent upon, British imperialism for survival, must of necessity become another pillar of alien domination'. Padmore suggested that Nigerians study the example of Burma, where the Burmese Anti-Fascist People's Freedom League had formed a 'common anti-imperialist front' out of a mix of ethnic groups. 'Unless Nigerians can build up a federally based political structure on the lines of Burma, Nigeria is bound to fall apart the day the British quit the country.'[17]

Whatever the difficulties in creating unity out of diversity, Padmore saw encouraging evidence that Africans could come together under the leadership of militant trade unions. Under the force of common economic cause, he believed, tribal differences would be seen for what they were – a 'retarding influence'. So long as African economies and governments were still controlled by foreigners, these unions could have more influence on development than they would have if Africa had its own strong capitalist class. Labour-powered nationalism was to Padmore more than a drive for self-government. It was an arena where diverse tribes came together to form a modern industrial state. Beyond national unity, Padmore hoped for a greater continental unity: 'the realization of the United States of Africa'.[18]

For all its factuality, *Africa: Britain's Third Empire* was a nationalist tract in the broader sense of nationalism: an assertion of Africans' right to rule themselves. As in previous books, Padmore had done what he could to undermine British moral authority – its claim to cultural and political superiority. He had presented Africa with a heroic past of struggle against the intruders; he had portrayed Africans as agents in their own history. He had held out a vision of a better Africa to come if the working masses and intelligentsia could join forces against the British and corrupt chiefs. He had, in short, offered African readers justification for political action and had suggested forms that action could take.

The moment seemed right for his message, and prospects for *Africa: Britain's Third Empire* seemed bright. Review copies had gone out to forty-five British, twenty-two African, one Indian, and six West Indian periodicals.[19] Responses covered a wide range. In the *Times Literary Supplement*, a former Gold Coast colonial administrator, G. N. N. Nunn (his identity concealed by the *TLS*'s policy of not naming reviewers), called the book '261 pages of glib, but embittered, writing and facts distorted by a race-consciousness'.[20] On the other hand, in the *Socialist Leader*, Padmore's longtime ally F. A. Ridley predictably called him 'a great African, whose contributions to the anti-imperialist struggle are part of the world history of our times. If there is a more dynamic critic of Imperialism in the British Empire, I do not know his name or whereabouts.'[21]

Azikiwe ordered five thousand copies for Nigeria. The whole first edition was sold out even before publication (which had been delayed by the printers)[22] and Dobson put out a paperback edition. But trouble took little time brewing. By the third week of March 1950, the book had been banned in Kenya and the Gold Coast, and banning was being considered in other British African colonies. Internal Colonial Office notes and commentaries document concern by Kenya, Gambia, and Gold Coast governors that the book would encourage 'hot heads' and stir up racial hostility. Commenting on their concern, 'J. G.' (presumably James Griffiths, Secretary of State for the Colonies) objected to overly enthusiastic endorsement of gubernatorial decisions to suppress the book. 'All my instincts are against banning books – particularly when I have had no opportunity of reading the book', he wrote.[23]

Shortly after, the American Embassy in London reported to the US Department of State that the book had been banned in Nigeria (where it had not) and in Kenya (where it had):

> and will probably be banned in most of Britain's other African colonies, although the decision will rest with the individual Governors in each case. It contains a wealth of material well fitted for either Communist or African nationalist propaganda against both the local authorities and the British Government.
>
> Officials of the Colonial Office classify George Padmore as a fellow traveller with strong Communist connections but hesitate to label him definitely as a Communist. They consider the book an extremely able collection of half-truths, entertainingly and provocatively written. There is some question in their minds as to whether it was wise to ban the book in the colonies since (1) banning the book will increase its influence among discontented elements in the colonies, (2) African students in London will be even more eager to read it, (3) censorship is against the British tradition, and (4) the great majority of colonial Africans are unable to read anyhow.

Although sales figures were not known (the American report continued), the British public seemed little interested in Africa, 'despite the exhortations of the Colonial Office'. On the other hand, Africans living in London would likely read the book, which thus might 'contribute somewhat to colonial discontent '.[24]

While the Embassy was wrong about Nigeria, the governor there did consider banning the book and cabled Griffiths for advice. Griffiths replied on 1 April 1950 that in his view, 'the disadvantages of banning this book ... are likely in the long run to outweigh any gain that there may be from taking that step'. Still, the decision was the Governor's, and, when parliamentary questions were raised, as Griffiths was sure they would be, he would respond 'that action has been taken by you under legal powers which entrust decision to you in your absolute discretion'. Copies of this telegram went to the governors of Sierra Leone, Gambia, and the Gold Coast.[25]

By late spring, the book had been banned in the Gold Coast, Gambia, Kenya, Uganda, and Tanganyika. It is not difficult to see why, given Padmore's account of nationalist movements in western, eastern, and southern Africa. After the recent upheaval in the Gold Coast, authorities there were not likely to welcome statements like the following, in a section on Gold Coast's Sedition Act: 'These are the sort of laws made by colonial dictators to trap innocent Africans and turn decent citizens into criminals.' Nor would the Kenyan government have welcomed Padmore's judgement that, in allowing white settlers more power in the Central Assembly than was earlier proposed, the Colonial Secretary had 'sacrificed the interests of the Africans to those of the settlers'.[26] Padmore's narrative of a 1945 revolt in Uganda and its aftermath could have worried authorities both in Uganda and other colonies. 'The uprising was brutally suppressed', he wrote, and after the Prime Minister Samwiri Wamala was arrested and banished, and a nationalist had shot the man who was put in his place, the assassin was hanged. 'The Government renewed the terror. Hundreds of people were arrested and exiled. Every Government department was purged. Anyone suspected of "dangerous thought" was dismissed.' After an investigation pinpointed flaws in the government's foreknowledge of the upheaval, there was talk of establishing a Special Branch to conduct surveillance. 'Who says that the secret police is abhorrent to the British and only operates behind the eastern European Iron Curtain?' Padmore asked. Editors had been imprisoned under a new press law and controls over assembly had tightened. 'The restrictions which these regulations place upon the nationalist movement, farmers' organisations, the African Press, and even trade union activities are obvious. They completely counteract any constitutional advance, and can quite readily be invoked to create any atmosphere of terror.'[27] Padmore did not actually write much about either Tanganyika or Gambia, the other colonies where the book was banned, although he said tersely of Gambia, 'It is the most primitive British territory on the continent. Many Gambians die yearly from semi-starvation, but the actual figure is not known, as no statistics are kept.'[28]

The bannings of *Africa: Britain's Third Empire* provoked a flurry of protests in Britain. After news of the Kenya ban appeared, an officer of the League of Coloured Peoples, M. Joseph-Mitchell, sent a letter of protest to Griffiths. Identifying Padmore as a League member, Joseph-Mitchell labelled the ban 'particularly arbitrary and high-handed in a Colony which is notorious for its controversial issues'. He noted that Griffiths's predecessor, Arthur Creech Jones, had actually lifted bans on other publications. Thus, allowing Kenya's governor to ban publications under the Colonial Office's jurisdiction would be a step backward. 'In our view this act is not just a violation of the Civil Liberties of the Colonial people, which is serious indeed, but an attempt to deride the oft-repeated pronouncements and declarations of the Labour Party and its government that they are desirous of fostering the free expression of opinion on matters of vital concern to us as Colonial peoples.'[29] The Secretary of State for the Colonies also received a protest from the National Council of Civil Liberties, which reported hearing from 'a number of coloured people' who said that, since no reasons had been given for the ban, they concluded 'an intellectual colour bar' was in effect. 'This Council has always believed that the banning of books of opinion is wrong and we are re-inforced in that opinion by Article 19 of the Universal Declaration of Human Rights.'[30]

Despite the criticism, Griffiths refused to countermand the governors' decision. In response to the League of Coloured Peoples and other critics, he explained that the governors had the power to ban the book as 'contrary to the public interest' and he would therefore not intervene.[31] He did, however, hold an internal meeting to discuss the bans of both Padmore's book and the communist *Daily Worker* and pointed out the publicity that banning brought to publications. Those at the meeting agreed to leave governors with the power to ban but require that the bans be placed by Governors-in-Council. They also agreed to point out to governors the variation in colonial governments' enthusiasm for bans, 'with a view to keeping the list as small as possible'. Focusing specifically on *Africa: Britain's Third Empire*, they wanted the Welfare Department's Colonial Liaison Officers to determine the effect banning Padmore's book had had on students and other colonial subjects living in London. Governors would then be informed of this study's results, presumably with an eye towards making them less eager to ban books in the future.[32]

Griffiths reiterated his position that bans on imports of publications generally caused more trouble than they were worth in a confidential reply to a Member of Parliament, Dr S. W. Jeger. Still, he said that each governor (or Governor-in-Council) had the power to make the decision since 'in practical cases, the decision on so delicate an issue depends to a very large extent on the particular local circumstances'.[33] Padmore did not give up the attempt to free his book from bans. After the former *New Leader* editor Fenner Brockway was elected to the House of Commons as a Labour Party member, Padmore paid a call on him, and Brockway took up his cause. He reminded Griffiths that he had told the House of Commons that he meant to read the book and hoped he had: 'I feel sure you would agree that it is a serious study and that it is contrary to "our way of life" to ban such a book.' Moreover, the ban was apparently not working: not only was the book getting through, it was selling in some areas at twice its list price. A second edition was about to be published and Padmore was writing a preface that criticised the ban. If the ban were lifted, 'he would then of course amend his preface so as to express his appreciation of this'.[34]

Despite the fact that the bans remained in place, Padmore pronounced the book 'a tremendous success' in a letter to Du Bois.[35] Du Bois had agreed to write a preface for an American edition if one materialised, but back in March, with the anti-communist movement in full swing in the United States, he cautioned, 'I do not know whether a publisher can be found; this country has gone stark crazy and our Civil Rights are only glimmering'.[36] After Padmore repeated the request on 21 August 1950, Du Bois replied, 'It is almost impossible to get any radical books published now in the United States'. Harcourt Brace had just turned down his own book on America and Russia. 'Sometime when this hysteria has passed, we will get back to normal attitudes in this country.'[37]

For Du Bois, worse was still to come. Two years earlier he had parted from the NAACP, which had fallen in line with the Truman Doctrine. With America leading a free world threatened by communism, there was little room for either Du Bois' brand of internationalism or his progressive politics. After losing his post at the NAACP, Du Bois moved into an office at the Council on African Affairs, recently weakened by a split occasioned by the complicated politics of the period.[38] After losing his column in the *Chicago Defender* for endorsing Progessive Party presidential candidate Henry Wallace, he began writing instead for the *National Guardian*, a new radical weekly. He also took on the job of organising a Peace Information Center to strengthen support for the Stockholm Peace Appeal for nuclear disarmament. In February 1951, he and four fellow members of the Peace Information Center were indicted for violating the Foreign Agents Registration Act.[39]

As soon as Padmore heard about the indictment, he drew on accounts in African-American newspapers to draft a news release which he sent to newspapers in Africa and the West Indies. To Du Bois he wrote, 'We are sorry to say it, but your country is fast losing its claims to be a civilised nation'.[40] A couple of months later, Padmore wrote again, promising Du Bois continued publicity 'in the African and Colonial Press' and enclosing clippings from West African newspapers. Cedric Dover and Peter Abrahams, both 'well known in the colonies', had sent out statements through Padmore's African Press Agency, and Dorothy Pizer had talked with political and trade union leaders about Du Bois' case when she went to the West Indies on holiday. Padmore promised Du Bois they would 'leave no stone unturned to voice our indignation and condemnation of the reactionary policies of the American authorities, who the colonial peoples everywhere consider the main bulwark of Colonialism in Asia, Africa and the West Indies today. What a tragedy for a nation which had its birth in the struggle against British Colonialism!'[41]

Meanwhile, Padmore had good news from Africa. The CPP had triumphed in the Gold Coast elections held under a new constitution in February, and Nkrumah had been released to take on the job of running the government.[42] He would be stopping in London on his way back from collecting an honorary doctorate degree from Lincoln University, his American alma mater, and Padmore told Du Bois that the two might travel together to the Gold Coast to lay the groundwork for another Pan-African Congress. That is not how events fell out, but

STRATEGIST, PUBLICIST

Padmore did go to the Gold Coast, which he had last seen two decades earlier when he traveling on behalf of the Communist International. The freedom tree he had watered for so many years had finally borne fruit, and he wanted to do what he could to help Nkrumah cultivate it.

Even before Padmore arrived in the Gold Coast in June 1951, his upcoming visit had received publicity suggesting its political importance. 'NKRUMAH TO BRING GEO. PADMORE', the *Accra Daily Echo* declared in a front-page banner headline on 6 June. A subhead added: 'Will Be Chief Adviser To C.P.P.' Both the party and Padmore quickly denied that report; Padmore said he was coming as a journalist on behalf of the *Pittsburgh Courier* and the *Crisis*. 'The Gold Coast Government seems to have done very well in their first three months. It would be an insult for me to tell Nkrumah how to manage things.' Of course, he acknowledged, both Nkrumah and Kojo Botsio were old friends and if they asked his advice he would give it.[43] Even before his arrival, Padmore and the press had begun what would prove to be a complicated dance over just who he was and why he was there. Was he a political adviser or a journalist? An outside observer or an old friend?

The confusion over his identity extended further. Reporting on his impending arrival in a report to the US State Department, the American consul identified him (inaccurately) as 'a Jamaican journalist' and (accurately) as 'a former Communist Party member' who 'still follows the Communist Party line'.[44] The United States had kept its eye on Padmore for years, as documents in US Department of State archives attest. Now, like Britain, the United States was watching for any signs that the Gold Coast, in the forefront of African colonies moving towards independence, might move towards the communist camp. Not surprisingly (given Padmore's communist past), the consul sent several reports on Padmore's visit back to the US Department of State. He noted that Padmore had received a warm welcome at the airport from Nkrumah and the crowd with him, although newspaper clips he enclosed suggest that Gold Coast journalists had at best a superficial knowledge of who Padmore was. One purpose of this visit was, surely, to introduce Padmore to the country. Whether or not Nkrumah had in mind a position for him down the line, Padmore could already play a useful political role. At a time when Nkrumah was under pressure from both the opposition and members of his party to push more forcefully for full self-government, Padmore could testify to Nkrumah's international renown as the man who had led the Gold Coast thus far.

Speaking that first day at the Accra Arena where mass political events were held, Padmore emphasised the progress the Gold Coast had already made under Nkrumah's leadership. When Padmore had arrived in the Gold Coast on his trip to West Africa twenty years earlier, no one had welcomed him; the thousands come to greet him on this day showed 'there are constitutional changes in your country'. Then, the *Gold Coast Express* reported,

> Kwame Nkrumah took the microphone amidst a thunderous ovation and in a very short and charming speech he traced his friendship with George Padmore and described him as one of the greatest advocates on the freedom of the African. He started with him in 1945 what is now the Liberation Movement and he has ever been proud of him ... Dr Kwame Nkrumah was cheered in several tongues as he finished his oration which was described by many people as 'wonderful and magical'.[45]

The next day, Nkrumah presented Padmore at a press conference as a Negro journalist from the New World. Padmore himself denied that he was either a communist or a politician. 'I am a journalist and author but with a touch of Marxism and Socialism', he said.[46] He told the journalists that other countries had a stake in the Gold Coast's success because (in the words of the *Post*'s reporter) 'if the Gold Coast failed it would affect Jamaica, Trinidad, Malaya and African peoples in other African territories'.[47] This was an important message, and one Padmore was uniquely qualified to deliver. Whether the Gold Coast press called him a 'West Indian journalist' or a 'Negro Journalist of International fame', he was a man from somewhere else, representing the larger African diaspora and the world freedom movement. He testified to the world's interest in the Gold Coast and, as a journalist, he would return to the world bearing news of 'the Gold Coast revolution'.

While his usefulness to Nkrumah was clear, Padmore's visit presented certain risks to Nkrumah. Although the British were inclined to support Nkrumah at this point as the lesser of possible evils, they kept a close eye on the author of *Africa: Britain's Third Empire*, which was still banned.[48] Padmore's letters to and from Pizer were intercepted throughout his stay in the Gold Coast, despite his attempts at subterfuge: Padmore instructed Pizer to address him as George Appiah while he addressed her as Dorothy Appiah, and he changed his cover address – useless strategies since they were communicated in letters that were being intercepted.[49] The fifty-nine items summarised in one intelligence document on his visit included a letter in which Padmore expressed concern about his relationship with Pizer, followed by another that was '[e]ssentially amorous'. The relationship that most concerned British officials, however, was Padmore's relationship with

Nkrumah, which would become a longstanding cause of concern and focus of surveillance.[50] Although they understood that Padmore had broken with the communists and was unlikely to join them again, he did remain a Marxist.[51] Sensitive to the problems his old alliances could cause, in a set of autobiographical facts he offered to journalists he apparently downplayed the Comintern part of his life; although he mentioned the *Negro Worker* and Moscow lectures he gave on colonial questions, he did not mention the Communist International. He closed the list of key events in his life with a reference to his banned *Africa: Britain's Third Empire*. He told the journalists that while he was in the Gold Coast he would lecture and gather information for another book, as well as newspaper articles.[52]

Though Padmore presented himself as a journalist and expert on colonialism, he seemed willing enough to play the politician as well. Privately, he worked on a draft of a CPP constitution that would strengthen discipline within the party; publicly, he condemned one-party rule but called on political parties to join together to achieve self-government.[53] In response to a question, he criticised as absurd Nkrumah opponent J. B. Danquah's motion for a committee of the Legislative Council to draft a new constitution. That remark would cause him no end of trouble. In its report of his comments on Danquah's motion, the opposition newspaper *Talking Drums* wrote that Padmore regarded Danquah's proposal as 'absurd in that it would be a waste of time. Given five days, he George Padmore could draft one.'[54] To that comment, the *Talking Drums* editorialised under the title 'Five-Day Constitution', 'We don't know how it is done in Padmore's beloved Russia; but we know for certain that there is no modern democratic country for which a constitution has been drawn up by one single person'.[55] The next day a *Talking Drums* columnist called Padmore a 'sensation monger' who, claiming to be a journalist, 'had the audacity to dabble in the deep realms of practical politics'.[56] In Kumasi, home of Padmore's London colleague Joe Appiah, the Asante Youth Association passed a resolution protesting against the *Drums*' attack 'on this man of integrity and fame'.[57] Padmore himself responded to the attack with an extended explanation of why he condemned Danquah's proposal.[58] To that, the *Drums* editor K. Y. Attoh fired back: little wonder, he said, that Padmore could not understand Danquah's motion since Padmore was 'an armchair politician' intruding upon 'practical politicians in the colonies his newspaper politics full of his untested dreams'.[59] That controversy died down, and then the opposition politician F. Awoonor-Williams, speaking at a United Gold Coast Convention conference, said Padmore had been brought in by 'certain people with Communistic outlook' and as a result the communist-averse USA might not give the Gold Coast funds for development.[60] A writer in the *Gold Coast Observer* asked how Padmore could deny he was a communist 'when chapter and verse could be quoted from his own book wherein he claims the distinction of being the first Negro to be elected a member of the Moscow Soviet'.[61] The Cold War was being fought on Gold Coast ground.

While opposition politicians and newspapers picked away at Padmore, sympathetic newspapers wrote about him in triumphal terms: 'G. Padmore Thrills Accra Audience with Powerful Historical Speech', 'George Padmore Storms Cape Coast', 'Packed House Hears George Padmore at Prempeh Assembly Hall'.[62] Forwarding these and other clips to the Department of State on 17 August, the American consul, Hyman Bloom, summed up Padmore's stay thus far:

> Since his arrival in the Gold Coast on July 1, George Padmore has travelled extensively, lectured practically every day before paying audiences made up for the most part of C.P.P. adherents, and has become the subject of heated controversy between the C.P.P. press and the opposition press. He never misses an opportunity to extol the virtues of Kwame Nkrumah and the C.P.P. and has definitely become a part of the local political picture. One opposition newspaper, 'The Daily Echo', actually suggests that he is seeking Gold Coast citizenship in order to take over the C.P.P. reins from Dr Nkrumah. The same paper thinks that Padmore plans to supervise a chain of newspapers in West Africa, to be organised by the C.P.P., to campaign for a Union of West Africa.[63]

Despite the political dust Padmore had kicked up, in a final report to the State Department after Padmore's departure on 21 September, the consul concluded, 'It is felt that George Padmore's presence and activities did not do Dr Nkrumah any harm. To the contrary, his being here probably benefited Nkrumah and the C.P.P.' Padmore himself seemed in good humour. Bloom reported that in response to Nkrumah's parting remarks 'Mr Padmore said Dr Nkrumah had used his 42 years in hunting imperialism and at last had rounded it up'.[64]

On Padmore's return (after a stop in Nigeria that made the front page of Azikiwe's *West African Pilot*), an editor's note to his *Socialist Leader* article on the 'Bloodless Revolution in the Gold Coast' assured readers, 'No man is more capable of giving a factual and impartial statement than George'.[65] Padmore was, of course, far from impartial. He had helped to foment the revolution he reported, and his Gold Coast visit helped solidify his position as Nkrumah's adviser and strategist. As became clear in letters Padmore wrote back to Nkrumah after his return home,[66] he had used this time in the Gold Coast for a good deal more than glorifying Nkrumah and educating CPP members. Familiarising himself with the conditions under which Nkrumah was working and the economic and political challenges Nkrumah faced, he had strengthened his ability to advise Nkrumah from London. In a stream of long letters, Padmore, sometimes speaking as 'we' – a pronoun that surely included Appiah and Pizer (both of whom would wind up with jobs in the Gold Coast office in London) but possibly others as well, advised Nkrumah on development decisions.[67] Most urgent was new housing, which mattered more to ordinary people than flashy projects like a new harbour. To build that housing, Swedish and Dutch companies were offering to build sawmills and cement factories in the Gold Coast, and that was what the Gold Coast needed – not imported lumber and cement. 'You must own and control. Only in that way we can lay the basis for a socialist economy and keep capitalists from exploiting us.'[68]

Handling negotiations with foreign companies was a tricky matter, especially with a political opposition poised to make the most of failure or signs of corruption. Padmore himself had an inconclusive brush with scandal.[69] As for failure, after a flap over a prospective deal with an American company, Padmore offered instruction on how to handle such situations in the future: avoid early press coverage. The press should receive a brief statement when firm representatives arrived for discussions and another at the end of discussions. Meanwhile, Padmore and Appiah would advise companies not to give interviews to the press.

> We told the American[s] that even after the failure of their mission they should not have given any statement to the Press that could be distorted and used as a whip against K. and the Govt. They saw our point and blamed Watu-Ofei of going through their papers when they were out. I doubt it. After all, they are smart businessmen who don't leave their papers unlocked in their hotel or boarding house. But that is no excuse. They talked too damn much.[70]

Although Padmore doubted that stolen papers were to blame in this case, he felt obliged, less than a week later, to caution Nkrumah to tell ministers not to keep these letters from London in their office files. 'What's wrong with them? ... [D]on't they realise that when they are out of the office, the white men are looking through their files ... This is a revolution we are fighting, not a game of musical chairs.'[71]

Nkrumah's London advisers worried that as Nkrumah made development decisions he would be too vulnerable to control by the British on the scene. Nkrumah ought not to take British advice on siting a proposed harbour; he ought to get the advice of independent consultants – Dutch or German engineers. And he ought to consider the political payoffs of siting the harbour in one place rather than another.[72] After consulting sympathetic MPs – Fenner Brockway and others – they counselled him, '[D]on't put your signature to anything until we have an opportunity over here of submitting to independent socialist minded experts these fishy reports'. They wanted copies of reports on banking, on the proposed harbour. 'I have discussed this matter with J several times, and he agrees with me that you must fight tooth and nail for the right of your development committee to recruit, either locally or abroad, the necessary technical staff, and don't depend upon these British', Padmore wrote on 15 November 1951.[73] 'For the more they smile and laugh with you, the more they will be stabbing you in the back. They are the real opposition, not the Danquahs, who are helpless.'[74] Urgently, Padmore returned to that theme a week later on 22 November: '[T]hey will stab you in the back every time while smiling in your face. I don't trust them Kwame, not even on my dying bed.'[75]

In these letters to Nkrumah, Padmore wrote with passion and impatience at the lack of progress and offered his own services to speed things along. '[W]e are disappointed that all the things we talked about [–] the foreign affairs committee, the co-operative committee, the education committee, to direct and organise political organisation through study circles in the branches, as well as the series of pamphlets to serve as directives to party officers have never been done.' If the material were sent to London, he said, 'we' would edit the pamphlets.[76] Unintimidated by Nkrumah's ascension to a position of power (his title would be upgraded to prime minister in March 1952), Padmore issued him orders as if, through the force of his certainty, he could guide events from afar. 'Under no condition accept the new salary scales and allowances for repatriates', he wrote 25 January 1952. 'I have discussed it with certain M.Ps, and they all agree that it is outrageous.' Yet his advice bordering on commands could be tinged with affection; their relationship was, as Nkrumah would write later, very close – an intimate political alliance. 'I warn you my dear brother', Padmore wrote on dealing with the opposition, 'it is better to go down fighting than to be stabbed in the back by one's allies. And that is what they intend to do. I shall read their so-called Plan through and send you a detailed reply.'[77]

After a long struggle to end imperial rule in Africa, Padmore felt the wind filling the sails. His old friend C. L. R. James once said that Padmore could 'sketch a programme for a country he had never seen'.[78] Now, after only a few weeks' first-hand acquaintance with the Gold Coast, Padmore offered a grand vision of 'a new society on libertarian socialist lines', with co-operatives as the building blocks. 'For the black man in this age of bankrupt capitalism as a social system will never have the capital and business apparatus to challenge U.A.C. and other giants. The history of the co-op in this country and Denmark and Sweden has proved that only salvation for the masses is self-help trading and marketing of their produce.'[79]

While Padmore kept up this stream of private advice to Nkrumah, he was also contributing articles to the *Accra Evening News*, which was edited by James Markham, who had studied economics in London.[80] A regular contributor, Padmore was not happy about the *News*'s delay in paying him. He was owed £21, he wrote to Nkrumah. 'If they can't run a paper which enjoys such popular support in a proper way, they may as well close down.'[81] Nevertheless, he kept on writing for the *Evening News* because, as its London correspondent, he could help to shape political events in Accra and maintain his political relationship with Nkrumah, such a promising political leader in the movement for African independence. When the opposition mounted an anti-CPP press campaign in Britain in mid-1952, he wrote Nkrumah, 'I shall expose the purpose behind the new anti-C.P.P. press campaign ... In a recent despatch to the "Evening News" I took up the gauntlet.'[82] A few months later, Nkrumah asked Padmore to counter critical *Daily Telegraph* articles with articles in the *Evening News* refuting them.[83] While in private Padmore was offering detailed counsel to Nkrumah, in public he was playing the role of foreign correspondent in stories that did not acknowledge his private advisory role. From this point until the Gold Coast's independence as Ghana, Padmore acted both as Nkrumah's policy adviser and propagandist.[84]

Given Padmore's intimate involvement in the Gold Coast revolution, the book he produced on it is something of a surprise. *The Gold Coast Revolution* was a detailed but dry account of the nationalist movement in the Gold Coast from the earliest struggles against European control up to the present. Padmore once wrote to Richard Wright that English publishers wanted 'books on colonial subjects to be seriously presented' so they could be sold like textbooks. His own publisher, Dobson, did not want 'slick writing'.[85] Thus, though *The Gold Coast Revolution* was a polemic, it was a polemic heavily dependent on official reports, memoranda, and British and Gold Coast newspaper accounts, which he carefully footnoted. He declared as the book's purpose 'to trace the evolution of Gold Coast nationalism from the foundation of the Ashanti Confederacy to the emergence of the Convention People's Party and after'.[86] Providing this long history, he established resistance to colonial rule as part of Gold Coast identity and authenticated the current movement by connecting it to the past.

He placed this movement within the larger struggle against European rule both through references to Asian nationalist movements and through his subtitle – 'The struggle of an African people from slavery to freedom'. He put that worldwide anti-colonial struggle in a Cold War frame: how could Western democracies 'denounce Soviet imperialism while they themselves maintain any vestige of colonialism'?[87]

He meant the book to be a handbook for its time, but its mode as sober history was ill suited to that end, and, while his explicit reliance on documentary sources gave the book one kind of authority, it rendered invisible the book's authority on other very solid ground: his relationship with Nkrumah. He did not mention the work they had done together on the Manchester Congress, noting instead that Nkrumah had helped formulate the congress's strategy under Du Bois' direction.[88] Except for this reference to the Manchester Congress, Padmore said nothing about Nkrumah's political activities in London. Padmore's only indication of his personal contact with the Gold Coast revolution came in a brief mention of his visit to the Gold Coast in 1951.[89] The fact that only a whisper of Padmore's own involvement in the Gold Coast revolution surfaced in the book itself suggests its status as propaganda despite its scholarly tone, yet his first-hand involvement heightens its interest as a primary record by an involved observer who drew information and understanding from conversations with Nkrumah and others, not only in the Gold Coast but in England after his return. 'You'd be surprised how difficult it is to put your finger on facts that are correct', Pizer told the Wrights. 'G[eorge] is doing quite a job for the future Gold Coast historian, by trying to bring [between] two covers the sequence of events in the country in some sort of order and historical relationship. When you read a single paragraph, it's quite difficult to appreciate the amount of research and reading which has gone into it.' Fortunately, some of the participants in the story were in London at the time and Padmore could check facts with them.[90]

Whatever the usefulness of these consultations, the resulting book appears more the work of a historian who has spent hours in the library than a behind-the-scenes account that would be useful to would-be revolutionaries elsewhere. Within the thicket of long quotations and lists of names, however, Padmore planted hints of the political world he and Nkrumah envisioned for the country that would take the name 'Ghana'. In this new 'democratic socialist society', the chiefs who had carried out British commands under the old system would be brought to heel, made accountable to the common people. This was the Gold Coast's 'bloodless revolution': not only a nationalist revolt but also a social revolution, upending class relations.[91] While in his introduction Padmore offered chiefs the possibility of an honoured place as counsellors and moral leaders in the 'modern democratic society', he also implied a threat: 'What they make of this new opportunity depends upon the chiefs themselves. For there is a substantial body of opinion among educated Africans, not only in the Gold Coast but elsewhere, that chieftaincy is a social anachronism that must adapt itself to the rapidly changing social order or disappear, if Africa is to take her place in the modern world.'[92] Thus he struck a blow in the political battlefield that Richard Rathbone has described in *Nkrumah and the Chiefs*, as Nkrumah and the CPP attempted to transform British indirect rule into a new kind of government wherein chiefs would have considerably less power than they once had.[93]

With Pizer's help, Padmore finished *The Gold Coast Revolution* two days before Christmas 1952. The manuscript done, the index came next – 'a horrid thankless job that always has to be done in a hurry and really needs plenty of time and care', Pizer wrote Ellen Wright. Pizer was presumably doing the index since she said Padmore was 'a little stuck for something to do, though he has his weekly press work for the colonial papers and to cope with sundry people who call with their troubles or for information and introductions to all parts of Africa and other colonial territories'. He was using his extra time and his book advance to spruce up their flat. '[I]t's not a bad thing to rewash the walls and paint the ceilings and get new curtains at this grey season of the year. It does put a new look on one's surroundings even if not in one's heart.'[94]

Although Padmore had told Dobson at one point that he meant to dedicate the book to Nkrumah, perhaps understanding the doubts such a dedication would raise about his impartiality he wound up dedicating it to Pizer, 'who encouraged me to write this account of the Gold Coast's struggle for Freedom'. Nkrumah appeared opposite the title page – smiling, regal, his Kente cloth draped over his shoulder. As for the author, the dust jacket description of Padmore mentioned his slave ancestry, his role in 'the Pan-African and Negro Labour movements', his work for the International Trade Union Committee of Negro Workers, his authorship of pamphlets and books on colonialism. Although his writings were said 'to have had a considerable influence on the younger generation of African intellectuals', as in the book itself no mention was made of his close political acquaintance with Nkrumah over the previous eight years.

Not many readers or reviewers would know just how close that relationship was, although a reviewer for *West Africa* noted that 'Mr Padmore writes like a partisan',[95] and reviewers for the *Daily Times* in Lagos and the *Daily Graphic* in Accra did take issue with Padmore's uncritical portrayal of the CPP,[96] while an anonymous WASU News

Service reviewer noted that the CPP had invited Padmore to the Gold Coast. That reviewer gave the book a solid bashing, criticising Padmore's adulatory portrayal of Nkrumah and 'uncouth' portrayal of CPP opponents. '[H]is opinion of Nkrumah borders on religious veneration.'[97] That may have been the impression Padmore gave in *The Gold Coast Revolution*, but in private, though he seemed to like and respect Nkrumah, he was less reverent, taking significant credit for setting Nkrumah on the right political path. Comparing Nkrumah to Azikiwe, Padmore once told Wright, 'K. N. is the only one who knows what it is all about. Thanks to Nello [James] who introduced him to Trotskyism and I knocked that nonsense out of him before his return. And put in its place Pan-Africanism (black nationalism plus socialism).'[98] In his own mind, at least, Padmore was more than the chief publicist for the Gold Coast revolution: he was also its hidden philosopher and strategist, a view entertained by British officials, who had tracked his relationship with Nkrumah at least since the trip to the Gold Coast. Now, as the culmination of that trip made its appearance, they worried about its impact. 'We have no information concerning the subject matter of this new book but can hazard a shrewd guess', the Security Liaison Officer in West Africa observed. Reporting that Nkrumah had authorised purchase of five thousand copies by the CPP, he further observed that, while there was still a Gold Coast ban on Padmore's *Africa: Britain's Third Empire*, that ban could not be replicated 'in present circumstances'.[99] In just three years, a seismic shift had occurred.

Notes

1 George Shepperson and St Clair Drake 'Fifth Pan-African Conference, 1945 and the All African People's Congress, 1958', *Contributions in Black Studies*, 8 (1986–87), 44–5.
2 Padmore, 'Murder on the Gold Coast', *Socialist Leader* (20 March 1948), 1.
3 Rukudzo Murapa, 'Padmore's Role in the African Liberation Movement'(Ph.D. dessertation, Northern Illinois University, 1974), p. 173; C. L. R. James made a similar comment in 'Notes on the Life of George Padmore', carbon copy typescript with author's corrections, microform (Chicago, IL: Center for Research Libraries, 1959), p. 44.
4 Padmore, 'Facts Behind the Gold Coast Riots', *Crisis*, 55: 7 (July 1948), 207. For the Watson Commission's findings, see [Watson Commission Report]: 'Minute by Mr Creech Jones to Mr Atlee', 19 July 1948, # 36, in Richard Rathbone (ed.), *British Documents on the Empire: Ghana*, Series B, Vol. 1, Part 1 – 1941–1952 (London: HMSO, 1992), p. 90; the report did say the UGCC had exploited the unrest but did not instigate it.
5 Marika Sherwood, 'Kwame Nkrumah: The London Years, 1945–47', in David Killingray (ed.), *Africans in Britain* (Ilford: Frank Cass and Company, 1994), p. 168.
6 Kwame Nkrumah, *Ghana: The Autobiography of Kwame Nkrumah* (New York: Thomas Nelson and Sons, 1957), pp. 93–4.
7 *Ibid.*, p. 109.

8   That straightforward march to action is Nkrumah's version of the story in *Ghana*, pp. 111–17. Bob Fitch and Mary Oppenheimer, in *Ghana: End of an Illusion* (New York, London: Monthly Review Press, 1966), p. 29, suggest that Nkrumah tried to delay the upcoming general strike announced by the Trade Union Congress.
9   Nkrumah, *Ghana*, pp. 118–26.
10 Nnamdi Azikiwe, *My Odyssey* (London: C. Hurst and Company, 1970), p. 177.
11 James R. Hooker, *Black Revolutionary: George Padmore's Path from Communism to Pan-Africanism* (New York, Washington and London: Praeger, 1970; first published 1967), p. 109.
12 James, 'Notes', p. 50.
13 George Padmore, *Pan-Africanism or Communism?* (London: Dennis Dobson, 1956), pp. 163–4, referring to West Africa.
14 George Padmore, *Africa: Britain's Third Empire* (London: Dennis Dobson, 1949), p. 114.
15 J. E. Appiah, 'Et Tu, Labour?, *Left*, 145 (December 1949), 216.
16 Partha Chatterjee, *Nationalist Thought and the Colonial World: A Derivative Discourse* (Minneapolis: University of Minnesota Press, 1986), p. 137.
17 Padmore, *Africa*, pp. 214–15; for what happened to Burma see Thant Myint-U, *The River of Lost Footsteps: Histories of Burma* (New York: Farrar, Straus and Giroux, 2006).
18 Padmore, *Africa*, pp. 216–18.
19 Hooker, *Black Revolutionary*, p. 111.
20 'African Problems', *Times Literary Supplement* (31 March 1950), 203; reviewers are identified in the online TLS Centenary Archive.
21 F. A. Ridley, 'Africa Calling!', *Socialist Leader* (18 March 1950), 7.
22 Hooker, *Black Revolutionary*, pp. 110–11.
23 UK/TNA, CO 537/6522. This discussion occurred on 21–2 March 1950.
24 US/NA, Department of State, 941.63/3–3050, Margaret Joy Tibbett, for Ambassador, to Department of State, No. 1570, 30 March 1950.
25 UK/TNA, CO 537/6523,Outward Telegram, Draft on 3/94077/1 Top Secret, to Nigeria, Sir J. Macpherson, 1 April 1950. This is identified as a draft but a note signed by J.G. approved it on 4 April.
26 Padmore, *Africa*, pp. 200, 235.
27 *Ibid.*, pp. 238–40.
28 *Ibid.*, p. 96.
29 UK/TNA, CO 537/6523, M. Joseph-Mitchell to James Griffith, 23 March 1950.
30 *Ibid.*, [indecipherable] A. Allen, to Secretary for the Colonies, 19 April 1950.
31 *Ibid.*, N.D. Watson, Private Secretary, 5 April 1950, to General and Travelling Secretary, League of Coloured Peoples.
32 *Ibid.*, 'Note of a Meeting Held on the 25th of April, 1950', Draft on 14253.
33 *Ibid.*, James Griffiths to S. W. Jeger, 8 May 1950.
34 *Ibid.*, Fenner Brockway to James Griffiths, 29 November 1950.
35 Padmore to Du Bois, 21 August 1950, in Herbert Aptheker (ed.), *Correspondence of W. E. B. Du Bois, III, Selections, 1944–1963* (Amhurst: University of Massachusetts Press, 1978), p. 290.
36 Du Bois to Padmore, 17 March 1950, in *Correspondence*, III, p. 280.
37 Du Bois to Padmore, 18 September 1950, in *Correspondence*, III, p. 290.
38 Penny M. Von Eschen, *Race Toward Empire: Black Americans and Anticolonialism, 1937–1957* (Ithaca, NY and London: Cornell University Press, 1997), p. 116.
39 David Levering Lewis, *W. E. B. Du Bois: The Fight for Equality and the American Century, 1919–1963* (New York: Henry Holt and Company, 2000), pp. 541, 546–8.
40 Padmore to Du Bois, 21 March 1951, in *Correspondence*, III, p. 312.
41 Padmore to Du Bois, 29 May 1951, in *Correspondence*, III, p. 316. The name of the press agency appears on a note 'To Whom It May Concern' that he wrote on Richard Wright's behalf 4 June 1953, in Wright Papers (G. Padmore).
42 Richard Rathbone, *Nkrumah and the Chiefs* (Accra: F. Reimmer; Athens: Ohio University Press; Oxford: James Currey, 2000), pp. 28–9.

43 US/NA, Department of State, 911.6245K/8-1751, clippings: 'Nkrumah to Bring Geo. Padmore', *Daily Echo* (6 June 1951); 'George Padmore Denies He Is Coming to be C.P.P. Adviser', *Daily Graphic* (9 June 1951); 'C.P.P. Secretary Makes Correction', *African Morning Post* (11 June 1951). These clippings and others listed in subsequent notes on Padmore's Gold Coast visit accompanied a letter from Hyman Bloom, American Consul, to Department of State, 17 August 1951, in the same file.

44 US/NA, Department of State, 911.6245K/6-1351, Hyman Bloom to Department of State, 13 June 1951.

45 US/NA, Department of State, 911.6245K/8-1751, 'George Padmore Addresses Anxious Crowd at Arena', *Express* (2 July 1951).

46 US/NA, Department of State, 911.6245K/8-1751, 'Not "Red Hot" Red, Say ...', *Spectator* (3 July 1951).

47 US/NA, Department of State, 911.6245K/8-1751, 'Mr Padmore Appreciates Determination of Ghana People in Press Talk', *African Morning Post* (3 July 1951).

48 US/NA, Department of State, 911.6245K/6-1351, Hyman Bloom to Department of State, 13 June 1951.

49 UK/TNA, KV2/1850/310289, summary, letter from Padmore to Pizer, 15 July 1951, in 'Correspondence relating to Padmore'; indecipherable signature at the bottom dated 8/2/51. Most of the fifty-nine items on the list are letters to or from Pizer and Padmore.

50 UK/TNA, KV 2/1850/310289 documents surveillance of Padmore, 1951–53, including reports from well-placed sources and intercepted letters and several expressions of concern about Padmore's Marxism and his influence over Nkrumah, for instance a letter to SLO West Africa, unsigned, 15 September 1953. This document is among a set of Security Service files involving African nationalists that were first made public in 2005.

51 For British understanding of his break with the communists see UK/TNA, KV 2/1850/310289, H. Loftus Brown to F.S., 5 July 1952.

52 US/NA, US Department of State, 911.6245k/6-751, Hyman Bloom to Department of State, 7 July 1951.

53 For his advising the CPP see UK/TNA, KV 2/1850/310289, 15 July 1951 letter to Pizer, summarised in 'Correspondence Relating to Padmore', and Office of the Commissioner, The Gold Coast Police Force, Accra, 16 October 1951, 'Special Branch Summary No. 32. September, 1951'.

54 US/NA, US Department of State, 911.6245K/8-1751, 'George Padmore Stands for ...', *Talking Drums* (3 July 1951), 1.

55 US/NA, US Department of State, 911.6245K/8-1751, 'Five-Day Constitution', *Talking Drums* (6 July 1951).

56 US/NA, US Department of State, 911.6245K/8-1751, 'George Padmore and Our Demand for Self Government', *Talking Drums* (7 July 1951).

57 US/NA, US Department of State, 911.6245K/8-1751, 'AYA Vehemently Protests Against Drums "Fetid Vituperations"', *Accra Evening News* (18 July 1951).

58 US/NA, US Department of State, 911.6245K/8-1751 , 'George Replies to "Drums" Attacks', *Talking Drums* (9 July 1951).

59 US/NA, Department of State, 911.6245K/8-1751, K. Y. Attoh, 'Padmore's Five-Day Constitution', *Talking Drums* (20 July 1951).

60 US/NA, Department of State, 911.6245K/8-1751, 'Awoonor-Williams Thinks Padmore's Presence May Deny Gold Coast of US Financial Help', *Ashanti Times* (7 August 1951).

61 US/NA, Department of State, 911.6245K/8-1751, 'At Random Notes', *Gold Coast Observer* (27 July 1951).

62 US/NA, Department of State, 911.6245K/8-1751, 'G. Padmore Thrills Accra Audience with Powerful Historical Speech', *Ashanti Pioneer* (5 July 1951); 'Packed House Hears George Padmore at Prempeh Assembly Hall', *Ashanti Pioneer* (1 August, 1951); 'George Padmore Storms Cape Coast', *Accra Evening News* (24 July 1951).

63 US/NA, 911.6245K/8-1751 Hyman Bloom, Consul, to Department of State, Activities of George Padmore, 17 August 1959.

64 US/NA, October 1951, 911.6245K/10–451, Bloom to Department of State, 'Departure of George Padmore', 4 October 1951.
65 Murapa mentions coverage of his Nigerian visit in 'Padmore's Role,', p. 191; Padmore, 'Bloodless Revolution in the Gold Coast: Crisis Facing Chieftainship', *Socialist Leader* (29 September 1951), 3
66 Typed copies of these letters or excerpts from them wound up as a set that the Nkrumah biographer June Milne turned over to the Moorland-Spingarn Research Center at Howard University, along with other papers apparently collected by Dorothy Pizer for the biography of Padmore that she hoped to write. In a 17 April 1968 letter to Drake, James said that he had gone to Ghana to look at Padmore's papers; he was unable to locate them but he found that 'when Dorothy died, Nkrumah examined them and took out what he wanted' (C. L. R. James Collection, University of the West Indies at St Augustine, Folder 194).
67 Appiah, *Joe Appiah*, p. 197. In a 30 August 1951 letter to Pizer from the Gold Coast, Padmore tells her the office will be set up and she will be on staff; letter summarised in UK/TNA, KV 2/1850/310289, 'Correspondence Relating to Padmore'.
68 Moorland-Spingarn Research Center, Howard University, Kwame Nkrumah Papers, Box 154–7, Folder 52 (Dorothy Padmore), unsigned, unaddressed typed copy of letter 9 November 1951; internal evidence suggests this letter may have been directed to CPP leaders rather than to Nkrumah himself.
69 Hooker, *Black Revolutionary*, p. 119.
70 Nkrumah Papers, Box 154–7, Folder 52, 9 November 1951.
71 *Ibid.*, 15 November 1951.
72 *Ibid.*, 22 November 1951.
73 *Ibid.*, 15 November 1951.
74 *Ibid.*
75 *Ibid.*, 22 November 1951.
76 *Ibid.*, 13 January 1952.
77 *Ibid.*, 25 January 1952.
78 James, 'George Padmore', *Tribune* (2 October 1964), 13.
79 Nkrumah Papers, Box 154–7, Folder 52, typed copy of letter [Padmore to Nkrumah], 21 July 1952.
80 Hooker, *Black Revolutionary*, p. 133.
81 Nkrumah Papers, Box 154–7, Folder 52, typed copy of letter [Padmore to Nkrumah], 21 July 1952.
82 *Ibid.*
83 UK/TNA, KV 2/1850/310289, for Director General to SLO West Africa, 2 September 1952.
84 Murapa describes Padmore's involvement in the CPP and his subsequent use of the *Evening News* to further CPP positions in 'Padmore's Role', pp. 193–202.
85 Wright Papers (George Padmore), Padmore to Wright, 28 June 1954.
86 Padmore, *The Gold Coast Revolution: The Struggle of an African People from Slavery to Freedom* (London: Dennis Dobson, 1953), p. 1.
87 *Ibid.*, p. 12.
88 *Ibid.*, p. 61.
89 *Ibid.*, p. 138.
90 Wright Papers (D. Padmore), Pizer to E. and R. Wright, Sunday, n.d.
91 Padmore, *Gold Coast Revolution*, pp. 129, 141.
92 *Ibid.*, p. 3.
93 Rathbone, *Nkrumah and the Chiefs*, pp. 40–7.
94 Wright Papers (D. Padmore), Pizer to E. Wright, 20 January 1953.
95 'West African Books in 1953', *West Africa*, 1923 (2 January 1954), 1235.
96 Murapa, 'Padmore's Role', pp. 188–9.
97 Hooker, *Black Revolutionary*, p. 117.
98 Wright Papers (G. Padmore), Padmore to R. Wright, 19 October 1955.
99 UK/TNA, KF 2/1851/310289 'Copy of a Letter from SLO West Africa Mentioning Nkrumah', 9 February 1953.

CHAPTER SIX

Acts of betrayal

While Padmore was writing *The Gold Coast Revolution*, Peter Abrahams was producing another and very different book: *Return to Goli*, an account of his return to Africa for the first time since the war. Unlike Padmore's dense narrative of Gold Coast history, *Return to Goli* was cast in the form of a travelogue, personal and enlivened by scenes, dialogue, and portrayals of individuals. Abrahams meant the book 'to reach the hearts and minds' of both 'whites' and 'non-whites' who lived in Africa.[1] To Padmore and Pizer, however, Abrahams's journey home had sinister overtones. On 26 May 1952, after Abrahams had left for South Africa, Pizer sent Richard Wright a couple of clippings 'relating to your one-time friend Peter Abrahams. G. is sending them both out to S. Africa immediately, where he is at this moment. I would like to see his hash settled by his own people. Once a coloured fellow gets on the B.B.C. in any other programme than a colonial or commonwealth one, you can know for sure that he's made his peace with the other side.'[2] The radio appearance to which she referred was on the BBC Third Programme, where Abrahams declared his intent to free himself from the burden of race. 'As a writer, my work demands this liberation if I am to see more clearly, to understand more wholly.' He acknowledged that he would probably 'be accused of being a Negro who is anti-Negro'.[3] Pizer commented: 'We hope he can maintain his "liberal" detachment in the very free air of Goli.'

A rift between Abrahams and the Padmore household had been widening for years. Abrahams had divorced his first wife, Dorothy, a political woman whom Padmore had apparently liked, and moved to France for a couple of years with his second wife, Daphne, an artist. There he concentrated on his growing family and his writing. He later wrote that, by the time he returned to live in England in 1950, he had 'lost regular contact with the Pan-African Federation'.[4] Focusing on his career as an author, Abrahams had published book after book about South African life – *Dark Testament, Song of the City, Mine Boy, Wild Conquest,* and *The Path of Thunder.* In a few short years he had made something of a name for himself, although his path to publication had not always been smooth. He was unable at first to find a British publisher for *The Path of Thunder.* Dorothy Crisp, the London publisher who had brought out *Song of the City* and *Mine Boy,* had gone out of business; Abrahams offered the book instead to George Allen and Unwin, the British publisher of his first book, *Dark Testament.* The response was negative. Allen and Unwin told Abrahams that novels had not been selling well in England; South Africa would thus need to supply most of the novel's sales and the book would most likely be banned there.[5] Published first by Harper in the United States, *The Path of Thunder* did not come out in Britain until 1952, the year the BBC broadcasts opened the way for Abrahams's return to Africa.

The trip's motivation was overtly political: under the sponsorship of the BBC Third Programme, the *Observer,* and the *New York Herald Tribune* in Paris, Abrahams was to travel first to South Africa, then to Kenya to test the argument made by some East African whites that what prevailed there was not a 'colour bar' but a 'culture bar'. As a westernised African, Abrahams could measure the truth of that argument.[6] Returning home to South Africa, he found the colour bar intact. When he visited his mother in Coloured Albertville, a bus 'For Coloured Persons Only' still ran. He also found continuing economic oppression along colour lines. In most of the Coloured areas he visited, he found people living crowded together, relying on bucket toilets.[7] Indians laboured for low wages in Natal sugar-cane fields and packed their families into single rooms in conditions even less sanitary than the Coloured slums of Albertville.[8] In the mines, Blacks worked for less than one-tenth the wages of whites. On the Reserves – land set aside for 'Natives' – a majority of Blacks had no land at all.[9]

In Johannesburg, Abrahams was given a temporary office at the *African Drum,* a new monthly where a Black South African he had known in London was assistant editor. At Abrahams's Hampstead flat, the two men had had long conversations about how Africa could change and about the part the press could play in that change. 'A critical detachment was needed to give the Africans who led the struggle for freedom some sense of balance', Abrahams wrote of the situation as his friend saw it. Africans needed 'a mirror in which the people could see themselves' and Abrahams envisioned the *African Drum* – a magazine financed by 'enlightened whites' – providing that mirror. Circulation had climbed past fifty thousand, and there were plans to put out editions targeted to West, Central, and East Africa. The magazine mixed pictures of beautiful women with stories about contract labour abuses or non-whites' housing and transportation problems. It carried reports on the non-white movements that were challenging apartheid and the political and economic powerlessness of Black, Coloured, and Indian South Africans.[10] Would Britain and other nations of the West follow India's lead in encouraging United Nations intervention to support this challenge to the colour bar? Or would communism turn out to be Blacks' only ally?[11] Despite this call for European solidarity with South Africa's people of colour, Abrahams expressed himself 'glad' to leave South Africa. What he saw in Africa weakened the resolution he had made in England to free himself from racial resentment. 'For six weeks I had lived with its sickness, its hatreds and its fears, and I was glad to get away. Yet I was also sorry to go, for I am a child of Goli.'[12] Such ambivalent feelings punctuate *Return to Goli*. Abrahams knew that flying away from Johannesburg would not free him from the knowledge of what went on there or moral responsibility for it, but he was glad to be gone.

In Kenya, to which he devoted only part of a single chapter at the end of the book, Abrahams saw the bitter fate of an old colleague who had returned to Africa and stayed: Jomo Kenyatta. In a conversation over drinks on Abrahams's first evening in Kenya, Kenyatta had shown to Abrahams the face of 'a lonely man', alienated by his Western experience from the country and culture of his youth. Unwilling to talk with whites who looked down on him and lacking peers among other Kenyan leaders, the author of *Facing Mount Kenya* had undergone a profound change.

> The fine scholarly brain I had respected so much in Europe had gone mouldy. Prejudice had taken the place of thought. In *Facing Mount Kenya* Kenyatta wrote: 'Europeans should realize that there is something to learn from the African.' When I saw him in Kenya he wanted to teach the European nothing and he wanted to learn nothing from the European. I think that Kenyatta has passed the point of creative possibility.[13]

Whatever the elements of truth and honesty in this bleak assessment, it could be seen as a betrayal of friendship, a public shaming of a pivotal political figure whose charismatic power derived from his connection to Kenya's people. Abrahams had actually not said all he could have. In a more detailed account published six years later in the American travel magazine *Holiday*, Abrahams described Kenyatta's abrupt departure from the chiefs' dinner welcoming Abrahams. Reluctant to offend the gathering, Abrahams hesitated, but Kenyatta insisted. '"I can't stand any more," he snapped. "Come!"' At Kenyatta's bookless home, with its sparse scattering of furniture, the two of them 'sat on the veranda and drank steadily and in silence until we were both miserably, depressingly drunk'. Kenyatta's discontent spilled out. 'He had no friends. There was no one in the tribe who could give him the intellectual companionship that had become so important to him in his years in Europe.'[14]

Here was a novelist's rendition of a painful human experience – a reading by a man who himself felt the loneliness of being 'a non-white Western man' in an African multi-racial society.[15] It was a compelling description and surely truthful, in its way. But it was not the whole truth: there was more to Kenyatta's anguish than the loneliness of a man uprooted from the home he had made in England and struggling to replant himself in his native soil. At the very time of Abrahams's visit, Kenyatta was already swept up in a battle to keep the Kenya African Union (KAU) from being undermined by Mau Mau, whose members swore oaths to fight physically for their rights. Struggling to retain his hold on the movement and forestall repression by the authorities, Kenyatta had launched a speaking campaign well before Abrahams's arrival in June. It started in April and peaked in July, when a crowd of fifty thousand heard Kenyatta disclaim the KAU's connection with Mau Mau. Although Kenyatta rejected violence and Mau Mau in his speeches, white settlers heard instead his calls for self-government. As rumours spread that a state of emergency would be declared, a secret central committee of the KAU began establishing bases in the forests. A small group of these young guerrillas-to-be met with Kenyatta in mid-August; at this point Kenyatta himself expected to be arrested. Invoking the example of Toussaint L'Ouverture, whose story he had heard from James, Kenyatta – less pacific in private than in public – told them, 'Everything in this world has to be paid for and we must buy our freedom with our blood'.[16]

In the midst of this tumult, Abrahams, back in England, gave a BBC Third Programme talk in which he warned of the coming troubles by describing an elegiac moment on a hill in Masai land with Kenyatta and Mbiyu (Peter) Koinange's father, a former Kikuyu chief who had lost his position because of his advocacy of Kikuyu land rights.[17] As the revolt that Abrahams had left undescribed simmered in the background, the former chief prayed to the 'God of Abraham and God of Isaac, God of our fathers, Father of all men' that their land not 'pass from us now' and, too, that they be led 'as you led your servant Moses out of bondage to freedom'. Abrahams left Kenya 'feeling there was desperately little time left for God to grant the old chief's prayer'. Including this story in *Return to Goli*, Abrahams downplayed the intensity of the crisis already in play while he was in Kenya. 'Though Mau Mau was mentioned in Kenya while I was there, no outrages had as yet been committed ... Kenya was then comparatively peaceful.'[18] Why did Abrahams miss the heart of this drama – Black Kenyans' movement to overthrow British dominance? It is possible that Kenyatta told him very little of what was actually going on. It is possible that Abrahams was exercising political caution. It is also possible that he reasonably feared that rapid political developments might outdate a more specific account by the time the slow wheels of publishing turned the book out. Whatever the reason (and Abrahams declined to respond to questions for this book on the ground that it would give him an advantage over those now deceased), and whether for this shortcoming or another, Abrahams confessed to the American editor who considered publishing *Return to Goli* there, 'It is not a book I am proud of'.[19]

By the time *Return to Goli* appeared in 1953, events in Kenya had indeed moved precipitously forward. On 24 August 1952, both Kenyatta and the elder Koinange spoke at a large well-publicised meeting held to denounce Mau Mau, but the crisis deepened with the murder of a chief who had openly opposed the Mau Mau's oathing movement. In London, Mbiyu Koinange and another KAU member had brought a petition to overturn land ordinances that benefited white Kenyans; Padmore believed that the publicity given the petition contributed to white settlers' calls to suppress the movement.[20] On 11 October, Padmore invoked the upheaval in Kenya in a letter to Nkrumah urging him to press for constitutional change in the Gold Coast. 'Now is the time to strike while Mau-Mau is spreading the fear of God among the imperialists here and in Kenya. Jomo! Jomo! Jomo! (laughter).'[21] On 20 October 1952 a new Governor of Kenya, Sir Evelyn Baring, proclaimed a state of emergency. Kenyatta was one of the first arrested.[22] Although historians have since cleared Kenyatta of involvement in Mau Mau, he was convicted and sentenced to seven years' hard labour. Reporting on the trial for an American political magazine, the *Nation*, Abrahams recalled Kenyatta saying when he had visited him the year before, 'Tell me, man, would it be such a crime if I, the leader of the majority in this country, were to be made Prime Minister?' While in the Gold Coast Nkrumah could be released from prison to govern the country, in Kenya the presence of forty thousand white settlers kept Kenyatta behind bars.[23]

Nkrumah's path at this point was not without obstacles, as Richard Wright discovered when he spent several weeks in the Gold Coast in mid-1953. Like Abrahams, Wright had wanted for years to make a trip to Africa – a return not to the continent of his youth but to the continent of his ancestors. He had mentioned this hope in an early letter to Padmore, and, when he finally made the journey in 1953, it was with Padmore's and Pizer's encouragement and assistance. Padmore gave Wright a helpful 'To whom it may concern' note under the return address of his African Press Agency, 22 Cranleigh House, and, when Wright expressed doubts about the welcome he would receive, Padmore and Pizer reassured him.[24] Given their reassurance and his own prominence as the world's most famous Black novelist (although lately that reputation had been slipping), Wright could be forgiven for expecting a warm welcome on his arrival in Ghana. Anticipating a flock of reporters present on his arrival he wrote out comments for them: 'I've come here to try to tell your story ... to report Ghana's rendezvous with the 20th Century'.[25]

In fact, when Wright disembarked from his ship at Takoradi on 16 June, no reporters met him at all – only one lone man, who put him on a bus to Accra. Nkrumah's secretary, Joyce Gittens – a friend of Padmore's and Pizer's – took him to his rest house above the city, which he explored the first day on his own, taking in the beggars, the street vendors, the crowds washing and filling their buckets at public hydrants. The following day he spent touring with Nkrumah as crowds swarmed round their car shouting 'Free-dooooom!' Finally he had an opportunity to deliver his comments at a rally: 'To a great and despoiled Africa, to an Africa awakening from its slumber, to an Africa indignant and militant, to an Africa burning with hope, I advise in the name of Jesus: TAKE UP YOUR BED AND WALK!' In response to those dramatic words, he heard only a scattering of applause. Perhaps his audience had not heard him? Or had not understood him? Afterwards, a reporter asked for a copy of his speech to publish in the *Daily Graphic*, the newspaper that had objected to Padmore's uncritical portrayal of the CPP in *The Gold Coast Revolution*. Turning to Nkrumah for an OK, Wright was surprised when Nkrumah took Wright's notes, studied them, then tucked them back in Wright's suit pocket. Wright wondered if he had said something wrong.[26]

Peter Abrahams happened to be in Accra on assignment from the *Observer* and the *Nation*,[27] and when the two men had breakfast one morning Abrahams had the impression that Wright found Africa 'bewildering'. Wright was put off by the openness towards sex that he saw around him; men holding hands and dancing together made him uneasy. In Wright, Abrahams found yet another black man alienated in Africa. When he wrote about their conversation for *Holiday* magazine, Abrahams said that the 'tribal African' was 'no Pan-African dreaming of a greater African glory when the white man is driven into the sea. The acute race consciousness of the American Negro, or of the black South African at the receiving end of Apartheid, is alien to him.' Africa was too large to 'inspire big continental dreams ... In terms of communications the man in the tribe lives in the Dark Ages.' To Wright's surprise, even Africans with education 'had not heard of him and were skeptical of a grown man earning his living by writing'.[28] A month after Wright's arrival, he sent Pizer and Padmore a long, disappointed letter filling them in on his visit. The CPP had not taken him in hand, as he had hoped; he had had to see the country on his own. As a result, he had to rethink the book he planned to write. He would not be able to concentrate on the political situation – instead, he would have to show how the people lived.[29]

It is not difficult to understand why the CPP had not opened its inner doors to Wright. He had arrived in the Gold Coast at a tricky turn in its road to independence. On 10 July, Wright watched as Nkrumah presented the government's White Paper on Constitutional Reform to the Gold Coast Assembly, along with a motion for independence. If the British government and Commonwealth countries accepted the terms of this White Paper, then the Gold Coast would become a self-governing nation within the Commonwealth.[30] But a split within Nkrumah's own party could slow the process. Asante CPP were pushing for more members in the new Legislature than their population would justify.[31] With the Gold Coast political ground so unsettled, it is not surprising that neither Nkrumah nor the CPP made Wright privy to their operations. Wright was not Padmore, whose loyalty to Nkrumah and the cause was unquestioned. Nor was Wright a charming journalist. By the evidence of his own writing as well as Abrahams's observations, Wright was discomfited by the Gold Coast, put off by the heat and the bugs and the tribal chiefs. As Wright's biographer Hazel Rowley writes, '[W]hy should his African cousins trust him? He did not trust them.'[32]

In addition to perceiving Wright's own prickly response to the place, Nkrumah and the CPP likely noticed Wright's repeated contacts with British and American officials in Accra. A British Information Service official treated him to dinner in his home and arranged a visit to the interior of the country. Wright's contacts with the Americans were even more frequent. The first day in town he introduced himself at the US Information Service, and, thereafter, USIS officials took him under their wing, driving him to a hospital to have an ear problem treated and, later, helping him find a hotel in Accra instead of outside of town where Nkrumah's secretary had deposited him. After three weeks in the Gold Coast, he actually moved in with the USIS's Eugene Sawyer. On several occasions the American consul William E. Cole invited Wright to his home.[33] Quite possibly, the CPP feared that Wright would tell whatever he learned from them to the Americans, who might then pass it on to the British.

That is in fact just what Wright did. Before he left the Gold Coast, Wright reported to the American consul some of the things he had learned about the CPP, including evidence of communist leanings. Hoping that the Gold Coast would set an example as a democratic country, the US consulate was watching for signs of which way the wind was blowing – towards the West or towards the communist bloc. Not long before Wright's trip to the Gold Coast, the consulate sent a despatch to Washington reporting Nkrumah's threat to dismiss the editor of the *Evening News* if he did not stop publishing 'pro-communist' items.[34] Thus, consul Cole welcomed information from Wright, who reported that he had encountered only one 'self-avowed member of the Communist Party': Bankole Renner, who had broken with the CPP but still held study group meetings. Wright attended one and came away convinced that, though the young intellectuals there were Marxist, they had no plans to organise a political party although they did hope to infiltrate the CPP. If the CPP 'rank and file' were to become dissatisfied with their current leaders, such infiltrators might be able to take over the party, which, after all, bore 'ideological and emotional similarities' to the Communist Party. Wright suggested one member, a journalist, who he thought might respond to 'discreet' requests for information about the group.

As for Nkrumah, he slept under a portrait of Lenin, 'his ideal', and had used Marxist organising techniques.[35] He had formed a Secret Circle, the CPP 'centre of power'. Wright listed their names. Although the CPP was not directly affiliated with communist organisations, leaders acknowledged modelling their party on the Russian Communist Party. 'In short, it is a Communist minded political party, borrowing Marxist concepts and applying them with a great deal of flexibility to local African social and economic conditions.' Wright then told a somewhat muddled story he had heard from Dzenkle Dzewu, a disaffected former deputy chairman of the CPP, who alleged that certain government ministers had been taking bribes (or 'commissions') for government contracts with foreign businesses. Other ministers learned about it when letters from Padmore 'fell into the hands of Party leaders who did not hold governmental positions'. Nkrumah's opponents were ready to publish Padmore's letters to prove corruption, and the fight over whether or not to publish them led seven members of the CPP's National Executive Committee to resign. Dzewu, Wright's informant, was among them. They then organised the Ghana Congress Party. 'In an interview with me', Wright reported, 'DD indicated a personal hatred of Nkrumah so strong and intense that he admits that he has given Scotland Yard all of the personal correspondence and all other documents relating to irregular activities of CPP political leaders'.

Wright described the present Secret Circle as 'composed of six members in Accra and one member in London, George Padmore. DD indicates that George Padmore has access to all confidential or secret documents of the C.P.P. and that he is an active adviser to Kwame Nkrumah and that a constant stream of communications flows between Padmore and Nkrumah.' Implying that the Secret Circle was, indeed, taking kickbacks from foreign companies, Wright identified a West Indian businessman in London who acted as an intermediary between the Secret Circle and foreign companies. Wright listed the six current Gold Coast members of this Secret Circle and said that they were in 'constant contact' with Appiah and Padmore. Then Wright provided information that told the Americans what the British already knew: that one intermediary for Padmore's letters to Nkrumah was a woman named Lucy Siedel, who worked for the Government Printing Office. The envelopes were addressed in 'a barely legible scrawl to mislead governmental censorship'. Wright said he understood there were other postal routes, too, 'through which this flow of communication is kept alive'.[36]

If Padmore had seen this document, he would no doubt have been astonished. Padmore had counselled Wright, visited him, confided in him, offered him hospitality in his own home, helped arrange this trip. Padmore gave every appearance of seeing Wright as a good friend with common political views. Why did Wright turn on him, and on Nkrumah, too, in this way? Wright's willingness to play the part of informer probably had several origins. One was his nervousness over the possibility of losing his passport. Passports had been denied to other Americans identified with communism and critical of US foreign policy; W. E. B. Du Bois and Paul Robeson had both lost theirs. The American consul in Paris, Agnes Schneider, was known to call in her fellow citizens, take their passports, drop them in a drawer, and present them with papers for their journey home.[37] Wright seriously did not want to abandon Paris to return to the United States. Not long after he returned from the Gold Coast, he signed an affidavit in the American Embassy naming people he had known when he was a member of the Communist Party.[38] Compounding his personal reasons for his report to the American consul in Accra was Wright's disappointment with the chilly reception he had received from the CPP. This was the explanation the American consul gave. 'Wright found he was not cordially received by the C.P.P.', the consul wrote in a cover letter. 'On the contrary he feels that he was ignored by them and that his reasonable requests for information were evaded.' Wright was also bitter that he was not generally received with the fanfare he had expected. When the NAACP labour director Herbert Hill ran into him in Paris not long after Wright returned from the Gold Coast, he found Wright in a state of shock. Wright had thought that he would be welcomed as a great man, and Africans did not even know who he was.[39] To these reasons Wright biographer Hazel Rowley adds another: a genuine fear of communist influence in Africa. 'Nevertheless', she has written, 'it was an act of betrayal ... Nkrumah was no pawn of Moscow, and George Padmore unequivocally shared Wright's hostility towards Communism. And yet, behind their backs, Wright was giving away black men's secrets.'[40]

Moreover, he kept on giving them away after he returned to Paris. In a 10 December 1953 report to the US Department of State, the American Embassy in Paris reported learning from the Accra consulate that Wright would 'be glad to tell someone in the Embassy of his meeting in London with George PADMORE, following his return from the Gold Coast'. After seeing Wright on two occasions, a reporting officer wrote a three-page single-spaced memorandum summing up what Wright had told him. In it, Wright described Padmore's meeting his train in London after the trip and put to rest rumours he had heard in the Gold Coast that Padmore was living in luxury in Kensington; Padmore still lived in his 'modest apartment' and his 'wife' still worked as a secretary. Wright told how they and Appiah tried to explain the CPP's coolness towards him as possibly embarrassment about the conditions in which CPP officials lived, although Pizer agreed that Wright might be correct in thinking the party had something to hide.

The most politically significant part of this second report was Wright's comment on Nkrumah's plan as Padmore had described it to him: first self-government, then a purge of the CPP's right wing and a move to the left; then a break with the Commonwealth and launching a West African movement. Also of interest to the Americans was Wright's assessment of Padmore's influence on Nkrumah. 'Wright considers that Nkrumah is very successful in arousing emotions and in haranguing but that essentially he is inarticulate ideologically and relies heavily on Padmore for guidance.' Padmore had told Wright that Nkrumah had even delayed the opening of the Legislative Assembly for more than a week 'because the speech which he had written for Nkrumah to deliver on that occasion had been mislaid. Padmore referred to the Gold Coast as a ship having a socialist captain but no crew'.[41]

With this report the Embassy enclosed, too, a typed copy of a pamphlet Padmore had loaned Wright: Nkrumah's *Towards Colonial Freedom – Africa in the Struggle Against World Imperialism*, written in the United States and later printed in England on a Communist Party press.[42] Padmore had told Wright the pamphlet reflected 'Nkrumah's basic philosophy and long term program'. In a letter introducing these materials, the Embassy counsellor Robert P. Joyce wrote, 'The figure of George Padmore emerges as a significant factor in the West African nationalist movement, if Wright's observations are valid.' He said, though, that a couple of English authorities with first-hand knowledge of the Colonial Office did not 'appear to share Wright's impression of the degree of influence which Padmore exercises over Nkrumah', although one thought 'that Padmore's influence in West African nationalist movements was perhaps underestimated in London'.

British intelligence records released in 2005 do not support that generalisation, nor do they suggest that the British would have learned much from Wright's reports, if the Americans passed them on. They demonstrate, rather, in compelling detail the British Security Service's knowledge that Nkrumah relied on Padmore, even recognising his hand in the speech Nkrumah gave to the assembly. At a time when Nkrumah was deciding whether or not to keep the Gold Coast in the Commonwealth, one report commented, 'it is not reassuring to think that PADMORE, the Pan-African Marxist, has lost none of his influence as NKRUMAH's guide and counsellor'.[43] Another report acknowledged that Padmore's influence extended beyond the Gold Coast, noting that Hastings Banda (who had attended the Manchester Congress) had asked Padmore to help publicise opposition to the Central African Federation.[44] To news that Banda was going to the Gold Coast, possibly permanently, there was speculation that he might become a liaison between Central and West Africa in a move towards Pan-Africanism, and Padmore might be invited in as adviser since he 'has long cherished the ideal of a Pan-African socialist union'. While such an alliance between Central and West Africa was considered hypothetical, opposition to Central African Federation could have more immediate consequences.[45]

In the context of what the British already knew, Wright's disclosures to the Americans seem unlikely to have damaged Padmore up to this point, although the Embassy counsellor held out the prospect of Wright as an ongoing source. 'The Embassy will maintain contact with Mr Wright who has shown every evidence of being most co-operative in passing along information on West African developments', he wrote. Ignorant of this possibility, Padmore kept on sharing with Wright confidential political information about Gold Coast affairs, along with suggestions for books and articles Wright ought to read. Letters continued to flow from London to Paris. Pizer wrote encouraging Wright to get his Gold Coast book finished as quickly as he could. If elections were held in February or March of 1954, there would undoubtedly be a push for independence soon after and the Gold Coast would be in the news: just the time for the book to come out.[46] On a return from Paris in the late summer of 1953, she filled the Wrights in on the reappearance of their mutual friend C. L. R. James.

The years apart had taken their toll on James's friendship with Padmore. When James was awaiting deportation on Ellis Island for overstaying his visa, James's American lawyer had appealed to Padmore for funds to help him return to England, and Padmore had written to James's friends on his behalf. Thanking economist Arthur Lewis for his contribution, Padmore wrote, 'It is our duty as his friends to extend him whatever support we can; for as West Indians, we are all indebted to him in some way or other'. He was pleased that 'Nello's fund' constituted a 'substantial sum'.[47] Yet Padmore had also replied to James's lawyer's letter with a letter noting the long time that had passed without any word from James. Padmore's letter hurt James deeply, to judge from his twelve-page impassioned response.

'Your whole letter startled me', James wrote, 'not only in what it actually said, but in its implications'. Since James had known Padmore as a man of 'constant good temper and self-control', he took seriously 'the implication that I have been pressing my personal problems on you and others of my friends after years of neglect'. But beyond that, James was disturbed by Padmore's response to the Melville book he had written, *Mariners, Renegades and Castaways*. Padmore had said that James's book had 'created anything but a good impression' in Britain. In case Padmore had just not understood him, James tried at considerable length to explain what he was trying to do in that book: to present Melville's classic novel *Moby-Dick* as a parable for the totalitarianism produced by American faith in capitalism – the hysterical anti-communism had swept across the United States on the wings of official American ideology: an uncritical faith in free enterprise and individualism.

In closing, James held out a hand of friendship: 'If I have been careless in writing, I am sorry. I have never had for you anything else but admiration and respect. You and I know more than most the long way we have travelled from the little capital in the little West Indian Island.' Now he saw before him a 'new field of work'. Even before his case arose, he had decided 'that my work in America for a period at least was over'. His goal now was to 'let European workers and intellectuals know that there was an America of which they knew little and that it was time they bothered themselves to know something about it'. He intended, then, to speak for America – to make America more real to Europe.[48] While Padmore had devoted his life to speaking for Africa, James had moved in a very different direction, appointing himself spokesman for America, and not only for American Negroes, not even only for American working people, but for the illusions and promise of this country that had apparently seized his heart and mind.

On the night in November 1953 when James had Pizer and Padmore over for dinner after so many years apart, he told them he had been to Paris to talk with a publisher but he had not contacted the Wrights, whom he had known in New York. As Pizer explained to them, James said he was

> 'fed up with Dick'. We didn't draw him, but he seemed most anxious to unburden himself on this subject, but G., in his so gentlemanly way, sidestepped the subject, but Nello would out one of his grievances, and that is that Dick although he has known him ten years, will not read his [Black] Jacobins. He feels that this is very strange, and that Dick won't do so because it will bring him up against some fundamental questions which he doesn't want to face! G. did tell him that you would like to hear from him and he should write you.

Pizer went on to say how sad she felt whenever she saw James, 'as each encounter emphasises more and more his wasted talents'. She apparently did not think well of his plan to write a book about America, and she found most 'pitiful' his delving around in past issues of the *Times Literary Supplement*. She and George had to work hard to keep up with the present.[49]

When James took a job covering cricket for the *Manchester Guardian*, Padmore wrote to Wright, 'That will take him out of his ivory tower and making his paper revolution based upon the "proletariat" of Detroit, where his faction operate'.[50] As Padmore saw it, James had drifted off in his American years into dialectical abstractions with his political study group in Detroit – a subgroup of the Workers Party called the Johnson–Forest Tendency after the political name he took in the US (J. R. Johnson) and the political name of Raya Dunayevskaya (Freddie Forest), a Russian-born theorist who had been Trotsky's secretary. Grace Lee Boggs, a third leading member of the group and holder of a Bryn Mawr Ph.D. in philosophy, has described the group's basic tenet: a faith in the spontaneous action of ordinary working-class people. Rather than a revolution led Lenin-style by a 'vanguard', the coming American Revolution would bubble up from the grassroots. What a small group of intellectuals like themselves could do to help it along was publish the experiences of ordinary people – their revolts and resistance.[51] That understanding of the intellectual's role comes through in a pamphlet Boggs helped the Kenyan Mbiyu Koinange produce when she spent four months in London in 1954.

She had come to work with James, she wrote in her autobiography, *Living for Change*, but like Pizer and Padmore she saw him 'at loose ends, trying to find his way after fifteen years out of the country'. She and James read the many newspapers he subscribed to – *The Times, Daily Telegraph, Manchester Guardian* – and they visited Ras Makonnen in Manchester, but most of her energy went into helping Koinange write *The People of Kenya Speak for Themselves*, in which the foremost Kenyan political leader to remain free and at large described the Kenyan history that led up to the emergency.[52] Another in the series of women who facilitated published works credited to men, Boggs appears to have put her stamp on this booklet: the preface that appeared under Koinange's name was in tune with the political approach the Johnson–Forest Tendency had adopted in Detroit – an emphasis on the common people as agents of their own destinies: 'In this pamphlet I want to tell people what my people were doing, of their energies, how they were doing for themselves what the Government should have been doing for them. It is when you suppress these energies, which are the driving force of any civilisation, that you have barbarism.'[53]

Boggs herself raised the money to bring out ten thousand copies of the book after her return to Detroit, where it was published under the imprint of the Kenya Publication Fund. Seven clergymen (including a rabbi and a Unitarian minister) signed a letter declaring their intention to introduce the book to their congregations.[54] The promotion plan succeeded. On 'Kenya Sunday', members of New Bethel, the church Boggs attended with her husband, Jimmy, bought more than four hundred copies, and several thousand more were sold elsewhere in the city. African-American newspapers across the country carried reviews, Grace Lee Boggs reported to the editor of the *Los Angeles Tribune* in a letter thanking her for her covering their fund-raising for the book.[55] Here was yet another collaborative effort emerging from diasporic relationships – in this case, a Chinese-American woman immersed in political work among African Americans, introduced to an African by a West Indian, helped to write, publish, and create an American audience for a book meant to stir support for an African independence movement.

While Boggs's contribution showed the potential for new energies rising from unexpected quarters, old bonds continued to fray. As Padmore had been critical of Peter Abrahams, Abrahams was frankly critical of Padmore when he gave a talk to members of the Royal Institute of International Affairs on 10 February 1954. Speaking to the institute's African Group, he offered a dim view of self-rule under Nkrumah and the CPP. With more than a trace of chauvinism, he said that 'social conditions in the Gold Coast ... are at least 50 years behind the social conditions of the Bantu in the Union of South Africa'. After three hundred years of occupation by Western Europeans, black South Africans were defending values he regarded as Western European – democracy, individuality. In the Gold Coast, on the other hand, he had found that '[t]he ideas of Western Europe had not conquered'. He had seen a lawyer argue a case like a European and then worship at ancestral shrines. Behind the modern façade of a parliamentary government in the Gold Coast stood a 'fundamentally tribal society'. It was all very well to mount a Volta project to escape the confines of an economy based on a single crop, cocoa, but 'before you can have an integrated society you must have a concept, a culture, something which would carry you over this frightfully difficult transition period, and I was looking for this, and I honestly could not find it'. Thus Abrahams had decided not 'to aid and abet this over-selling of the Gold Coast'. Friends had cautioned him that Africa's enemies would use any criticism 'to condemn this experiment in self-government', but he doubted the British would block independence. He was more concerned that seeing only what was good in the Gold Coast and ignoring the problems would turn Africans into spoiled children who had to be rescued by the British. '[M]y over-riding impression is that things are not as easy as they have been made out in the Gold Coast, and there are an awful number of terribly ugly things, and it should be brought to the attention of the leaders of the countries.'

In offering this cautionary view of the Gold Coast as it moved towards independence, Abrahams dissented from the current 'exaggerated respect' for Nkrumah, who he predicted would be 'the Prime Minister of the transition'. He took aim particularly at Padmore's rosier outlook. 'Mr Padmore wrote a book called "The Gold Coast Revolution" which I suspect many of you have read, in which he talked about the Gold Coast developing in the form of a Welfare State. Well again, before a country can work out as a Welfare State it has to accept certain fundamental things.'[56] He elaborated on that point in the July 1954 issue of the Institute's journal, *International Affairs*, where he pointed out the difficulty of building a welfare state when tribal customs would undermine the honesty of the civil service. He noted Padmore's mention of a plan for a Dutch firm to produce prefabricated housing for the Gold Coast. When he enquired about the plan, he heard 'distressing tales of corruption, and no houses'. He predicted 'a head-on collision between the government and the chiefs'.[57]

That collision between tribal power and a nationalist leader dedicated to transforming his country into a modern industrial state became the topic of Abrahams's next novel, *A Wreath for Udomo*.

A *roman à clef*, *A Wreath for Udomo* featured characters based on members of the London political circle of which Abrahams had been a part – not only Padmore, Nkrumah, Kenyatta, and Appiah but also the Englishwomen who helped and loved them. The novel's main character, Michael Udomo, modelled chiefly on Nkrumah (but with a touch of Kenyatta), goes back home to Panafrica after years abroad to lead his people to independence from British rule. Like Nkrumah, he starts a newspaper to summon support for revolt; like Nkrumah, he is imprisoned. He nevertheless triumphs, becoming his country's first prime minister. There the parallels to Nkrumah's life up to this point end. In return for technical assistance from white-governed Pluralia (a country very like South Africa), Udomo betrays one of his London comrades, David Mhendi, a Pluralian nationalist whose uprising echoes Kenya's Mau Mau. By delivering Mhendi to his enemies, Nkrumah buys white Pluralian support for a hydroelectric project comparable to the Gold Coast's proposed Volta dam. His eyes fixed on a modern future, Udomo goes on using white money and expertise, angering former allies who had helped him to power. In the end, undone by the 'fear and blood and darkness' that Abrahams associated with tribalism in his 1954 article for *International Affairs*,[58] Udomo dies in what Abrahams described in a letter to his Knopf editor (who had encouraged him to make Udomo's death more dramatic) as 'a full-blooded tribalistic ritual murder scene'.[59] Published in 1956, the year before Ghana's independence was to mark the start of a new era for Africa, *A Wreath for Udomo* struck an ominous chord.

While Abrahams presented himself as a hard-headed realist, even before *Udomo*'s publication Padmore regarded him as something else: a man who had sold his political soul for money and fame. On 28 June 1954, four months after Abrahams's talk to the Royal Institute, Padmore said of Abrahams and George Lamming, another West Indian writer, 'I avoid these pretentious upstarts like the plague'. In a letter to Wright, Padmore continued, 'Since Peter was taken up by his ofay [white] friends and dropped after they had made enough use of him to tell the spades back home how to behave as "black Englishmen" – no bitterness – I have not seen the lad in years. He has deserted all his poor friends who helped him out when he was even poorer than they. May God help him to prosper and end up in Hollywood. I can even provide him with a title: "From Johannesburg Slum to Paradise".'[60] Just a few months before *Udomo* appeared, Padmore wrote of Abrahams again with palpable disgust, responding to the news that Abrahams had gone to Jamaica to write a book for the Colonial Office. 'What a little rat ... His mother and sisters are rotting in Johannesburg and he is whitewashing their oppressors for a few dollars.'[61]

If Abrahams had any inkling of Padmore's sharp distaste for him, he gave no hint of it in his later autobiography, but in *A Wreath for Udomo* he created a devastating fictional portrait of Padmore: Tom Lanwood, 'the greatest political writer and fighter Panafrica had produced'. In London, Lanwood led a 'brains trust behind the various colonial organisations in this country',[62] but, brought by Udomo from London to Panafrica, he finds himself a fish out of water. He no sooner arrives than he begins to lecture whoever will listen. '"[W]hat are we to do with him? He just doesn't fit here"', Udomo wonders. He suggests that Lanwood write a book that the party will publish but Lanwood declines the offer. If he writes a book, it won't be helpful there, in Panafrica. '"Only white folk will read it."' Besides, he adds, '"I've had a chance to see that the real Africa is not the Africa I wrote about in my books ... I don't understand this tribal business and I don't want to ... I've been in Europe too long".'[63] Abrahams was working the material of real possibility. Nkrumah had told him he hoped to bring Padmore to the Gold Coast to work, and Abrahams imagined his way into that eventuality. He also pinpointed accurately Padmore's distaste for tribal culture and his preference for life in Europe. 'I hate primitiveness', Padmore once wrote to Richard Wright. 'Me, go native? Not on your life. I will fight for a free Africa and Asia, not live there (*laughter*).[64] While Padmore was the obvious model for Lanwood, there was something in Lanwood, too, of Richard Wright, who had found that his blackness did not make him understand Africa. Lanwood had learned that 'colour isn't an automatic passport to Africa',[65] an echo of a comment by Wright in *Black Power*, the book he wrote out of his trip to the Gold Coast: 'I was black and they were black but it did not help me.' Quoting Wright's comment in his 1959 article for *Holiday*, Abrahams said of Wright's inability to understand Africans, 'My sympathies were all with Wright'.[66] There was something in Lanwood, then, of Abrahams himself. Like Abrahams, Lanwood was a 'creole' – a man of mixed ancestry, not African in the way the others in the novel are African. Unlike Padmore but like Abrahams, Lanwood had grown up in Africa; like Abrahams, he had stayed away from Africa a long time. Abrahams surely poured into Lanwood's distress some of his own distress on his return trips to Africa in 1952 and 1953. Along with Padmore and Wright, Abrahams had no patience with tribal ways, which he believed stifled the individual human personality. In his talk to the Royal Institute, Abrahams pronounced himself 'irritated very much' by the low value assigned to individuals and 'revolted' by 'a man having to go and wriggle his way on his belly to a Chief'. He imagined himself into this world and turned away: 'it would be like going back in time for me to go and live in the Gold Coast, for me to go there and participate in these struggles out of the inward tribal society when my own origin is the outward world culture type of society'.[67]

A Wreath for Udomo closes with a condemnation of tribalism and an effort to justify Udomo for doing what had to be done to move Africa into the modern world. The character who is the most obvious stand-in for Abrahams, the artist Paul Mabi, sees his own adherence to 'private moralities' as somehow a dream next to the 'reality' that Udomo had brought into their lives.[68] Mabi's *mea culpa* suggests that the book may in part be an effort to work out Abrahams's own conflicts and confusions about the freedom struggle and his role in it. While former comrades like Padmore, Nkrumah, and Kenyatta were engaged directly in political work to free West and East Africa from white rule, he, Abrahams, had chosen to focus his energies on writing novels and personal journalism that would bring the plight of apartheid South Africa to the world's attention. Moreover, unlike Nkrumah and Kenyatta, he had left Africa for good. Transplanted to England and France, married to a white Englishwoman, fathering children who were the product of multiple cultures, he faced the practical problem of finding a place where they could all live together in dignity and peace. Not long after *A Wreath for Udomo* was published, he moved his family to Jamaica, which became his permanent home.

Writing a political memoir there many years later, Abrahams justified his criticism of nationalist movements over the years as a writer's proper work. 'This looking inward, this holding up of a mirror, critically, harshly at times, but always with love, is, for me, the most important function of the writer.' In his own mind, he was doing the honest intellectual labour that modernisation of Africa required. Those who interpreted his criticism as pessimism were wrong. 'They were still trying to divide and rule. They did the same when I published *A Wreath for Udomo*. Kwame Nkrumah got word to me ... to express his disturbed appreciation.'[69]

For Nkrumah, *Udomo* must have seemed a simplified abstraction of the real political fray. Despite the novel's transparency as a *roman à clef* with characters based on identifiable individuals, Abrahams made no attempt to capture the political complexity of what was happening in the Gold Coast. Nor, ignoring his real-life model, did he frame Udomo's 'bloodless' revolution as socialist in intent. Although he identified Lanwood as a former communist and referred once to Lanwood's 'anti-capitalism', the political goal for Lanwood and Udomo was, more simply, 'freedom'. Simplifying the political picture is understandable in a novel, but why did Abrahams erase socialism from his imagined African future? He may have had Cold War sensitivities in mind, or he may have been trying to present a book that would appeal to a broad American and British audience with little knowledge of Africa – a book focused on the human feelings and relationships of an African generation caught between two worlds.

That, apparently, was the book his publishers wanted. In his initial response to the manuscript, Knopf's Harold Strauss expressed appreciation for the book's politics as 'representative' and 'not too explicit'.[70] Strauss was hoping to frame the novel as a literary rather than a political work. As *A Wreath for Udomo* moved towards publication by his American and British publishers, Strauss lamented to Faber and Faber's Peter du Sautoy the 'tendency for book review editors to have novels reviewed by specialists in their subject rather than by literary critics'. To forestall that, might du Sautoy obtain an 'advance comment by someone of very high literary reputation'? Du Sautoy came up with Joyce Cary, who had written a novel, *Mister Johnson*, out of his experience as a colonial administrator in Nigeria. Cary called Abrahams's novel '[a] good study of African nationalism, valuable in revealing both the conscious and unconscious motives at work in a movement which gathers momentum a great deal faster than Europe realizes'. On the carbon of du Sautoy's letter forwarding Cary's statement to Knopf, someone wrote that 'S.' (presumably Sautoy) expressed the wish that Cary had said more about *Udomo* as a novel. 'We are trying to avoid treating the book as a treatise on African nationalism.'[71] Strauss's own comment on Cary's blurb: 'of dubious value'.[72] In the end, reviews were mixed on both sides of the Atlantic. Foreseeing low sales, Strauss told Abrahams's New York agent that the book did not 'seem to have created any excitement even among those people whom one would normally expect to be excited about the new book by Peter Abrahams'.[73]

Richard Wright's own contribution to the expanding political literature on the Gold Coast arrived at the Padmore flat on 29 September 1954.[74] Padmore had suggested that Wright change the title of his Gold Coast book from *Black Power* to *Black Freedom* because 'after all', Padmore wrote, 'G.C. is more after Freedom than power. What power will they ever have in this atomic age.'[75] But *Black Power* it was – a forceful phrase undercut by the subtitle: 'A Record of Reactions in a Land of Pathos'. The book Wright had produced, so distant from the one he had hoped to write, was as much about his own ambivalent encounter with Africa as it was about the Gold Coast. Like the novelist he was, Wright had created a protagonist – Richard Wright, an African-American writer who comes to Africa with illusions and dreams and watches them melt into the African soil, like gin poured in ritual welcome. Again and again, in the early part of the book, Wright hazards interpretations of what he sees, only, a few pages later, to turn back: he has not understood at all. Yet he is not able to restrain himself from believing that he understands. He can describe markets and jungles with his novelist's sensitive touch, then break into a harangue about what is wrong with Africa – the influence of missionaries, the oppression of the British, or, most often, African culture itself. Brushing aside the limitations he has felt in himself only a few pages earlier, he forges on, as much the overconfident westerner as any British colonial administrator.

In his final pages, in an act of unapologetic hubris, Wright offers advice to Kwame Nkrumah, who, having given him an initial tour, has largely disappeared from Wright's immediate vicinity but cannot so easily escape. Here, in these closing pages, reflecting on the Gold Coast's historical moment through the lens of psychology, Wright tells Nkrumah what he thinks: that Nkrumah needs to do nothing less than reorganise the African personality. '[T]here is too much cloudiness in the African's mentality, a kind of sodden vagueness that makes for lack of confidence, an absence of focus that renders that mentality incapable of grasping the workaday world.' To bridge 'the tribal and the industrial ways of life', Wright issues this command to Nkrumah: 'AFRICAN LIFE MUST BE MILITARIZED! ... not for war, but for peace; not for destruction, but for service; not for aggression, but for production, not for despotism, but to free minds from mumbo-jumbo.'[76]

Wright's prescription might have been mistaken for the strategies used by communist countries, a deduction more likely given Wright's own communist past. At the request of the chairman of Harper and Brothers' board, Wright added to his introduction a disclaimer of any identification with communism.[77] Although he still used Marxist analysis, he wrote, he was not necessarily committed to Marxist programmes.[78] Indeed, like Abrahams in *Return to Goli*, Wright argued that communists' hand would be strengthened if the West failed to support the drive for freedom among people of colour. At the same time, in his conclusion he urged Nkrumah not to beg the West for development money, which would come attached to 'degrading conditions'. Instead, Nkrumah should organise his people to build a new world with the sweat of their own brows. 'Beware of a Volta Project by foreign money', he said. 'Build your own Volta, and build it out of the sheer lives and bodies of your people!'[79] Pizer told Wright that both she and Padmore liked this closing letter to Nkrumah,[80] and Padmore offered to send a copy of the book to Nkrumah by someone flying soon to the Gold Coast.[81] Whether in that way or another, Nkrumah did get a copy. He was not favourably impressed, except on one count: the closing letter. When St Clair Drake asked him about it not long after the book was published, Nkrumah said, 'Sometimes I think that Dick Wright is right'. Among others Drake talked with in Ghana (where he taught in the late 1950s), reaction was 'uniformly negative'.[82]

The reviewer for the progressive American political magazine, the *Nation*, where Abrahams himself had published, was less pleased. Joyce Cary – who had supplied a promotional blurb for the book he was now reviewing – agreed that, in an unindustrialised country where most of the population was illiterate and poor, Nkrumah would 'have to be a dictator whether he likes it or not'. Yet Cary approved of Britain's long practice of encouraging change under chiefs' rule and doubted the wisdom of Wright's closing prescription: militarism. Like other reviewers, Cary noted that while Wright had left the party, he still thought like a communist. 'He imagines that violence, cruelty, injustice, and some clever lying can achieve a new civilization.'[83]

At the other end of the political spectrum, Du Bois sent Padmore a blistering response to *Black Power*. 'Naturally I did not like Richard Wright's book', Du Bois wrote. 'Some of his descriptions were splendid but his logic is lousy. He starts out to save Africa from Communism and then makes an attack on British capitalism which is devastating. How he reconciles these two attitudes I cannot see.'[84] There was a sharp logic to Du Bois' judgement, shaped as it was by his intensifying sympathy with communism; the brilliant elder scholar had put his finger on a slipperiness in Wright's political analysis. A self-educated man without the advantage of Du Bois' Harvard training, Wright had attempted during his French years to turn his writing in an intellectual direction. He had associated with the existentialists Simone de Beauvoir and Jean-Paul Sartre and written his own existentialist novel, *The Outsider*. But the power of his work when it was powerful came not from expansive thought but from deeper passions and intuitions. *Black Power*'s force derived more from what the book revealed about Richard Wright, a man struggling with and rejecting his own ancestral heritage, than from what it said about what was happening and should happen in the Gold Coast.

In the weeks that followed *Black Power*'s publication in America, Padmore advised Wright on British publication. One publisher was interested in bringing it out but with cuts. 'Personally', Padmore wrote to Wright,

> we think it will be a pity to have to mutilate it. We certainly don't see anything anti-British in it. I have been hitting them with sledge hammers for years with no literary disguise and I have always found an outlet. Quite true I have never been able to get on the bandwagon of the big boys with a powerful publicity machinery outlet to push my books, but I consider myself lucky to find an outlet for my anti-British, anti-

imperialist views. And you have certainly not said anything about John Bull and missionaries that have not been said before.

Padmore's own publisher, Dobson, had told him that Muller, the publisher that wanted cuts, was once a progressive firm, but under new Australian owners was 'more British than the English'. Padmore advised Wright not to accept Muller's terms; Dobson would bring out *Black Power* as it was. Dobson, however, was experiencing financial problems, which had put a new book Padmore was writing on hold and left Dobson owing Padmore £400. If Dobson recovered his footing and if Wright could not find another publisher, Wright could turn to Dobson (who did eventually publish *Black Power*). But, Padmore said, 'I would prefer you to find a publisher with *money*. It is enough that I write for nothing.' Not for the first time, Padmore let slip out his bitterness over the meagre financial rewards he received for his work. 'We can't all be suckers for these people', he said.[85] He did not, however, want to look for another publisher for his own new book on Pan-Africanism, despite Dobson's financial troubles. 'They have been decent folk in the past, so what can I do ... [M]ost of these Britishers are afraid to handle "hot political stuff".'[86] He told Wright that Dobson never asked him to cut anything – 'and I specialize in giving the British hell'.[87]

Over the past several months, Padmore had been 'giving the British hell' in three articles in *Socialist Asia*, published by the Asian Socialist Conference in Rangoon. The articles provoked British officials to make worried efforts to counter his influence. The first, in May, criticised a British Parliamentary delegation's suggestion that Kenyans involved in Mau Mau had inexplicably 'reverted' to savagery. There was nothing inexplicable about it, Padmore said. Colonial administrators had given Black Kenyan colonial police 'unbridled licence to practice brutality, corruption, and bribery'. While Padmore did not doubt Mau Mau's use of 'revolting methods', he accused European police officers of encouraging African policemen to carry out tribal vendettas against the rebellious Kikuyus. '[T]he system is so repressive that unless the Africans resort to direct action, their rulers just refuse to recognise – much less redress – their grievances.'[88] Padmore's June article on the Gold Coast revolution took a more positive turn,[89] but in August he addressed the less happy topic of the 'Anglo-Egyptian Conflict in the Sudan'. The Sudan had been promised independence by Britain and Egypt, Sudan's co-governors, who were now engaged in a tug-of-war to decide who would have influence over an independent Sudan. The outcome of their combat could be a decay of civil order that, Padmore said, 'would suit the British nicely' as evidence 'that the Sudanese are not yet ready for self-government'.[90]

The British Embassy at Rangoon was worried enough about the Asian impact of these articles to bring them up to Morgan Phillips, chairman of the Socialist International, when he visited Rangoon as part of a Labour Party Delegation. The Embassy reported to the Foreign Office that Phillips 'undertook to see whether something could be done to undermine Padmore's position'. He suggested getting the International Secretary of the Labour Party, Saul Rose, to write to the Asian Socialist Bureau 'to try to persuade them that articles by Padmore should no longer be accepted by their magazine'. The Embassy did not think it ought to intervene since 'we should not like to let it be thought that the Labour Party was taking action at our bidding'.[91] The department's minutes on this letter concluded that 'it is most unlikely that the Asian Socialists will drop Padmore – anti-colonialism is, when all is said done, after socialism their main plank. The most I think we shall get, and what the Labour Party can fairly press for, is a reasoned statement in *Socialist Asia* of their view on British policy.' The writer asked that someone pass on this suggestion to Saul Rose.

The October issue of *Socialist Asia* subsequently carried Labour Party statements on colonial policy, but it also included a one-page message from George Padmore, chairman, Pan-African Federation, that the Embassy in Rangoon found 'thoroughly offensive to the British Labour Party'. His 'Freedom-Message', appearing on the second page of this special issue on colonialism, pre-empted the subsequent three pieces laying out the Labour Party view on independence for the colonies: essentially, that independence should come after a period of training in democracy, especially in Central and East Africa where too rapid self-government would lead either to continued white domination or to chaos. One of the writers, Rita Hinden, secretary of the Fabian Colonial Bureau and joint-editor of *Socialist Commentary*, spoke of the racial fears that had been stirred not only by the white nationalist government in South Africa but also by 'Dr Nkrumah's black nationalist government', which she said had 'curdled the fears of white people that they will be dispossessed and governments on the hated "Gold Coast model" will dominate the whole of Africa'.[92] While the Labour Party had eleven pages to Padmore's one, the lead position of his 'Freedom-Message' gave him the powerful first word, a sweeping rejection of Western claims to know what was best for Africa. Centuries of dominating Asia and Africa had left westerners with the notion that 'guidance and direction can come from the West alone', he said, and warned of the dangers of 'partnership' with a West convinced of the inability of former colonies to make their own decisions. Partnership without equality would be a partnership 'between the rider and the horse'. In a specific rebuke to the Labour Party, he alluded to 'all the pious resolutions passed by European so-called socialist parties when they are not in power but who follow decidedly imperialist policies when in Office'.[93]

The British Embassy at Rangoon again suggested that the Foreign Office intervene to silence Padmore. Reporting to the Foreign Office on 24 November 1954, the Embassy wondered 'whether the time has now come to raise once more with Morgan Phillips the whole question of Padmore's position as a contributor of articles to "Socialist Asia". Padmore's articles are undoubtedly doing great harm here and anything the Labour Party can do to persuade the Asian Socialists that they should no longer publish them would be very useful.'[94] Someone from the Foreign Office did speak to Rose, who expressed the hope that *Socialist Asia* would stop publishing Padmore. However, the Foreign Office's Information Research Department (in charge of anti-communist propaganda) told the Embassy that Rose thought the matter was 'too delicate' to be brought up in writing. He would raise the issue in person with members of the Asian Socialist Bureau on their upcoming visit to Britain.[95] There the correspondence ends, closing this window on behind-the-scene efforts to silence George Padmore. Whether because of these efforts or for other reasons, he did not appear again in the issues of *Socialist Asia* that came out only sporadically over the next year. Meanwhile, an announcement on the last page of the October colonialism issue reported the Kenyan government's ban of *Socialist Asia*, an ironic postscript to the claim that Britain was training its colonies in the ways of democracy.[96]

Despite the turmoil of 1954, Padmore ended the year on a note of optimism. In a 3 December letter to Du Bois, he tallied the victories: Azikiwe's NCNC party had won in Nigeria. Uganda was moving towards status as an independent state, and in Kenya, if the independence movement there could hold out one more year, he believed the whites would give in. He lamented African-American newspapers' indifference to the struggle – his articles were no longer appearing in the *Courier* and *Defender*. Nevertheless he had a hefty writing project on his hands: a new book that would be his most enduring work as an author.[97]

Notes

1 Peter Abrahams, *Return to Goli* (London: Faber and Faber, 1953), p. 29.
2 Wright papers (D. Padmore), Pizer to R. Wright, 26 May 1952.
3 Abrahams, *Return to Goli*, p. 19.
4 Peter Abrahams, *The Black Experience in the 20th Century* (Bloomington: Indiana University Press, 2000), p. 111.
5 Allen and Unwin – AUC 385-1, for George Allen and Unwin to Abrahams, 30 March 1949.

6 Abrahams, *Black Experience*, p. 121.
7 Abrahams, *Return to Goli*, pp. 52, 55.
8 Ibid., pp. 86–7.
9 Ibid., 107.
10 Ibid., pp. 119–45.
11 Ibid., p. 198, 203.
12 Ibid., 203.
13 Ibid., pp. 205–6.
14 Peter Abrahams, 'Nkrumah, Kenyatta, and the Old Order', in Jacob Drachler (ed.), *African Heritage* (New York: Crowell-Collier Press, 1963), pp. 142–3; originally published as 'Blacks', *Holiday*, 25: 4 (April 1959), which included a long closing section in which Abrahams described a scene with a witch doctor and portrayed 'tribal man' as 'hemmed in, imprisoned by his ancestors' (p. 126). Abrahams offered a more analytic rendering of Kenyatta's position as a 'detribalized man' in 'The Conflict of Culture in Africa', *International Affairs*, 30: 3 (July 1954), 304–12.
15 Abrahams, "Conflict of Culture', p. 307.
16 Jeremy Murray-Brown, *Kenyatta*, Second edition (London: George Allen and Unwin, 1979), pp. 243–6.
17 Fenner Brockway, *Outside the Right* (London: George Allen and Unwin, 1963), p. 46.
18 Abrahams, *Return to Goli*, pp. 206–8, 217; the talk also appeared in the *Listener* (August 1952), 288–9.
19 Harry Ransom Humanities Research Center, The University of Texas at Austin, Alfred A. Knopf, Inc., Records, Box 161, Folder 2, Abrahams to Harold Strauss, 30 December 1954.
20 Padmore, 'Behind the Mau Mau', *Phylon*, 14: 4 (Fourth Quarter, 1953), 364.
21 Nkrumah Papers, Box 154-7, Folder 52, Padmore to Nkrumah, 11 October 1952.
22 Murray-Brown, *Kenyatta*, p. 253.
23 Abrahams, 'Colonialism on Trial', *Nation* [New York] (11 July 1953), 32.
24 Wright Papers (G. Padmore), Padmore to R. Wright, 19 September 1946; Padmore wrote to Frank Leach, Gold Coast Commissioner, 30 May 1953, protesting against Leach's treatment of him when Wright sought a visa; Padmore to 'To Whom It may Concern', 4 May 1953; Pizer (D. Padmore) promises he will be welcomed in an undated [1952] letter and offers information on ship passage in letters of 15 April 1953 and 21 April 1953. In the opening chapter of *Black Power*, Wright attributes the idea of a trip to Africa to Pizer (London: Dennis Dobson, 1954), p. 9.
25 Wright Papers, Box 22, Folder 340, Wright's travel diary, pp. 48–54.
26 Wright, *Black Power*, pp. 34–79.
27 Knopf Records, Box 161, Folder 2, Memo to HS [Harold Strauss?] from SC for BWK, 20 July 1953, mentions Abrahams's forthcoming trip to the Gold Coast.
28 Peter Abrahams, 'Nkrumah, Kenyatta, and the Old Order', pp. 133–5.
29 Wright Papers (G. Padmore), carbon copy, Wright to Padmore and Pizer, 16 July 1953.
30 Kwame Nkrumah, *Ghana: The Autobiography of Kwame Nkrumah* (New York: Thomas Nelson and Sons, 1957), pp. 187–204; also Richard Rathbone (ed.), *British Documents on the End of Empire: Ghana*, Series B, Vol. 1, Part 1 – 1941–1952 (London: HMSO, 1992), p. 63.
31 Richard Rathbone, *Nkrumah and the Chiefs* (Accra: F. Reimmer; Athens: Ohio University Press; Oxford: James Currey, 2000), pp. 63–4.
32 Hazel Rowley, *Richard Wright: The Life and Times* (New York: Henry Holt and Company, 2001), p. 429.
33 Rowley, *Richard Wright*, pp. 421–2, 424–5, 427, 431, 436.
34 Ebere Nwaubani, *United States and Decolonization in West Africa, 1950–1960* (Rochester, NY: University of Rochester Press, 2001), p. 121.
35 In *Black Power* Wright quotes Nkrumah identifying himself as a 'Marxist Socialist' (p. 62).
36 US/NA, Department of State Decimal File, 745K.00/9-1553, 'Transmitting

Memorandum on Left-Wing Politics in the Gold Coast', Despatch No. 42 from Accra, 15 September 1953.
37 Rowley, *Richard Wright*, p. 452.
38 Addison Gayle, *Richard Wright: Ordeal of a Native Son* (Garden City, NY: Anchor Press/Doubleday, 1980), pp. 244, 250–2.
39 Herbert Hill told me this on 1 February 2001.
40 Rowley, *Richard Wright*, p. 437.
41 US/NA, General Records of the Department of State (Record Group 59), 1950–54 Decimal File, Box 3582, 250/40/06/4, Despatch 1533 from Paris to the Department of State.
42 It was printed without a publisher's imprint; see Marika Sherwood, *Kwame Nkrumah: The Years Abroad* (Legon, Ghana: Freedom Publications, 1996), p. 168.
43 UK/TNA, KV 2/1851/310289, letter from Loftus Brown to P. M. Kirby Green, SLO West Africa, 15 May 1953. Comments on Padmore's hand in Nkrumah's speech appear in same file in a letter from H. Loftus Brown to C. J. J. T. Barton, Colonial Office, 26 May 1953 and from P. M. Kirby Green to Brown, 13 July 1953.
44 UK/TNA, KV 2/1851/310289, Brown to Barton, 26 May 1953.
45 *Ibid.*, 1 July 1953.
46 Wright Papers (D. Padmore), Pizer to R. and E. Wright, 2 November 1953.
47 Seeley G. Mudd Manuscript Library, Princeton University, Princeton, NJ, W. Arthur Lewis Papers, Box 10, Folder 6, Padmore to Arthur [Lewis], 1 October 1952.
48 Wright Papers (G. Padmore), James to Padmore, 22 June 1953.
49 Wright Papers (D. Padmore), Pizer to E. and R. Wright, 2 November 1953.
50 Wright Papers (G. Padmore) Padmore to R. Wright, 24 May 1954.
51 Grace Lee Boggs, *Living for Change: An Autobiography* (Minneapolis, London: University of Minnesota Press, 1998), pp. 61, 67.
52 *Ibid.*, p. 69.
53 Mbiyu Koinange, *The People of Kenya Speak for Themselves* (Detroit, MI: Kenya Publication Fund, 1955), p. 1.
54 *Ibid.*, p. 115.
55 Boggs, *Living for Change*, p. 69; University of West Indies–St Augustine, James Collection, Box 7, Folder 196, carbon copy, [Boggs] to Almena Lomax, editor, *The Tribune*, 19 February 1955.
56 Royal Institute of International Affairs, 8/2284, carbon, 'Report of a meeting on 10 February 1954 to hear Peter Abrahams speak on "Some Impressions of the Gold Coast Today"', pp. 1–5.
57 Peter Abrahams, 'Conflict of Culture', p. 311; this article was republished in the African American journal *Phylon*, XVI: 4 (Fourth Quarter 1955), 387–96.
58 Abrahams, 'Conflict of Culture', p. 307.
59 Knopf Records, Box 161, Folder 2, Abrahams to Strauss, 30 August 1955; Strauss to Abrahams, 11 August 1955.
60 Wright Papers (G. Padmore), Padmore to R. Wright, 28 June 1954.
61 *Ibid.*, Padmore to R. Wright, 19 October 1955.
62 Peter Abrahams, *A Wreath for Udomo* (New York: Alfred A. Knopf, 1956), pp. 7, 16.
63 *Ibid.*, pp. 232, 275–6.
64 Abrahams, *The Black Experience in the 20th Century*, p. 125; Wright Papers (G. Padmore), Padmore to R. Wright, 23 August 1955.
65 Abrahams, *Udomo*, p. 294.
66 Abrahams, 'Nkrumah, Kenyatta, and the Old Order', *African Heritage*, pp. 134–5.
67 Abrahams, 'Report of a meeting', p. 2.
68 Abrahams, *Udomo*, pp. 356–7.
69 Abrahams, *Black Experience*, pp. 61–2.
70 Knopf Records, Box 161, Folder 2, Harold Strauss to Abrahams, 11 August 1955; a carbon copy to Peter du Sautoy is in the Faber Archive, London, Box 7, Folder 21.
71 The Faber Archive, London, Box 7, Folder 21, du Sautoy to Strauss, 28 February 1956; since the comment was written on the carbon in the Faber and Faber archive,

it would seem to have been made by someone at Faber and Faber.
72 Knopf Records, Box 178, Folder 3, HS [Harold Strauss] written in margin of typescript, 2 March 1956.
73 Knopf Records, Box 178, Folder 3, Harold Strauss to Abrahams, 4 June 1956; Harold Strauss to Jo Stewart, 5 June 1956; Abrahams to Strauss, 8 June 1956.
74 Wright Papers (G. Padmore), Padmore to R. Wright, 29 September 1954.
75 *Ibid.*, Padmore to R. Wright, 28 June 1954.
76 The closing letter appears in Wright, *Black Power*, pp. 342–51.
77 Constance Webb, *Richard Wright* (New York: G. P. Putnam's Sons, 1968), pp. 336–7.
78 Wright, *Black Power*, p. 3.
79 *Ibid.*, p. 349.
80 Wright Papers (D. Padmore), Pizer to R. Wright, 19 October 1954.
81 Wright Papers (G. Padmore), Padmore to R. Wright, 29 September 1954.
82 Drake in Shepperson and Drake, 'Fifth Pan-African Conference', p. 57.
83 Joyce Cary, 'Catching Up with History', in *The Case for African Freedom and Other Writings on Africa* (New York, Toronto, London: McGraw-Hill, 1964), pp. 221–3.
84 Du Bois to Padmore, 10 December 1954, *Correspondence, III*, p. 374.
85 Wright Papers (G. Padmore), Padmore to R. Wright, 27 October 1954.
86 *Ibid.*, Padmore to R. Wright, 29 September 1954.
87 *Ibid.*, Padmore to R. Wright, 24 May 1954.
88 Padmore, 'British Parliamentary Report on Kenya', *Socialist Asia*, 3: 1 (May 1954), 16–18.
89 Padmore, 'The Gold Coast Revolution', *Socialist Asia*, 3: 2 (June 1954), 14–18.
90 Padmore, 'Anglo-Eyptian Conflict in the Sudan', *Socialist Asia*, 3: 4 (August 1954), 21.
91 UK/TNA, FO 1110/693, Chancery, British Embassy, Rangoon to Information Research Department, Foreign Office, 27 September 1954.
92 Rita Hinden, 'British Socialists Think Twice', *Socialist Asia*, 3–4: 6–7 (October 1954), 15.
93 George Padmore, 'Freedom-Message', *Socialist Asia*, 3–4: 6–7 (October 1954), 2.
94 UK/TNA, FO 1110/693, Chancery, British Embassy, Rangoon, to Information Research Department, Foreign Office, 24 November 1954.
95 UK/TNA, FO 1110/693, Information Research Department/Foreign Office, to Chancery, Rangoon, 7 December 1954.
96 Ba Swe, 'Statement on Ban of "Socialist Asia" in Kenya', *Socialist Asia*, 3–4: 6–7 (October 1954), 32.
97 Padmore to Du Bois, 3 December 1954 in Du Bois, *Correspondence, III*, pp. 373–4.

CHAPTER SEVEN

Their own histories

'When I started I did not know quite the line of approach', Padmore wrote to Richard Wright in July 1954 about the book he meant to call 'Black Zionism, Pan-Africanism and Communism', 'but it developed as I went along'. Countering Cold War allegations that African independence movements were communist-inspired, he hoped 'to give a coherent picture of the ideals and movements which have arisen among black folk independent of the C[ommunist] P[arty]'.[1] The notion that communists initiated 'every manifestation of political awakening in Africa' was 'gross hypocrisy',[2] he said in his introduction, then rolled out a history of African nationalism, from the establishment of Sierra Leone and Liberia through Garvey's Black Zionism, the Pan-African congresses organised by W. E. B. Du Bois, the work in which Padmore himself had been involved in London, and a survey of colonial systems in Africa. 'I have traced the whole history of the Pan-African movement down to Nkrumahism', he told Wright. In July 1954, he had only the last chapter to write – 'on the C.P. tactics as a warning to the boys in Africa'.[3]

While he finished most of the manuscript in a spurt of energy over four weeks that summer of 1954, the last chapter dragged on. He was still at it the following April, pouring out his stored-up knowledge of communists' efforts to recruit the world's 'darker peoples'. Although at times communists had played a positive role in anti-colonial movements, at other times they had engaged in deception and betrayal. They were still playing the same game in the 1950s that they had played in the 1930s, Padmore believed. He predicted another shift in communist policy should 'the East and West settle their differences'. Then the Soviet Union would no longer need 'the African liberation movement as a whip against the main spearhead of anti-Communism and defenders of the colonial *status quo*'.[4]

From this scornful characterisation of communists as hypocritical

[145]

opportunists on whom African nationalists could not rely, he turned to his own political programme for Africa – one that would appeal to capitalist anti-communists in one way but not in another. 'The only force capable of containing Communism in Asia and Africa is dynamic nationalism based upon a socialist programme of industrialisation and co-operative methods of agricultural production', he wrote. In one sentence, he upheld the Western campaign to 'contain' communism while at the same time offering as an alternative not free-market capitalism but 'a socialist programme ... and co-operative methods'. Rebuilding African economies along these lines required 'setting the colonies immediately on the road to self-government, since only popularly elected leaders can harness the emotions and loyalties of the common people of town and country'.[5]

Often in his letters Padmore demonstrated a sardonic humour, which he sometimes emphasised for his correspondent by placing the word 'laughter' in parentheses. You can almost hear his own quiet laughter to himself as he used the current campaign against communism, so often turned against Nkrumah's CPP, to hoist Western capitalists on their own petard in the book his publisher insisted he call, simply, *Pan-Africanism or Communism?* 'If the Western Powers are really afraid of Communism and want to defeat it, the remedy lies in their own hands. First, it is necessary to keep one step ahead of the Communists by removing the grievances of the so-called backward peoples, which the Communists everywhere seek to exploit for their own ends.'[6] The communist movement that had been Padmore's vehicle for anti-imperialism in his early years had once again become useful, this time in a different way – as a threat. To save the colonial world from communism, colonial powers would have to let their colonies go.

Then independent colonies could join in socialist federations and, with Pan-Africanism as a 'beacon light', a socialist United States of Africa, a goal Nkrumah shared.[7] As he wrote to Nkrumah on 5 August 1955, 'Brother, they are going to be in a fix as to what to do with "Pan-Africanism". It exposes the role of the communists on the one hand and that the imperialists will like, but on the other they will hate the ideas of Pan-Africanism – black nationalism plus socialism.'[8] In the book itself, he identified himself as 'a socialist and democrat', praised Nkrumah's 'wise and constructive socialist leadership',[9] and wrote that 'Pan-Africanism subscribes to the fundamental objectives of Democratic Socialism' and 'stands for the liberty of the subject within the law'. Thus, it 'sets out to fulfill the socio-economic mission of Communism under a libertarian political system'.[10] In a later letter to Wright, Padmore said that 'Nkrumah and Co.' hoped to use this 'program of "PanAfrican Socialism", to mark themselves off from Western Social Democracy and Eastern European Communism'.[11]

Although Padmore offered Pan-African socialism as a distinctive African path towards the future, he was still promoting a predominantly Western vision, with no place in it for tribal chiefs. Like more academic modernisation theorists in the 1950s, Padmore believed that the task facing Africans at this historic moment was to transform their traditional societies into modern societies. 'The traditional African way of life needs a cataclysm to free it from its own decay. It is the newly emancipated younger generation of Africans with a detribalized outlook, who, under the stimulus of Western political ideas and technocracy, alone can bring about the necessary regeneration.'[12] He laid out for this young generation a blueprint: the state should control development of the national economy's key sectors because only the state could come up with the resources needed for big projects (although he suggested the United States pay for the Volta River project to compensate the Gold Coast for the slaves taken from the Guinea coast).[13] Padmore's vision for Africa was not that different from Nehru's socialist vision for India – industrialised, rationalised, modernised – with a strong national state.[14] There was this key difference, however, between Padmore and Nehru: Nehru felt an obligation towards India's ancient culture that Padmore did not feel for Africa's. As Partha Chatterjee has pointed out in *Nationalist Thought and the Colonial World* (1986), Nehru went to some trouble in *The Discovery of India* (1946) to demonstrate that India could modernise without losing its Indian soul.[15] In contrast, Padmore – who was not African and casually dropped contemptuous remarks about African 'mumbo-jumbo' in his letters to Wright – felt no compunctions about calling for a 'cataclysm' to sweep aside the 'traditional African way of life'.

Strengthening the tie between independence movements in Asia and Africa, Padmore published sections of his new book in a special June 1955 issue on Africa that he edited for an Indian periodical, *United Asia*, and included, too, a speech by Nkrumah, along with Wright's letter to Nkrumah from *Black Power*. The issue was timely, appearing on the heels of the Bandung Conference that brought together newly independent Asian and African nations. Wright had attended that conference with the financial help of the Congress for Cultural Freedom (CCF), an organisation secretly funded by the US Central Intelligence Agency. Three CCF magazines published excerpts from *Black Power*, and four CCF magazines would publish excerpts from Wright's book on Bandung.[16] Padmore tried to find a British publisher for Wright's Bandung report, *The Colour Curtain*, but it was not an easy sell. While promising to bring out Wright's *Black Power*, Dobson was 'not so keen on Bandung', Padmore told Wright.

> [T]heir excuse is that the public here is not interested ... Oh boy, they may not be interested but the coloured folk are making them sit up. Africa is really in ferment. They don't know what to do. They have even indirectly approach[ed] me to see if I can help them save their rotten empire. To hell with them.
>
> They are worried stiff about the effect of Pan-Africanism or Communism. They know that the C.P. is bankrupt but black nationalism cannot be suppressed even with guns. We are feeding the flames. Don't know how long the French will let me back in after the book appears. I have stripped them nacked [sic].[17]

While British leaders across a political range agreed that Britain should be preparing colonies for independence, the French had no such goal in mind. Before the war, they had offered colonial elites assimilation as French citizens, with 'careers and opportunities denied to the unassimilated natives', Padmore wrote in *Pan-Africanism or Communism?* As the war neared its end, the French government in exile abandoned assimilation as a goal and adopted instead the goal of 'closer association' without any promise of self-government. The French would remain in firm control of this 'indivisible French Union'. Inspired by the movement for self-government in British West African colonies, however, French radicals like Leopold Senghor were rebelling against French political control, preparing the way for both 'self-determination and the federation of all West African territories'.[18]

That vision of unity was theoretical at this point. Even within the single West African nation that Padmore was most closely associated with – the Gold Coast – there were fierce divisions. Chiefs losing power under the CPP had joined forces with cocoa farmers unsettled by a government decision to hold payments for cocoa steady while international prices rose.[19] Asante was the heart of the cocoa region, and among Asante CPP members who defected to the opposition National Liberation Movement (NLM) was Joe Appiah, who had served as Nkrumah's official representative in England and invited Nkrumah to be his best man when he married Peggy Cripps, daughter of Sir Stafford Cripps (when Nkrumah could not come, Padmore stood in for him). Despite these close ties, just a few months after returning to the Gold Coast, Appiah had defected from the CPP to the NLM.[20] Eight months later, on 19 October 1955, Padmore wrote to Wright about a story he had sent to the *Evening News*. 'I am exposing Joe [Appiah] and the Ashanti chiefs and their game is up ... Penny papers were sold on the streets of Accra at 2 shillings. By the time I am through with them they will all cut their throats to water the stools of their ancestors.'[21] With his letter he sent Wright a copy of the federal constitution that the opposition had proposed to the Colonial Office; the NLM's plan would assign significant power to chiefs and regional units. Although in *Africa: Britain's Third Empire* Padmore had favoured a federalist system for Nigeria, he now regarded its adoption in either Nigeria or the Gold Coast as a disaster. By giving tribal-based regions more autonomy, federalism would undermine the strength of the national government. 'The whole G[old] C[oast] are calling them traitors.'[22]

Padmore fought Nkrumah's opposition through the press. He obtained a copy of a secret document implicating foreign companies in the opposition movement and thought of trying to place the story in Claude Bourdet's French weekly, *France-Observateur*, where he had published before. 'The stuff is so hot I would have to come and bring the documents myself', he wrote to Wright on 5 October 1955.[23] Three days later on the front page of the *Ghana Evening News*, where Padmore's London despatches appeared regularly, he reported payments to Gold Coast trade unions 'from big business sources to carry on activities against Nkrumah Government by inciting the trade unions against the C.P.P.'[24] In a succession of front-page stories in the *Evening News*, he relayed from London to Accra reports of scandal in the Gold Coast and support for Nkrumah in London. After a trip to Paris, he reported French fears that independence for the Gold Coast would embolden French colonies to demand the same.[25] Writing for Gold Coast readers, he put the Gold Coast forward as the leader of the continent. The Uganda National Congress, demanding self-government, was using *The Gold Coast Revolution* as a guidebook, he told Wright.[26]

By the end of 1955, with *Pan-Africanism or Communism?* in final page proofs, Padmore was nearly breathless from the speed of the Empire's unravelling. 'Brother, what changes are taking place before our eyes', he wrote to Wright on 5 December 1955. 'I never expected such moves ten years ago. The west is beaten.'[27] They were reaching the triumphal moment, Padmore and Wright, writers who, so far as Padmore knew, had fought side by side in the political trenches. Wright began his Foreword to *Pan-Africanism or Communism?* with these words, which, given what he had told American diplomatic officials about Padmore, were weighted with irony: 'Concerning George Padmore I am biased, for he is my friend'.[28] In a letter of 5 March 1956 Padmore expressed his appreciation both for the introduction and for Wright's 'friendship and sincerity'. Reciprocating the favour, he promised to review the English edition of Wright's new book, *The Colour Curtain*, which Dobson had published after all, and provided Dobson with a list of Asian booksellers who might handle it. The Egyptian Embassy was interested in translating Padmore's *Africa: Britain's Third Empire,* and Padmore had suggested translating Wright's book, too.

In a postscript, he touched on their next joint project: the writers' conference that the *Présence africaine* was organising for that September. More than once in his letters to Wright, Padmore expressed disdain for the French-speaking Africans involved in publishing the *Présence africaine;* he thought their preoccupation with culture distracted them from the political work they ought to be doing. Now, alluding to the revolt in Algeria, he said, 'While the Arabs fight these boys spend their time in café talking culture'.[29] Nevertheless, he joined Wright in helping to plan the conference, though he asked Wright to see that the names of conferees coming from England be left off the public list; he feared the French might prevent them from entering France.[30]

Pan-Africanism or Communism? The Coming Struggle for Africa appeared the month before the Paris conference. It had been long delayed by Dobson's financial troubles, printing strikes, and Padmore's own slowness in completing the index. The delay was too long, Padmore's French socialist friend Daniel Guérin wrote to him – too many things had happened, outdating parts of the book. There were other things Guérin did not like about *Pan-Africanism or Communism?,* and he spoke frankly. He had known Padmore at least since 1946. They had offered each other mutual aid in placing articles and books with publishers, and Pizer and Padmore had stayed in Guérin's apartment on visits to Paris. Responding to *Pan-Africanism or Communism?,* Guérin reassured Padmore that the book was 'brilliant', but he levelled tough criticism at Padmore's anti-communism. 'I am afraid that you mix up communism (or Marxism) with Stalinism and that sometimes your justified hate against Stalinism makes you too indulgent towards the *reactionary* anticommunist forces.' Unfairly, he accused Padmore of not saying frankly that socialism (or Marxism or communism – although not Stalinism) was the answer; he worried that '"Pan-Africanism" without economical contents is hollow'.[31]

In response, Padmore wrote that, if Guérin thought his concept of Pan-Africanism had no economic content, then Guérin had not read the book carefully. Nor had he meant to denounce Marxism; he had meant to denounce 'the opportunism of the Communist International and its sections'. On the other hand, he did not accept the idea that Europeans could impose their ideologies on Africans. To another objection by Guérin – that he had spoken too well of the Moral Rearmamament movement, which Guérin correctly linked to the CIA – Padmore responded with an explanation that suggested how Guérin ought to read *Pan-Africanism or Communism?*: as a strategic document.

African nationalists used Moral Rearmament to get passports so they could travel to Europe; '[t]here is a good reason why I mentioned them in my book'.³²

While Guérin criticised Padmore for sounding too anti-communist, a reviewer for the CIA-backed *Encounter* (to which Dobson had unsuccessfully offered an excerpt of the book)³³ criticised Padmore for sounding too much like a communist. *Encounter's* reviewer, Rita Hinden, who had contributed one of the Labour Party pieces to *Socialist Asia* that Padmore had debunked, classified him among those 'who have revolted against Communist conduct and cynicism, but can never free themselves from Communist ideology'.³⁴ Hinden was apparently carefully chosen to write this critical review. Michael Josselson, the CIA agent who handled the Congress for Cultural Freedom (CCF), had told the *Encounter* editor Irving Kristol that he should run a review of *Pan-Africanism or Communism?* 'by one of "our" people'. That description fitted Hinden, whom Josselson elsewhere described as 'one of us'.³⁵ A South African who had studied at the London School of Economics, she had been a longtime leader in the Fabian anti-colonial movement, which favoured reformism rather than radical action. The journal she edited, *Socialist Commentary*, showcased the views of the Labour Party's right wing and met CCF approval: the CCF solicited subscriptions for it in Asia and Africa.³⁶ If there was a CCF party line on Padmore, Hinden had the credentials to express it, though the fierceness of her hostility – 'This is an infuriating book' – may have been fuelled by Padmore's long-running criticism of the Labour Party and other political differences – she told James Hooker that Padmore was a 'near-communist or Trotskyist'.³⁷ While *Pan-Africanism or Communism?* was not anti-communist enough for Hinden, G. N. N. Nunn, the *Times Literary Supplement* reviewer who had skewered Padmore's two preceding books, appreciated Padmore's 'powerful exposure of the cynicism and perfidy of Communist African policy'.³⁸ Ironically, in a colonial edition printed up for release by Azikiwe's Zik Press in Nigeria, Padmore omitted Wright's militant introduction and 'Communism' disappeared from the title, which became, simply, *Pan-Africanism*.³⁹

Meanwhile, another inspirational record of the African struggle for independence was in the works – Nkrumah's autobiography, *Ghana* – and Padmore and Pizer had a hand it shaping it. On 28 June 1955, Pizer had written to Nkrumah on Padmore's behalf to outline a plan for the book: not a 'straightforward narrative' but 'a sociological history, told in terms of yourself, your environment, the influences which moulded your thinking and ideas'. She then laid out a step-by-step blueprint:

'[Y]ou should open with the life of the family and village in which you were born and lived – Nzima, and relate it, as far as you can, to the rest of the country. Set out the social forces and relationships which existed, the different strata of which the local society was made up; as far as possible denote the influence of outside forces.' Then Nkrumah should describe his higher schooling, his experience in America and Britain, and his return to the Gold Coast – always aware of varying social forces in these varying situations. His section on building the Gold Coast movement would take up 'the clash of African attitudes; the old outlooks against the new', but he should also include useful information on how he organised people in rural areas, 'for this is of particular interest to the young organisations which are forming in Africa (it was raised by the leading spirits of the Uganda National Congress on Sunday at our house)'.[40]

Within a few weeks, Nkrumah was at work on the book. He took his English secretary Erica Powell and her typewriter along on a Dutch ship for an August holiday excursion along the West African coast. Powell would claim credit, later, for giving Nkrumah the idea of writing the book: others had offered to write it for him but she had told him he ought to do it himself. Actually, Nkrumah had thought of producing an autobiography as far back as 1948, when he asked the WANS secretary Margot Parrish to write it for him. She suggested he put in 'a few years of work' in the Gold Coast first.[41] He had done that now, and his current secretary, Erica Powell, became a close collaborator, at least, if not in some sense the book's writer. She accompanied him on a visit to the village where he was born in an effort to pin down his birthdate, and over the coming months Nkrumah dictated sections of the book to her. When the book came out, he included a prominent acknowledgement of 'the many hours of her spare time she devoted to the compilation of the manuscript'.[42]

The plan Pizer had outlined would be only occasionally visible in the published book. Nkrumah followed it for the early part of his story – his education in the Gold Coast and the United States. As he moved into the years of growing political power, though, his account became increasingly bureaucratic, packed with verbatim speeches and dry accounts of political twists and turns. He largely ignored Pizer's detailed request for description of how he organised the rural people. What Padmore and Pizer were looking for was a handbook that would be useful to other Africans seeking independence. Instead, perhaps with his eye on British and American readers, perhaps as a result of Powell's influence, Nkrumah emerged less as a firebrand and more as a genial statesman.

He did conclude the book on a note consistent with Pizer's advice to present 'the future – yours and that of Ghana, linked up with that of Pan-Africa – the final objective'. Working his way towards his final scene, he wrote,

> I have never regarded the struggle for the Independence of the Gold Coast as an isolated incident but always as a part of a general world historical pattern. The African in every territory of this vast continent has been awakened and the struggle for freedom will go on. It is our duty as the vanguard force to offer what assistance we can to those now engaged in the battles that we ourselves have fought and won. Our task is not done and our safety is not assured until the last vestiges of colonialism have been swept away from Africa.

He closed with an image of himself standing on a ship's bridge sailing into 'the hazards of the high seas'.[43]

Nkrumah had already had ample experience on stormy seas by the time the manuscript was completed. The opposition NLM had so effectively resisted moving forward under the 1954 constitution that London had intervened. The Secretary of State ordered another general election before independence.[44] Just before the election, Powell set sail for a home leave. While she was there, she handled a delicate complication in the book's progress towards publication. Nkrumah and Powell had started the book without a contract with a publisher, although the Edinburgh publisher Thomas Nelson and Sons had stepped in after its overseas editor, Van Milne, met with Nkrumah on a visit to the Gold Coast. As Powell told the story, Milne read the first couple of chapters and saw the book's promise, especially if publication coincided with independence. Now, back home in Britain and close to that deadline, she and Milne talked to the publisher's legal adviser about passages that he believed could invite libel action. She presented the problem to Nkrumah in a telephone call from Edinburgh. He balked at making the cuts. If Thomas Nelson would not publish the book, somebody else would, he told Powell, and (as she later recalled) 'hung up without saying goodbye'.[45]

A letter the publisher's office sent to Nkrumah 20 August 1956 diplomatically leaves a somewhat different impression. Alluding to Powell's telephone conversation with Nkrumah, the letter expresses satisfaction that Nkrumah was willing to delay publication until February or March so he could go over the manuscript with Milne and add a final chapter on the election. The publisher and its New York counterpart would have more time, too, to produce the book and get it out to reviewers and stores with the expectation of 'a great deal of excitement' inside and outside of Africa. 'Every responsible (and many an irresponsible!) reviewer in Britain will have to and will want to concern himself with it, and it is my belief that it will help thousands of people outside Africa to understand and therefore to assess the greatness and singularity of your achievements.'[46] Fortuitously, the day Powell left for the Gold Coast the Governor had relayed a message from the British government: independence was set for 6 March 1957. Elated by the news, Nkrumah in the end did not object to the deletions Nelson's lawyer had proposed.[47] Thomas Nelson made good on its goal: reviews appeared in the United Kingdom and the United States just as the Gold Coast's independence as Ghana became a top news story around the world. Nkrumah had more than 30 pounds of newspaper cuttings, Padmore told Wright. The book's first edition of ten thousand sold out.[48]

In the *Crisis*, Padmore's review of Nkrumah's *Ghana* opened an entire April issue devoted to Ghana. The issue also included a tribute to Padmore himself: 'Ghana's Silent Hero'. In yet another twist of Padmore's protean identity, a brief biography of Padmore identified him as a European, a label commonly used in West Africa for anyone not African. Describing him as 'mentor and political guide to most of Africa's nationalists' and 'a figure venerated and respected throughout black Africa', the short tribute closed with a quote from Richard Wright's introduction to *Pan-Africanism or Communism?*: 'George is, in my opinion, the greatest living authority on the fervent nationalist movements sweeping Black Africa today.'[49]

Although Padmore had earlier told Wright he could not afford to make the trip to Ghana's independence celebration 'just to see spades dance', in the end he and Pizer went, and Padmore wore Kente cloth for the occasion.[50] Wright, to his disappointment, was not invited and, Pizer wrote to Ellen Wright, should have been, 'particularly considering the invitations sent to certain people who could very well have been left off the list without offence or detriment to the general good. Nello [James] was there.' James left after just two weeks but 'got to see that the "permanent revolution" was taking place in Africa, and that he, after all, had been instrumental in bringing [it] about', Pizer wrote. 'I am being a bit catty … What a poseur he is.'[51]

James himself told a story about this visit suggesting his willingness to pose, in this case as George Padmore. When Padmore was not well enough to travel in Nkrumah's car on independence night, James rode in it himself. 'As the big car drove slowly through the packed crowds', James later wrote,

> people recognized it as the Prime Minister's and pressed close to greet him. They saw me sitting in the front and one after another they began to say 'Hello, Mr Padmore!' 'How are you, Mr Padmore,' 'Good Evening,

Mr Padmore.' If a black stranger was in the Prime Minister's car on a night like this, then of course it was Mr Padmore. I had neither the heart nor the courage to disappoint them. So I accepted the greetings and smiled and shook hands on behalf of George.[52]

James took on Padmore's identity in another way, as historian of the Gold Coast revolution. In a letter written from Ghana on 3 March 1957, James told friends that Nkrumah had encouraged him to write about the building of the Convention Peoples Party. 'N told me that his autobiography told the story but nobody yet had "philosophized it".' James had no apparent doubt that he was the man for the job – with the assistance of Grace Lee Boggs, who had been his close associate in the United States. He sketched in his theory that, while Western political parties were failing, the CPP's organisation of illiterate peasants and market women provided a model for African political parties *at this stage*. A challenge would rise, however, when the Volta project produced fifty thousand industrial workers. 'Can they integrate the totality?' He and Boggs working together would provide guidance – 'pose shopfloor organisations, etc. etc., analyse what they have done, show that for Africa ... this is the form for the next generation, and leave the future open for them. They may have something to show the West. We shall pose the problem. History moves. You do your work. Opportunities arise. Let us do this.'[53]

The idea of bringing Boggs in on the project appears not to have been solely James's – in this letter from Accra, James wrote, 'N says, how to get G here.' James suggested she be invited to give philosophy lectures, and Nkrumah agreed. Boggs had known Nkrumah from his New York days, and after he left the US he wrote to her, even making an unexpected proposal of marriage. She had declined, she wrote in her autobiography, 'because I couldn't imagine myself being politically active in a country where I was totally ignorant of the history, geography, and culture'. She married the African American Jimmy Boggs instead. Years later, when she finally did visit Nkrumah with her husband, Nkrumah made a remark that suggested to Boggs the political motivation behind his proposal: '[I]f Grace had married me we would have changed all Africa.'[54] The new book project was another way to enlist Boggs's astute political help in the project of changing Africa. James encouraged her: 'We are in a beautiful position to do it', he wrote to his friends in the United States. 'Now G [Grace] must get his book, read it and do a job on it and send me letters. Let us give it all we have.' As he wrote in a later letter, the book 'simply has to be done. The world-wide concentration on Ghana makes it a natural, for US too.' Too many people, including American Negroes, equated whites with 'culture and civilization'; that belief 'must be blown sky-high'.[55] He saw only one problem: Padmore – who Nkrumah thought had failed to 'philosophize' the party's rise –had been 'left behind. It is very sad. N. wants more than GP can give. He may be bitter and fight us.'[56] His belief that Padmore failed to understand the 'Gold Coast revolution' surfaced again in a letter 25 March, when he pointed out that, in *Africa: Britain's Third Empire*, Padmore had shown no evidence of understanding the mass movement that the CPP would soon unleash.[57]

Ironically, when James eventually published *Nkrumah and the Ghana Revolution* (without Boggs's help),[58] he offered as chief among his credentials his relationship with Padmore. '[W]hat I wrote in the history expressed, I believed, what our circle, which had lived with the African question for over twenty years, thought of the future of the struggle for African independence at the time of its first success.'[59] This claim to authority was actually weak: James had stepped out of the circle concerning itself with African independence when he moved to the United States. Although Padmore sent him documents from time to time, he had not been present at the pivotal Manchester Congress, and *Nkrumah and the Ghana Revolution* reflects only a vague grasp of the organisational changes the England-based movement passed through in the early postwar years. Nor does he mention Padmore's book *The Gold Coast Revolution* though he does refer to Padmore's 'accurate, though condensed, account of the Ghana revolution' in *Pan-Africanism or Communism?*,[60] implying that his own book was the more complete rendering.

Omitting reference to Padmore's history of the Gold Coast revolution in his own, James keyed his analysis, as planned, to Nkrumah's autobiography. From the platform of Nkrumah's narrative, James launched the Ghana movement as more than a nationalist movement from independence rule: it was a social revolution, bent on transforming the relations not only between Ghana and Great Britain but also among Ghanaians themselves. While Padmore had compared the Gold Coast movement to other contemporary nationalist movements (India's, Ceylon's), James set the Ghana revolution beside great revolutions of the past: Haitian, French, Russian. He set Nkrumah beside Lenin as a revolutionary leader who had mobilised the people. To make them aware of themselves as a nation, Nkrumah and the CPP had convinced Ghanaians that they were 'the vanguard of a new world'.[61]

James was in the midst of writing the book when he accepted an invitation from his former student Eric Williams to edit the People's National Movement's political weekly, the *Nation*, in Trinidad, where Williams was leading the transition to independence. Relocated in Trinidad, James brought the Trinidad movement into his Ghana book, describing Williams's lectures to thousands of people at Woodford Square – an illustration of the power James believed cosmopolitan intellectuals like Williams could have when they brought home what they had learned about Western civilisation, the birthplace not only of capitalism and imperialism but also of those thinkers like Marx, Lenin, and Trotsky who understood capitalism and imperialism. Offering 'political disquisitions which with little change he could have delivered to students at the American university at which he was formerly a professor', Williams defied colonial administrators' assumption that colonial subjects had to be gradually educated for self-government.[62]

To James, enlightenment could come quickly to a people prepared for it. 'With the ordinary working man a good article in the paper, a pamphlet, is an event of some significance in his intellectual life. Workers think over it, pass it around, they remember it, they check events by it and it by events.' He pointed out how many doors one of Nkrumah's messages to his countrymen opened to other worlds, packed as it was with references to 'Calvary, Garibaldi, Battle of Britain, campaigns of East Africa, Burma and India, Shakespeare's *Julius Caesar*'. Even those who could not read could profit from the published word. 'One man reads and the others who do not read listen. Then would come the elucidation of the various points and references. It can last for days.' He reached back to a memory of Kenyatta telling him how in the 1920s one Kenyan would translate an article by Marcus Garvey while others listened and then would travel to other places to repeat the performance to other listeners. Garvey, he noted, 'wrote a vast deal of nonsense and many lies, but at any rate with a phenomenal energy he conveyed the idea that Africa should belong to the Africans'. This, too, was Nkrumah's message, and he had brought it so 'magnificently' that 'nothing like it has been seen anywhere since the first years of the Russian revolution'.[63]

Reflecting half a century later on James's application of Marxist–Leninist thought to Africa, Grace Lee Boggs portrayed him as trapped in the dominant radical frame of his time. Coming himself from a westernised colony, comfortably at home with Shakespeare and Thackeray, James shared with the other West Indians involved in the African nationalist movements an inability 'to understand that Africa was something very different'. Revisiting the past in a conversation in her Detroit home in 2007, Boggs said that James, so willing to tell Nkrumah what to do, 'had not the faintest notion about how to run a country, he had not the faintest notion about Africa. He had written the *History of Negro Revolt*. He did a lot of brilliant stuff, but it was essentially the brilliance of a historian and of a man who was a lover of books.'[64]

As it turned out, James's analysis of Ghana's political situation at the time of independence had no impact at all on the fortunes of the new nation of Ghana since it would not be published until 1977, and then, necessarily, with added accounts of the unfortunate turn the Ghana revolution had taken. James had initially thought he would have no trouble publishing the book, which he had intended for a 'bourgeois publisher'.[65] During his 1957 visit to Accra for the independence celebration, he had talked with two Nelson and Sons representatives at a ceremony held for Nkrumah's autobiography. He had told them he was writing 'a critical study of N's book' and they invited him to submit it to Nelson. But James was distracted by other developments – when Boggs arrived in London in 1957 at his invitation, she found him caught up in enthusiasm for the Hungarian Revolution and writing *Facing Reality*.[66] Then came his work in Trinidad, which ended when James returned to London after a political break with Eric Williams, who, following colonial tradition, later banned books by both James and himself.[67] James's book on the Ghana revolution would not be published for twenty years.

It is perhaps just as well that James's book was not published as Ghana began its life as a nation. As Boggs observed, James's theory about what was happening in Ghana was stronger than his grip on the reality of the situation. Padmore, a much more intimate confidant and adviser of Nkrumah, had a significantly more detailed understanding of the challenges faced by Nkrumah and other African leaders. *Pan-Africanism or Communism?* was barely out when he was already working on a new and far gloomier book than James had in mind: 'on tribalism as a disintegrating force in Africa', as Pizer described it in a letter to Ellen Wright. Writing about the project on 30 September 1957, Pizer said that Padmore planned to use Nigeria as 'the supreme example'.[68] While he presented the book in letters to Dobson as something he wanted to do for Nigeria and Azikiwe,[69] he had a larger purpose in mind: a guide for countries across Africa. He had been reading in the British Museum and had already mapped out his argument, Pizer told Ellen Wright: 'no possibility of resolving the tribalist fragmentation within a democratic set-up; the Soviet administrative set-up the only means of resolving the problem'.[70]

This was the strategy Nkrumah had put forth in the preface to his autobiography and would follow after independence: 'Capitalism is too complicated a system for a newly independent nation. Hence the need for a socialistic society. But even a system based on social justice and a democratic constitution may need backing up, during the period following independence, by emergency measures of a totalitarian kind.'[71] Despite Padmore's longstanding advocacy of democratic socialism for Ghana,[72] he now agreed with Nkrumah. Tribalism was 'as bad as religion', he wrote in a letter to Wright on 29 January 1957. 'Only Stalinism can smash this mess and liberate these people. After that, it will be time for de-Stalinism and democracy. K. [Kwame] feels the same way, but has to pay lip service to western clap-trap. Note his hint about totalitarism! [sic].'[73] Writing from Ghana on 22 April 1957, Padmore made the point again: Nkrumah 'has endorsed our line that it will be necessary to impose a transition period of "benevolent dictatorship" if Ghana is to get started on the road to civilization. There is so much to do at all levels; and so much mess to be cleaned up that no other way but strong govt. can even essay the task.'[74]

Nkrumah was urging Padmore to join him in transforming the country, and they had discussed development projects, among them ordering small generators for villages: 'Give the people light and ju-ju will retreat into the bush', Padmore believed. Meanwhile, he told Wright, he was meeting secretly with 'Young Turks' from Ivory Coast. By November, Padmore had a contract to work for Nkrumah in Ghana.[75] He was to leave Britain by end of the year, with Pizer following soon after. They settled into a spacious two-storey house with flamboyant trees and bougainvillea in the garden, but her letters to Ellen Wright suggest her own loneliness in Accra and Padmore's frustration in his new job.[76] Other high-level officials resented his presence. Ras Makonnen, who also moved to Ghana, would recall the scorn heaped by British-trained Africans who looked down both on Nkrumah and on the West Indians he had brought to Ghana: '"Who is this upstart, this Nzima boy, this goldsmith's son (Kwame)? He is not part of the old Oxford brigade; he is one of these damned American-educated types. Look at these strange people – these Makonnens and Padmores – he has dug up and brought into our Ghana. We don't even know their ancestry."'[77] According to Makonnen, Padmore encouraged Nkrumah to let him head a separate branch to deal with African affairs without the interference of British-trained Ghanaian civil servants suspicious that these West Indians might be communist.[78] Pizer told Wright that Nkrumah made the appointment 'grudgingly' after pressure from 'the most politically conscious younger men'. Opposition to the appointment came, significantly, from the head of the Ghana Foreign Service, A. L. Adu, who noted that 'Padmore had never lived in Africa nor had he been involved in any of the African nationalist movements within Africa'. Adu dropped his objection when he saw the virtue of Nkrumah's appointing someone outside the civil service 'to carry through his policy for the emancipation of those parts of Africa still under foreign rule', but Adu's relations with Padmore remained uneasy for a time.[79] Indicative of his awkward status, Padmore had a small budget and a small office, and, since he was given no private secretary, Pizer handled his confidential affairs.[80]

However disappointing his position in Ghana, Padmore did travel widely with Nkrumah and joined him in planning the first Conference of Independent African States, held in April 1958. Eight nations came together, with those to the north of the Sahara outnumbering those to the south. Describing the conference, St Clair Drake noted that of the eight only two, Liberia and Ghana, were 'indubitably black'. Organising this conference and the All African People's Conference in Accra later that year altered Nkrumah's and Padmore's plan for achieving Pan-African unity, Drake observed. In *Pan-Africanism or Communism?* Padmore had proposed regional federations leading to a united continent, but now he and Nkrumah believed such federations would perpetuate 'colonial balkanization – the separation between French and British areas being a major threat to united continental action'.[81]

Drake was present at the All African People's Conference (he had taken a teaching job at Ghana's University College), but missed the address by the delegate from Algeria, Frantz Fanon, who denounced the conference's espousal of non-violence in the light of Algeria's desperate struggle for independence. Moved by the words of the future author of *The Wretched of the Earth* (1963), the conferees passed a resolution justifying violence by nationalists when violence was thrust upon them; during the discussion a floor demonstration called for Kenyatta's release.[82] Kenyatta's was a notable absence in an array of future leaders of their independent countries – Julius Nyerere of Tanganyika (later Tanzania), Kenneth Kaunda from Northern Rhodesia (later Zambia), Hastings Banda of Nyasaland (later Malawi), and Patrice Lumumba of the Congo. To Drake, a longtime observer of the Padmore circle, this conference was 'the high point of influence of the Pan-African group', in part because Nigeria's independence two years later cost Ghana its dominance as a leader.[83] Even earlier, though, Makonnen saw the efforts to use Ghana as a base for Pan-African revolution thwarted by dissension among tribal groups within Ghana itself. 'You couldn't expect much dedication to pan-Africanism abroad when at home the Fanti boys were working to establish their fellow Fantis, and the Ewes and others were doing likewise', Makonnen later wrote. 'It angered George a great deal and he used to come to me and say: "These damn fellows, they're very chauvinistic".'[84] The Pan-Africanist, returned home, found there contentious allegiances to local identities.

As an arena for redirecting young Ghanaians on the broader socialist path, the National Association of Socialist Student Organisations became a place where both Padmore and Makonnen could wield influence,[85] but that organisation was just a corner of a broad, unruly political scene. Nkrumah and the CPP faced rising opposition from a diverse array of political enemies. Attempting to control the jostling for power, the CPP stripped chiefs of their authority, banned tribally based parties, and outlawed false and critical statements about the government. The Stalinist scenario Padmore had favoured before independence was put into play. Given Padmore's longtime assault on such laws in the colonies, the irony was deep: as a member of the Cabinet's National Defence Council he reviewed Special Branch reports on the opposition – the kind of reports that British officials had once filed on himself and his circle in London.[86]

While Padmore was neither as pitiful nor ineffectual as Tom Lanwood in *A Wreath for Udomo*, he did suffer the disillusion of that armchair revolutionary. He was not alone. Nkrumah's economic adviser, the West Indian Arthur Lewis, serving a two-year appointment under United Nations auspices, was optimistic when he arrived in Ghana, but fourteen months later he described his frustrations in a letter to the UN official Hugh Keenleyside: 'There is a limit to what one can take, and I get tired of sticking around just to play nursemaid to grown men.'[87] Lewis had built a sturdy reputation as a development economist since 1938 when he contributed a pamphlet to Padmore's IASB series. He had taught at the London School of Economics and the University of Manchester, served on the Colonial Economic and Development Council, and produced a body of work that set him on a path to the 1979 Nobel Prize. He had also moved in political circles that Padmore criticised. Involved with the Fabian Colonial Bureau, which worked hand-in-glove with the Labour Party, Lewis advised the bureau's Rita Hinden before a 1946 conference to invite critics of Labour's colonial policy, for instance George Padmore, 'whose widely publicised writings are a possible source of trouble',[88] a comment that hinted at the gulf between the two men. In 1952, Padmore wrote to Lewis to express his concern that British investment in the massive Volta River dam project would allow Britain to perpetuate its power in Ghana after political independence. Lewis responded that any investment, even British, could increase a country's wealth.[89] Pizer probably expressed Padmore's opinion when, two years later, she lamented Lewis's advocacy of foreign investment as the best route for industrialising Ghana. 'What is the use of exchanging political domination for economic dependence?'[90]

Despite their political and economic differences, Padmore and Lewis did share a faith in socialism as the best path for developing nations. Padmore quoted Lewis at some length in *The Gold Coast Revolution* to make the point that the government needed to take an active role in developing colonial economies.[91] In a 1959 essay (not published until later) Padmore offered economic proposals consistent with Lewis's. Both favoured mixed economies with investment by government and private capitalists; both advocated an emphasis on food production and agricultural development; both promoted small-scale industrial projects producing goods for the Ghana market; both mistrusted premature investment in expensive showcase projects like the Volta dam that Nkrumah wanted to build.[92] Yet politically they took separate paths once they were in Ghana: while Padmore participated in the security clampdown, Lewis was sickened by it. He wrote to Keenleyside, 'The fascist state is in full process of creation, and I find it hard to live in a a country where I cannot protest against imprisonment without trial or the new legislation prohibiting strikes and destroying trade union independence.' Out of patience with Accra's political atmosphere and frustrated by his inability to rein in wasteful projects, Lewis abandoned his position at the end of 1958 before his two-year term was up.[93]

Padmore, for his part, was 'continually being criticized by some C.P.P. leaders', the US Embassy in Accra reported to the Department of State on 9 August 1958.[94] In an unflattering article published in *Encounter* after Padmore's death, Russell Warren Howe, a stringer for *Newsweek* who had ties to the CIA, referred to a 'revolt of other African leaders' against Padmore at the All African People's Conference. Howe portrayed Padmore as contemptuous of Africans, 'appallingly British' – a 'rather terrifying figure' who had ordered Howe out of Ghana after Howe reported a Padmore power play in the *Sunday Times*. Howe claimed familiarity with Padmore ('I sat many times on his stoep'), but Howe's CIA association and the identifiable errors of fact and interpretation in his article undermine its credibility.[95] It is clear from other evidence, however, that Padmore found working conditions in Ghana difficult – so difficult that he planned to move to the West Indies, according to Makonnen, although another report had him considering relocation in the Sudan.[96] Wherever he thought of going, barely a year after his arrival Padmore told Nkrumah he wanted to leave. Nkrumah talked him out of it.[97] Yet when an interviewer spoke with him in early 1959, Padmore put an optimistic face on affairs. Ghana would leap from feudalism to Pan-Africanism socialism, he said, and there would 'be a United States of Africa, in our own lifetime, in all Africa'.[98]

Just a few months later, Padmore, his health unsteady for some time, fell ill during a trip to Liberia and left for London for medical treatment. Hospitalised for cirrhosis of the liver, he died on 23 September 1959. Rumours that he was poisoned would circulate, but within days Pizer had typed up a five and a half page statement to correct 'certain misunderstandings' about his death. She said that his liver condition had deteriorated over the previous nine months and, by the time he sought medical care from his old friend Dr C. Belfield Clarke in London, it had become serious enough to provoke the haemorrhages that led to a coma and then death, despite the attentive medical care he had received at a London hospital. 'I was with George when he died, painlessly and without knowing that he was going out of life.'[99] To Nancy Cunard, she wrote, 'Dear Nancy, I know the blow of George's death is one you will find it difficult to surmount, as I know how much you loved him'.[100]

In Ghana, Nkrumah broadcast a tribute. 'One day, the whole of Africa will surely be free and united and when the final tale is told, the significance of George Padmore's work will be revealed.'[101] In the *Pittsburgh Courier*, George S. Schuyler spoke of Padmore's 'many books, pamphlets, articles and news releases' as 'an inspiration to the men who dreamed of a free Africa' but feared that with Padmore's death went 'the high hopes for a politically united Africa'.[102] In Port of Spain, James wrote an eleven-part series on Padmore for the *Nation*. In London Padmore's longtime physician and friend, Cedric Belfield Clarke, wrote Padmore's obituary for the *Times*. Although Clarke mentioned Padmore's role in the Pan-African Congress and Nkrumah's administration, his warmest words were devoted to Padmore as a writer who collected books and newspaper cuttings, studied and marked them up, wrote his books on Africa, and loved English literature.[103] A funeral service was held for Padmore at a crematorium in London, and his ashes were returned to Ghana for interment at Christiansborg Castle.

St Clair Drake sat in the crowd as, from the castle's veranda, Nkrumah said, 'Who knows but from this very spot his ancestors were carried out across the ocean there while the kinsmen stood weeping here as silent sentinels. We have brought his ashes "home to rest".'[104] Then, Drake said, Nkrumah slammed the ashes into the wall, took out his handkerchief, and wept.[105] The American broadcasting network NBC telecast the ceremony.[106] Afterwards, Pizer wrote to Wright, 'When I saw the urn in which George's ashes had been placed, I thought how strange that the remains of so tremendous a personality, so great a man, could be put into so small a compass.'[107]

After Padmore's death, Pizer stayed on in Accra, in a job Nkrumah arranged for her and in the house where she and Padmore had lived. She wrote a preface for the *Présence africaine*'s French edition of *Pan-Africanism or Communism?*, which Padmore had hoped would stiffen the political backbone of nationalists from the French colonies.[108] She also began collecting material for a biography of Padmore, reaching out to people who had known him around the world at different stages of his life. She enlisted James; his wife, Selma; Cunard, Wright, and others in that effort.[109] She told Wright she meant to write a simple version that would be released by the CPP, without her name on it, and then a fuller version like one Padmore himself might have produced: 'an interpretation of an epoch which linked him with the two great movements – the Communist and Pan-Africanism'.[110] She wrote Cunard, 'He was so much part of an epoch and mixed with so many of the names that have made history. It's his development during a developing era that I want to bring out. But where is my material? He was always destroying papers and he did not talk about the past.'[111] She died in 1965 without writing her book, though at least some of the documents she collected wound up in a collection of Nkrumah's papers at the Moorland-Spingarn Research Center at Howard University, and a copy of the recollections Cunard wrote out for Pizer survives in the Harry Ransom Humanities Research Center at Austin.

Wright, himself in ill health and low on financial resources, gave up his newest project – a book on French Africa, still dangling between full independence and alliance with France.[112] A little more than a year after Padmore's death, Wright died of a heart attack in a Paris clinic under cloudy circumstances. In 1961, W. E. B. Du Bois moved to Ghana, where he died in 1963; he was buried outside the walls of Christiansborg Castle where Padmore's ashes were interred. Meanwhile, Nkrumah's regime stiffened its control of printed speech, detaining editors, nationalising newspapers, censoring press reports going out of the country, banning imported publications 'contrary to public interest', and, in 1963, requiring that newspapers be licenced.[113] In 1966, Nkrumah was overthrown in a military coup. In exile in Conakry, Guinea, he continued his political career chiefly by writing books; he, too, considered writing a biography of Padmore.[114]

James attempted for years to write and publish his own biography of Padmore. Writing on 8 April 1963 to update the New York bookseller Walter Goldwater on his activities, James mentioned a new edition of *The Black Jacobins* coming out from Vintage Press, his book on cricket, *Beyond the Boundary*, to be published by Hutchinson's, and Dobson's acceptance of his proposal for the Padmore biography. He was trying to find copies of *International African Opinion*, the periodical he had edited, and wondered if Goldwater had any of the African Bureau publications.[115] A year later, James received word from Goldwater that a Michigan State University professor, James R. Hooker, was writing a Padmore biography. 'Of course my first feeling was that he had no business writing life of George at all, while your work is still in process', Goldwater wrote. '[I]f he gets his book done before you find a publisher for yours, there probably will be no market for yours.'[116] Hooker's biography appeared in 1967, and James judged it 'a scrupulous distillation of a mass of material'. He did think Hooker had not paid enough attention to Pizer, who had contributed so much to Padmore's work, or to Makonnen's 'tremendous organisational work' during the British years.[117] James did not give up on his memoir of Padmore and continued to collect miscellaneous documents (later archived at the University of West Indies at St Augustine), but in the end he seems to have produced only a slim biographical manuscript fragment, 'Notes on the Life of George Padmore'.[118]

It took James years to get his book on Ghana published. On 10 June 1965, before Nkrumah's overthrow, he wrote to Goldwater that he had completed the manuscript of 'Nkrumah Then and Now' and it was 'magnificent', but publishers were 'afraid to touch it', presumably (Goldwater told an American publisher he pitched it to), because it was too critical.[119] Nkrumah's overthrow the following February did not, however, improve the book's publishing prospects. Not until 1977 did *Nkrumah and the Ghana Revolution* emerge from Lawrence Hill and Company in the United States and Allison and Busby in the United Kingdom. To the book he had written right after Ghana became independent James had added reprints of several other pieces that chronicled Nkrumah's subsequent troubles and fall.

By that time, disappointment in the consequences of African independence was rampant. In 1969, when a small American publisher reissued James's 1938 book *A History of Negro Revolt*, retitled *A History of Pan-African Revolt*, James added to it an epilogue explaining the 'rapid decline of African nationalism'. To the customary explanation that the Western industrial nations still controlled African economies he added this: 'the newly independent African state was little more than the old imperialist state only now administered and controlled by black nationalists'. As Frantz Fanon had seen, James wrote, 'these men, western-educated and western-oriented, had or would have little that was nationalist or African to contribute to the establishment of a truly new and truly African order'.[120] Yet James was unwilling to give up his attempt to link African nationalists to the Western revolutionary tradition. In Julius Nyerere's efforts to build a socialist Tanzania, he saw a continuation of a Leninist faith in the peasantry and a reliance on local rather than central leadership. Socialism as practised by Tanzania 'can fertilise and reawaken the mortuary that is socialist theory and practice in the advanced countries'.[121]

Critical of James's limited understanding of Africa and what she saw as his misguided attempt to frame African experience in Western terms, his longtime political intimate Grace Lee Boggs nevertheless retained a respect for the efforts of James, Padmore, Nkrumah, and the others who have been the subject of this book. Reflecting on their limitations, Boggs also counselled seeing those limitations in the context of a time when 'we are learning, we are developing, we are maturing, we don't really have a serious Black movement, we don't have a serious independence movement, a Third World movement, until the twentieth century. So there's a lot of hit and misses, a lot of trial and error, and I think we have to see each one of these individuals as part of the developing movement, playing their particular role, making their particular contribution.'[122]

Others who made their particular contributions as sometime members of the Padmore circle have set their memories and assessments down in memoirs and autobiographies: Nnamdi Azikiwe, who became president of Nigeria (and, like Nkrumah, proved less than a champion of press freedom),[123] in *My Odyssey: An Autobiography*; Peter Abrahams in *The Black Experience in the 20th Century*; Eric Williams in *Inward Hunger: The Education of a Prime Minister*, and Joe Appiah in *The Autobiography of an African Patriot*. St Clair Drake drew on his personal knowledge of the London circle in his several reflections on the African diaspora.[124] Fenner Brockway, the Englishman who had been a useful ally to Padmore, Nkrumah, and Kenyatta had surprisingly little to say about their London days in his memoirs and books on Africa, although in *The Colonial Revolution* he did describe Padmore as 'a leading constructive influence in African liberation' and wrote that 'his death was a great loss to African unity and Nkrumah's subsequent course might have been different had he lived'.[125] Yet in *African Socialism*, published in 1963, Brockway attributed the popularity of socialism in newly independent African nations more generally to the popularity of socialism in Europe towards the end of the Second World War, when leading African nationalists were completing their European studies; he omitted the significant role of the circle around Padmore and its prewar origins in the international communist movement.[126]

The most intimate history of the London-based political community to which Padmore belonged came from Ras Makonnen, who had always been more of a financier, organiser, and publisher but at the end of their story came into his own as a narrator. An active participant in Nkrumah's Pan-African initiatives both before and after Padmore's death, Makonnen sometimes lost his way in the political intrigues of what he characterised as Ghana's Machiavellian society.[127] After Nkrumah's overthrow, he was imprisoned in Ghana. Pleading for his release, the American writer Julian Mayfield, himself lately a resident of Ghana and editor of the *African Review*, wrote to Lieutenant-General

J. A. Ankrah, chairman of the National Liberation Council, that he had met no man during his five years in Ghana 'more keenly aware of the deficiencies of the former government'; indeed, Makonnen had told him before the coup that he was preparing to leave the country. Mayfield made an eloquent plea for the release of this 'old Pan-Africanist pioneer who, although born in the West Indies, has always been a foremost champion of the struggle for African freedom'.[128] Makonnen was released, and his old ally Jomo Kenyatta assigned him to a post in Kenya's Ministry of Tourism. A professor at the University of Nairobi, Kenneth King, had heard about Makonnen's life in Kenya from St Clair Drake, and proposed that they work on a textbook for King's course on Africa and the African diaspora. King interviewed Makonnen over nine months, then transcribed his tapes and reorganised the material.[129]

In part because the book emerged from Makonnen's conversations with a knowledgeable interviewer who could probe for explanations and detail, Makonnen's *Pan-Africanism from Within* provides a nuanced and sometimes gossipy account, not always accurate in its details but memorable for its intricate weave and blunt evaluation of the Ghana revolution. Unlike Padmore, James, and Nkrumah, whose histories of the anti-colonial movement seem firmly locked within a purposeful frame, Makonnen spoke spontaneously, recalling not only events but also his and others' often conflicting thoughts and feelings about those events. In his own book on the Ghana revolution, James wrote, 'Too often these events are summarised in books so that the reader cannot get the feeling of what happened'.[130] That could not be said of Makonnen's personable memoir, which conveys the feeling of the life he had lived in British Guiana, the United States, England, Ghana, and Kenya. Usually a secondary player in historians' summaries of the London circle, Makonnen emerges in his own book as a hero, not only of his own story but of the larger story he tells: the twists and turns of the Black diaspora's relation to the African liberation movement.

New Africa's failure to offer a better life to her people after the transfers of power does not negate the contribution of all these who tried to write a better world into being, even when they were in part responsible for that failure. Their books stand as evidence of a will to speak, re-envisioning Africa's past and future: Kenyatta's *Facing Mount Kenya*, Nkrumah's *Ghana*, James's *Nkrumah and the Ghana Revolution*, Abrahams's novels and memoirs, Padmore's *Pan-Africanism or Communism?* These books endure, lingering on bookshelves in every corner of the world. Their authors' periodical publications have remained less visible, their little papers and pamphlets hidden away in archives and intelligence files, many of Padmore's cascade of news items lost in the diverse array of publications where they appeared. Faded, crumbling, these chronicles of old battles still have their story to tell: of writers who believed they could change the world with their words, and did.

While historians have commonly seen the Pan-Africanists around Padmore as a political community, seeing them as a writers' community cautions us not to oversimplify the relationship between their writing and their political ends. They shared a common political ground, but only to a certain extent. While they sometimes worked together to publish their own short-lived periodicals, while there were times when they helped each other on pamphlets and books, while they might have agreed on manifestos or resolutions when they came together in conferences, they also struck out on their own as independent writers beholden not to the creed of any organisation but to their particular understanding. Each of the books mentioned above emanated from an individual mind and life experience. All these individuals saw themselves not only as political figures but also as intellectuals: their writing was not only political work, though it was that; it was intellectual work, and, in the case of James and Abrahams, artistic work as well. Abrahams spoke of Kenyatta's 'fine scholarly brain'. Padmore referred to his own book on Russia as 'one of the best pieces of sociological work' he had done. Nkrumah spent years living a scholar's life in the United States and made a serious attempt, first as Ghana's head of state and then as its overthrown leader in exile, to establish Nkrumahism as a political philosophy. None exceeded James's devotion to merging intellectual and political into one life. As political intellectuals these men walked in the footsteps of Marx and Lenin; they believed in the power of ideas to remake the world. Their writing ought not be seen, then, merely as instrument of their politics; it was both a crucible for their politics and sometimes, when they disagreed with one another, a battleground. There was a remarkable reflexivity about their work: writing about each other, whether in agreement or contention, they expanded the space they occupied. Writing was itself a political act.

We might even entertain the idea that their politics served their writing as well as the other way round. Motivated to make their voices heard in the world, they found in the political realm a forum. A man who loved literature and wrote an early novel and later a book on Melville's *Moby-Dick*, James found his earliest success in the political history *Black Jacobins*. Abrahams's novels caught publishers' and reviewers' attention because they dealt with one of the hottest political issues of this time: race. In a period when black authors were rare, asserting themselves as writers was easier if they asserted themselves as political writers, the voices of an unheard people. Thus the reader for Allen and Unwin thought Abrahams's *Dark Testament* on the lives and Coloured peoples in South Africa would be worth publishing if he were indeed Negro; then his book would have social significance. Without questioning the sincerity of these writers' desire to be free of colonial rule, we may consider the likelihood that this shared political desire had specific origins in their own particular desires to live in a world where, as individuals, they could speak and be heard. Thus to see them as primarily Pan-Africanists using writing as propaganda to accomplish their goals is to oversimplify their lives and the work that they did. Let us at least consider the possibility that they spent so much time and energy on writing not only in the hope that it would have its effect but also because they wanted, simply, to write and be published.

This is not to say that they did not have specific political ends. Padmore wrote *How Britain Rules Africa* to counter proposed Labour Party policy. He wrote *Africa: Britain's Third Empire* to provide fuel for the fire that the attenders of the Manchester Congress hoped to light in Africa. He hoped *The Gold Coast Revolution* would inspire and guide movements elsewhere in Africa. He certainly saw Wright's *Black Power* and Nkrumah's autobiography as useful publicity for the Ghana movement. James, too, began *Nkrumah and the Ghana Revolution* with the idea of presenting a model for organising the next generation of revolutions. Abrahams had a specific political motive when he wrote *A Wreath for Udomo*: to counter Padmore's too rosy view of Ghana's future. In *Facing Mount Kenya*, Kenyatta made an argument for the land claims that had brought him to England. Yet these works not only served political ends; they were also themselves political ends, claiming a space in the public sphere for voices that had had been excluded from it.

The fact that this was a transnational public sphere is significant. Publishing or distributing their publications across the world, these writers conjured up an 'imagined community' of colonised people of colour bound together by a common cause. That community proved fragile with geographic dispersal – the ties that bound them together in London loosened when Kenyatta returned to Kenya and Nkrumah to the Gold Coast, which became more and more the focus of Padmore's concern. The international fight against colonial powers gave way to efforts to build individual nations.

A logical continuation of the work in London would have been to launch a Pan-African publishing venture based in Africa, but in the decades after independence the new governments placed their focus instead on restricting publication in their own countries to undermine opposition. Nkrumah's control of the press was the most notorious, but in 1977, not long before Kenyatta's death, the Kenyan government arrested novelist Ngugi wa Thiong'o, an advocate of publication in Gikuyu and a critic of multinational corporations; Ngugi spent a year in prison.[131] Ten years earlier in Nigeria, the writer Wole Soyinka was arrested after he attempted to prevent civil war when Biafra seceded; he spent nearly two years in prison without trial and has repeatedly gone into exile, the course taken by many of Africa's writers. Some who have stayed have suffered the darkest fate: Nigeria's Ken Saro Wiwa was executed in 1995 for his advocacy of the rights of his Ogoni people, their homeland stripped and desecrated for its oil.[132]

Half a century after Ghana's independence, African publishers produced an infinitesimal number of the world's books. As Charles R. Larson has pointed out in *The Ordeal of the African Writer* (2001), despite the efforts of agencies and determined individuals, this large continent's publishing industry remained frail, its readers still heavily dependent on books imported from Europe and the United States and written in the languages of the former colonial rulers, and many of its writers scattered beyond the continent to the cities of the West where, like Padmore and his allies, they had more freedom and better access to publishing resources.[133] Magazines and journals that focused on Africa were more often than not published outside the continent, and, although individual African localities had lively and courageous newspapers, what Padmore said in the mid-1930s was still true at the start of the next century: 'Blacks have no powerful press ... ' While his London circle did much to advance the right asserted by Chinua Achebe – 'the right of a people to take back their own narrative' – they did not complete that work.[134] It still awaits the attention of new generations.

Notes

1. Wright Papers (G. Padmore), Padmore to Wright, 21 July 1954.
2. George Padmore, *Pan-Africanism or Communism?* (London: Dennis Dobson, 1956), p. 15.
3. Wright Papers (G. Padmore), Padmore to R. Wright, 21 July 1954.
4. Padmore, *Pan-Africanism*, p. 338.
5. *Ibid.*, p. 339.
6. *Ibid.*, p. 339.
7. *Ibid.*, pp. 22 and 118, where he uses the alternative term Pan-African Federation of United States; Wright Papers (G. Padmore), Padmore to R. Wright, 21 July 1954, 28 June 1954.
8. Nkrumah Papers, Box 154–7, Folder 52, typescript copy of letter [Padmore to Nkrumah], 5 August 1955.
9. Padmore, *Pan-Africanism*, pp. 371, 345.
10. *Ibid.*, pp. 21–2.
11. Wright Papers (G. Padmore), Padmore to Wright, 5 March 1956.

12 Padmore, *Pan-Africanism*, p. 373; for a description of modernisation theory, see Robert L. Tignor, *W. Arthur Lewis and the Birth of Development Economics* (Princeton, NJ and Oxford: Princeton University Press, 2006), p. 93.
13 Padmore, *Pan-Africanism*, pp. 376–7.
14 Partha Chatterjee, *Nationalist Thought and the Colonial World: A Derivative Discourse* (Minneapolis: University of Minnesota Press, 1986), p. 133.
15 *Ibid.*, pp. 133–8.
16 Hazel Rowley, *Richard Wright: The Life and Times* (New York: Henry Holt, 2001), pp. 452–3, 468.
17 Wright Papers (G. Padmore), Padmore to R. Wright, 23 August 1955.
18 Padmore, *Pan-Africanism*, pp. 195, 197, 203, 207.
19 Dennis Austin, *Politics in Ghana: 1946–1960* (London, New York, Toronto: Oxford University Press, 1964), p. 265.
20 Appiah explained why he left the CPP in Joseph Appiah, *Joe Appiah: The Autobiography of an African Patriot* (New York: Praeger, 1990), pp. 237–42.
21 Wright Papers (G. Padmore), Padmore to R. Wright, 19 October 1955.
22 *Ibid.*, Padmore to R. Wright, 19 October 1955.
23 Wright Papers (G. Padmore), Padmore to R. Wright, 5 October 1955.
24 Padmore, 'Padmore Exposes £5,000 Deal Behind the WFTU-Federalist Labour Intrigues / Money Freely Distributed to Pull Down Nkrumah & Sabotage Independence', *Ghana Evening News* (8 October 1955), 1, 4. Padmore mentioned writing an article on the Gold Coast constitution for Bourdet's weekly in a letter to Wright, 21 [no month] 1954.
25 Padmore, 'French Worried over G.C. Independence', *Ghana Evening News* (15 August 1955), 1.
26 Wright Papers (G. Padmore), Padmore to R. Wright, 19 October 1955.
27 *Ibid.*, Padmore to R. Wright, 5 December 1955.
28 Wright, 'Foreword', *Pan-Africanism*, p. 11.
29 Wright Papers (G. Padmore), Padmore to R. Wright, 5 March 1956.
30 *Ibid.*, Padmore to R. Wright, 13 March 1956.
31 Daniel Guérin, Mémoires, 1904–1988/F RES 688-19/Folder 2, Daniel Guérin to Padmore, 18 September 1956.
32 *Ibid.*, 26 September 1956, Padmore to Guérin.
33 Pizer said Dobson offered chapters to *Encounter* in her letter to Wright, Wright Papers (D. Padmore), 14 December 1955; no excerpt appeared in the magazine.
34 Rita Hinden, 'The White Man's Pride', *Encounter*, 7: 6 (December 1956), 85–6.
35 Frances Stonor Saunders, *The Cultural Cold War: The CIA and the World of Arts and Letters* (New York: New Press, 1999), pp. 323, 330.
36 Hugh Wilford, '"Unwitting Assets?": British Intellectuals and the Congress for Cultural Freedom', *Twentieth Century British History*, 11:1 (2000), p. 50; Stephen Howe, *Anticolonialism in British Politics* (Oxford: Clarendon Press, 1993), pp. 135–6.
37 James R. Hooker, *Black Revolutionary: George Padmore's Path from Communism to Pan-Africanism* (New York: Praeger Publishers, 1967), p. 105.
38 'Aspects of African Nationalism', *Times Literary Supplement* (21 September 1956), 555.
39 Hooker, *Black Revolutionary*, pp. 124, 127.
40 Nkrumah Papers, Box 154-7, Folder 52, retyped letter [Pizer to Nkrumah], 28 June 1955.
41 Marika Sherwood, *Kwame Nkrumah: The Years Abroad* (Legon, Ghana: Freedom Publications, 1996), pp. 150–1.
42 Erica Powell, *Private Secretary (Female) / Gold Coast* (New York: St Martin's Press, 1984), pp. 81–90; 'Acknowledgement', Nkrumah, *Ghana*.
43 Kwame Nkrumah, *Ghana: The Autobiography of Kwame Nkrumah* (New York: Thomas Nelson and Sons, 1957), p. 288.
44 Austin, *Politics in Ghana*, p. 308.
45 Powell, *Private Secretary*, pp. 99–101.

46 Edinburgh University Library, Special Collections, Thomas Nelson and Sons, Ltd, Records, 1861–1960, unsigned carbon, letter to Nkrumah, 20 August 1956.
47 Powell, *Private Secretary*, pp. 101–2.
48 Wright Papers (G. Padmore), Padmore to R. Wright, 22 April 1957.
49 Padmore, 'The Birth of a Nation', *Crisis*, 64: 4 (April 1957), 196–207; 'Ghana's Silent Hero', 214, 253.
50 Wright Papers (G. Padmore), Padmore to R. Wright, 29 January 1957; James, 'Notes', p. 55.
51 Wright Papers (D. Padmore), Pizer to E. Wright, 9 April 1957.
52 James, 'Notes', p. 45.
53 Lilly Library, Indiana University, James Mss, Folder 1, carbon, letter James to Friends, 3 March 1957.
54 Grace Lee Boggs, *Living for Change: An Autobiography* (Minneapolis and London: University of Minnesota Press, 1998), pp. 72–3.
55 Lilly Library, James Mss, Folder 1, carbon, letter James to Friends, carbon copy, letter from James, recipients not identified but probably the same 'Friends' to whom he wrote the earlier letter, 11 March 1957.
56 Lilly Library, James Mss, Folder 1, carbon copy, J[ames] to Friends, 3 March 1957.
57 Ibid., Folder 4, James to Friends, 25 March 1957.
58 Grace Lee Boggs told me this on 12 August 2007.
59 James, *Nkrumah and the Ghana Revolution* (Westport, CT: Lawrence Hill and Company, 1977), pp. 6–8.
60 Ibid., p. 64.
61 Ibid., p. 86.
62 Ibid., p. 121.
63 Ibid., pp. 123–4.
64 Conversation with me, 12 August 2007.
65 Lilly Library, James Mss, Folder 1, carbon copy, James to Friends, 3 March 1957.
66 Conversation with me, 12 August 2007.
67 Farrukh Dhondy, *C. L. R. James* (New York: Pantheon Books, 2001), p. 142.
68 Wright Papers (D. Padmore), Pizer to E. Wright, 30 September 1957.
69 Hooker, *Black Revolutionary*, pp. 131–2.
70 Wright Papers (D. Padmore), Pizer to E. Wright, 30 September 1957.
71 Nkrumah, *Ghana*, p. xvi.
72 See, for example, Nkrumah Papers, Box 154–7, Folder 52, typed copy, [Padmore to Nkrumah], 10 May 1954.
73 Wright Papers (G. Padmore), Padmore to R. Wright, 29 January 1957.
74 Ibid., Padmore to R. Wright, 22 April 1957.
75 Wright Papers (D. Padmore), Pizer to E. Wright, 27 November 1957.
76 The house is described in 'George Padmore: Mr Pan-Africa', *Contact* (21 March 1959), 15.
77 Ras Makonnen, *Pan-Africanism from Within*, recorded and edited by Kenneth King (Nairobi, London and New York: Oxford University Press, 1973), p. 203.
78 Ibid., p. 258.
79 Michael Dei-Anang, *The Administration of Ghana's Foreign Relations, 1956–1965: A Personal Memoir* (London: The Athlone Press, 1975), p. 13.
80 Wright Papers (D. Padmore), Pizer to R. Wright, 31 October 1959.
81 George Shepperson and St Clair Drake, 'The Fifth Pan-African Conference, 1945 and the All African People's Congress, 1958', *Contributions in Black Studies*, 8 (1986–87), 49–50.
82 Ibid., pp. 50–1.
83 Ibid., pp. 50–1.
84 Makonnen, *Pan-Africanism*, p. 259.
85 Legum, 'Socialism in Ghana', in William H. Friedland, Carl G. Rosberg, Jr (eds), *African Socialism* (Stanford, CA: Stanford University Press, 1964), p. 137.
86 Rathbone, *Nkrumah and the Chiefs*, pp. 150–3; Fitch and Oppenheimer, *Ghana*, pp. 53–4.

87 Quoted by Tignor, *W. Arthur Lewis*, p. 172.
88 Tignor, *W. Arthur Lewis*, p. 110.
89 *Ibid.*, pp. 195–6.
90 Wright Papers (D. Padmore), Pizer to R. Wright, 19 October 1954.
91 George Padmore, *The Gold Coast Revolution* (London: Dennis Dobson, 1953), pp. 217–18.
92 For Lewis's views on Ghana development see Tignor, pp. 124–5, 154–63, 195–201; for Padmore's see his 'A Guide to Pan-African Socialism', a 1959 essay first published in *African Socialism*, pp. 230, 233–4.
93 Tignor, *W. Arthur Lewis*, pp. 172–3, 179.
94 US/NA 770.00/8-958 HBS, American Embassy, Accra, to Department of State, 'Comments of Observers from Ghana to Cotonou Congress', 9 August 1958.
95 Russell Warren Howe, 'George Padmore', *Encounter*, 13: 6 (December 1959), 52–6. A couple of years later, editors at the *Reporter*, an American magazine, asked Howe to write a piece countering the tendency of some Americans 'to romanticize and idealize African nationalism', and Howe obliged, though the result was, in one editor's opinion, 'a mish-mash'. The magazine cut it heavily and used it anyway. See Carol Polsgrove, *Divided Minds: Intellectuals and the Civil Rights Movement* (New York: W. W. Norton and Company, 2001), pp. 143–6.
96 Makonnen, *Pan-Africanism*, p. 259; Hooker, *Black Revolutionary*, p. 133.
97 Wright Papers (D. Padmore), Pizer to R. Wright, 31 October 1959.
98 'George Padmore: Mr Pan-Africa', *Contact* (21 March 1959), 15.
99 Nkrumah Papers, 154-7/52, untitled, unsigned typescript that begins, 'There are certain misunderstandings about the death of George Padmore ... '
100 Nancy Cunard Collection, Box 17, Folder 10, D. Padmore [Pizer] to Cunard, 9 October 1959.
101 James, Foreword, 'Notes on the Life of George Padmore'.
102 George S. Schuyler, 'Views and Reviews', *Pittsburgh Courier* (31 October 1959), A4.
103 'Mr George Padmore / Political Adviser to Dr Nkrumah,' *The Times* (25 September 1959), 8.
104 St Clair Drake, 'Diaspora Studies and Pan-Africanism', in Joseph E. Harris (ed.), *Global Dimensions of the African Diaspora*, Second edition (Washington, DC: Howard University Press, 1993), pp. 460–1.
105 Drake in Shepperson and Drake, 'Fifth Pan-African Conference', p. 63.
106 C. L. R. James, 'George Padmore', *Tribune* (2 October 1964), 13.
107 Wright Papers (D. Padmore), Pizer to R. Wright, 31 October 1959.
108 George Padmore, *Panafricanisme ou Communisme? La prochaine lutte pour l'Afrique*, trans. Thomas Diop (Paris: Présence Africaine, 1960).
109 James, 'Notes', pp. 60–1; Cunard Collection, Box 17, Folder 10, D. Padmore to Cunard, 24 October 1959; Wright Papers (D. Padmore), Pizer to R. Wright, 16 February 1960.
110 Wright Papers (D. Padmore), Pizer to R. Wright, 20 October 1959.
111 Cunard Collection, Box 17, Folder 10, D. Padmore to Cunard, 24 October 1959.
112 Wright enlisted Gunnar Myrdal's help as he tried to raise funds to write this book; see Wright Papers, Gunnar and Alva Myrdal – Box 101, folder 1481, G. Myrdal to Ira and Edita Morris, 17 September 1959; Gunnar Myrdal to R. Wright, 2 November 1959; see also Pizer to R. Wright, 16 February 1960, for his decision to abandon the book.
113 Gunilla L. Faringer, *Press Freedom in Africa* (New York; Westport, CT; London: Praeger, 1991), pp. 45–6.
114 Letter, Nkrumah to June Milne, 21 August 1967, in June Milne (ed.) *Kwame Nkrumah: The Conakry Years* (London: Panaf, 1990), p. 172.
115 James Mss, Folder 2, James to Walter [Goldwater], 8 April 1963.
116 *Ibid.*, unsigned carbon to Nello [James], 23 May 1964.
117 UWI-St Augustine, James Collection, Box 10, Folder 243, typescript of an unpublished review of James R. Hooker's *Black Revolutionary*.

118 Robert Hill, executor of the James estate, confirmed that this manuscript and an eighty-page manuscript with the same title at the Institute of Commonwealth Studies, University of London, are the only known versions of James's manuscript for a book on Padmore.
119 Lilly, James Mss, Folder 2, Goldwater to Frederick Praeger Co., 22 June 1965.
120 James, *A History of Pan-African Revolt* (Washington, DC: Drum and Spear Press, 1969), pp. 115–16.
121 *Ibid.*, p. 143.
122 Conversation with me, 12 August 2007.
123 Charles R. Larson, *The Ordeal of the African Writer* (London, New York: Zed Books, 2001), pp. 51–3.
124 See, for instance, Drake in Shepperson and Drake, 'The Fifth Pan-African Conference'. For more on Drake's role as publicist and defender of Padmore, Nkrumah, and their fellow pan-Africanists, see Kevin K. Gaines, *American Africans in Ghana: Black Expatriates in the Civil Rights Era* (Chapel Hill: University of North Carolina Press, 2006), pp. 91, 164, 215–17.
125 Fenner Brockway, *The Colonial Revolution* (New York: St Martin's Press, 1973), p. 51, note 2.
126 Fenner Brockway, *African Socialism* (London: Bodley Head, 1963), p. 18.
127 Makonnen, *Pan-Africanism*, p. 234.
128 Schomburg Center for Research in Black Culture, Julian Mayfield Papers, Box 7, Folder 4, Julian Mayfield to J. A. Ankrah, 24 October 1966
129 Kenneth King, 'Introduction,' Makonnen, *Pan-Africanism*, p. xxi.
130 James, *Nkrumah*, p. 183.
131 Larson, *Ordeal of the African Writer*, pp. 133–4.
132 *Ibid.*, p. 140.
133 See also Sanya Osha, 'Writing in a Continent Under Siege', *Research in African Literatures*, 29: 1 (Spring 1998), pp. 174–8; James Gibbs and Jack Mapanje (eds), *The African Writers' Handbook* (Oxford: African Books Collective, 1999), especially Paul Tiyame Zeleza, 'A Social Contract for Books', pp. 3–14.
134 Chinua Achebe, *Home and Exile* (Oxford and New York: Oxford University Press, 2000), p. 44.

SELECT BIBLIOGRAPHY

(Periodical articles cited in the notes are not repeated here.)

Manuscript collections and archives

Records of Allen and Unwin, Ltd. Reading University. Reading, UK.
Nancy Cunard Collection. Harry Ransom Humanities Research Center, University of Texas at Austin, USA.
St Clair Drake Papers. Schomburg Center for Research in Black Culture, New York Public Library, USA.
Faber Archive, London, UK.
Daniel Guérin, Mémoires. Bibliothèque de documentation internationale contemporaine, Universite Paris – X Nanterre, France.
INCOMKA Project: Communist International (Comintern) Archives Project, a selection of digitised files of the Communist International at the Russian State Archives of Socio-Political History (RGASPI), Moscow. Available in the European Reading Room of the Library of Congress, Washington, DC.
C. L. R. James Collection. University of the West Indies at St Augustine, Trinidad and Tobago.
C. L. R. James Mss. Lilly Library, Indiana University, USA.
Alfred A. Knopf, Inc., Records. Harry Ransom Center, University of Texas at Austin, USA.
W. Arthur Lewis Papers. Seeley G. Mudd Manuscript Library, Princeton University. Princeton, NJ, USA.
Alain LeRoy Locke Papers. Moorland-Spingarn Research Center, Howard University, Washington, DC, USA.
Thomas Nelson and Sons, Ltd, Records. Special Collections, Edinburgh University Library, UK.
Kwame Nkrumah Papers. Moorland Spingarn Research Center, Howard University, Washington, DC, USA.
George Padmore Papers. Schomburg Center for Research in Black Culture, New York Public Library, USA.
Routledge and Kegan Paul Ltd. Records. Reading University, Reading, UK.
Royal Institute of International Affairs. Chatham House, London, UK.
Louise Morgan and Otto Theis Papers. General Collection, Beinecke Rare Book and Manuscript Library, Yale University, New Haven, Connecticut, USA.
United Kingdom Colonial Office, Metropolitan Police, Foreign Office, and Security Service Records. The National Archives, Kew, UK (UK/TNA).
United States Department of State. National Archives, College Park, Maryland (US/NA).
Eric Williams Memorial Collection. University of the West Indies, St Augustine, Trinidad and Tobago.

SELECT BIBLIOGRAPHY

Lawrence and Wishart Archive. Beinecke Rare Book and Manuscript Library, Yale University, New Haven, Connecticut, USA.

Richard Wright Papers. Yale Collection of American Literature, Beinecke Rare Book and Manuscript Library, Yale University, New Haven, Connecticut, USA.

Memoirs, published letters, and selected works by principal figures

Abrahams, Peter. *The Black Experience in the 20th Century: An Autobiography and Meditation*. Bloomington: Indiana University Press, 2000.

___. *Dark Testament*. London: George Allen and Unwin, 1942.

___. 'Nkrumah, Kenyatta, and the Old Order', in Jacob Drachler (ed.), *African Heritage*. New York: Crowell-Collier Press, 1963.

___. *Return to Goli*. London: Faber and Faber, 1953.

___. *A Wreath for Udomo*. New York: Alfred A. Knopf, 1956.

Appiah, Joseph. *Joe Appiah: The Autobiography of an African Patriot*. New York: Praeger, 1990.

Azikiwe, Nnamdi. *My Odyssey*. London: C. Hurst and Company, 1970.

___. *Suppression of the Press in British West Africa*. Onitsha, Nigeria: African Book Company, 1946.

Boggs, Grace Lee. *Living for Change: An Autobiography*. Minneapolis, London: University of Minnesota Press, 1998.

Brockway, Fenner. *African Socialism*. London: Bodley Head, 1963.

___. *The Colonial Revolution*. New York: St Martin's Press, 1973.

___. *Inside the Left*. London: George Allen and Unwin, 1942.

___. *Outside the Right*. London: George Allen and Unwin, 1963.

___. *Towards Tomorrow*. London: Hart-Davis, MacGibbon, 1977.

Buhle, Paul (ed.). *C. L. R. James: His Life and Work*. London, New York: Allison and Busby, 1986.

Chisholm, Anne. *Nancy Cunard*. New York: Alfred A. Knopf, 1979.

Cripps, Louise. *C. L. R. James: Memories and Commentaries*. New York, London: Cornwall Books, 1997.

Dei-Anang, Michael. *The Administration of Ghana's Foreign Relations, 1956–1965: A Personal Memoir*. London: The Athlone Press, 1975.

Drake, St Clair. 'Diaspora Studies and Pan-Africanism', in Joseph E. Harris (ed.), *Global Dimensions of the African Diaspora*, Second edition. Washington, DC: Howard University Press, 1993.

___. 'Mbiyu Koinange and the Pan-African Movement', in Robert A. Hill (ed.), *Pan-African Biography*, Los Angeles: African Studies Center, University of California/Crossroads Press, 1987.

Du Bois, W. E. B. *The Correspondence of W. E. B. Du Bois, III, Selections, 1944–1963*, ed. Herbert Aptheker. Amherst: University of Massachusetts Press, 1978.

Gayle, Addison. *Richard Wright: Ordeal of a Native Son*. Garden City, NY: Anchor Press/Doubleday, 1980.

SELECT BIBLIOGRAPHY

James, C. L. R. *At the Rendezvous of Victory: Selected Writings*. London: Allison and Busby, 1984.
___. *Beyond a Boundary*. Durham: Duke University Press, 1993.
___. *The Black Jacobins: Toussaint L'Ouverture and the San Domingo Revolution*. London: Allison and Busby, 1994 (reprint of 1980 edition).
___. *The C. L. R. James Reader*, ed. Anna Grimshaw. Oxford; Cambridge, MA: Blackwell, 1992.
___. *The Case for West-Indian Self Government*. London: Hogarth Press, 1933.
___. *A History of Negro Revolt*. New York: Haskell House, 1938.
___. *Nkrumah and the Ghana Revolution*. Westport, CT: Lawrence Hill and Company, 1977.
___. 'Notes on the Life of George Padmore' (microform of typescript carbon). Chicago, IL: Center for Research Libraries, 1959.
___. *World Revolution, 1916–1936*. Westport, CT: Hyperion Press, 1973; reprint of London: Martin Secker and Warburg, 1937.
Kenyatta, Jomo. *Facing Mount Kenya: The Tribal Life of the Gikuyu*. London: Secker and Warburg, 1959; first published 1938.
Koinange, Mbiyu. *The People of Kenya Speak for Themselves*. Detroit, MI: Kenya Publication Fund, 1955.
Makonnen, Ras. *Pan-Africanism from Within*. Kenneth King (ed.). Nairobi, London, New York: Oxford University Press, 1973.
Nkrumah, Kwame. *Ghana: The Autobiography of Kwame Nkrumah*. New York: Thomas Nelson and Sons, 1957.
___. *Kwame Nkrumah: The Conakry Years: His Life and Letters*, ed. June Milne. London: Zed Press, 1990.
Padmore, George. *Africa and World Peace*. London: Secker and Warburg, 1937.
___. *Africa: Britain's Third Empire*. London: Dennis Dobson, 1949.
___. *Afrika: Unter dem Joch der Weissen*. Erlenbach-Zürich, Leipzig: Rotapfel-Verlag, n.d. [1936]).
___. *The Gold Coast Revolution*. London: Dennis Dobson, 1953.
___. *How Britain Rules Africa*. London: Wishart Books, 1936.
___. *Life and Struggles of Negro Toilers*. London: Red International of Labour Unions, 1931.
___. *Pan-Africanism or Communism?* London: Dennis Dobson, 1956.
___. *Panafricanisme ou Communisme? La prochaine lutte pour l'Afrique*, trans. Thomas Diop. Paris: Présence Africaine, 1960.
___ (ed.), *The Voice of Coloured Labour: Speeches and Reports of Colonial Delegates to the World Trade Union Conference – 1945*. Manchester: PanAf Service, 1945.
___ and Nancy Cunard. *The White Man's Duty*. London: W. H. Allen, 1942.
___ with Dorothy Pizer. *How Russia Transformed Her Colonial Empire: A Challenge to the Imperialist Powers*. London: Dennis Dobson, 1946.
Powell, Erica. *Private Secretary (Female) / Gold Coast*. New York: St Martin's Press, 1984.
Warburg, Fredric. *An Occupation for Gentlemen*. Boston: Houghton Mifflin Company; Cambridge: The Riverside Press, 1960.

SELECT BIBLIOGRAPHY

Woolf, Leonard. *The Journey Not the Arrival Matters*. New York: Harcourt, Brace and World, 1970.

Williams, Eric. *Inward Hunger: The Education of a Prime Minister*. London: André Deutsch, 1969.

___. *The Negro in the Caribbean*, International African Service Bureau Publications, No. 5. Manchester: Panaf Service Ltd, nd.

Wright, Richard. *Black Power*. London: Dennis Dobson, 1954.

Selected secondary sources

Achebe, Chinua. *Home and Exile*. Oxford, New York: Oxford University Press, 2000.

Adi, Hakim. *West Africans in Britain, 1900–1960: Nationalism, Pan-Africanism and Communism*. London: Lawrence and Wishart, 1998.

Adi, Hakim, and Marika Sherwood. *The 1945 Manchester Pan-African Congress Revisited, with Colonial and Coloured Unity*, ed. by George Padmore. London and Port-of-Spain: New Beacon Books, 1995.

Anderson, Benedict. *Imagined Communities: Reflections on the Origin and Spread of Nationalism*. London, New York: Verso, 1983.

Anderson, Paul (ed.). *Orwell in* Tribune. London: Politico's, 2006.

Austin, Dennis. *Politics in Ghana: 1946–1960*. London, New York, Toronto: Oxford University Press, 1964.

Baptiste, Fitzroy and Rupert Lewis (eds). *George Padmore: Pan-African Revolutionary*. Kingston, Miami: Ian Randle Publishers, 2009.

Berman, Bruce. 'Ethnography as Politics, Politics as Ethnography: Kenyatta, Malinowski, and the Making of *Facing Mount Kenya*', *Canadian Journal of African Studies*, 30: 3 (1996), 313–44

Cary, Joyce. *The Case for African Freedom and Other Writings on Africa*. New York, Toronto, London: McGraw-Hill, 1964.

Chatterjee, Partha. *Nationalist Thought and the Colonial World: A Derivative Discourse*. Minneapolis: University of Minnesota Press, 1986.

Chisholm, Anne. *Nancy Cunard*. New York: Alfred A. Knopf, 1979.

Dhondy, Farrukh. *C. L. R. James*. New York: Pantheon Books, 2001.

Douglas, Roy. *Liquidation of Empire: The Decline of the British Empire*. New York: Palgrave Macmillan, 2002.

Drake, St Clair. 'Diaspora Studies and Pan-Africanism' in Joseph E. Harris (ed.), *Global Dimensions of the African Diaspora*. Second edition. Washington, DC: Howard University Press, 1993.

Edmonson, Locksley. *George Padmore's Place in the Study of Pan-Africanism*. Thesis, Kampala, Uganda: Makerere University College, 1968.

Edwards, Brent Hayes. *The Practice of Diaspora: Literature, Translation, and the Rise of Black Internationalism*. Cambridge, MA and London: Harvard University Press, 2003.

Esedebe, P. Olisanwuche. *Pan-Africanism: The Idea and Movement, 1776–1991*. Second edition. Washington, DC: Howard University Press, 1994.

Faringer, Gunilla L. *Press Freedom in Africa*. New York and Westport, CT;

SELECT BIBLIOGRAPHY

London: Praeger, 1991.

Fitch, Bob and Mary Oppenheimer. *Ghana: End of an Illusion*. New York, London: Monthly Review Press, 1966.

Friedland, William H. and Carl G. Rosberg, Jr, (eds), *African Socialism*. Stanford, CA: Stanford University Press, 1964.

Gaines, Kevin K. *American Africans in Ghana: Black Expatriates and the Civil Rights Era*. Chapel Hill: University of North Carolina, 2006.

Geiss, Imanuel. *The Pan-African Movement*, trans. Ann Keep. New York: Africana Publishing Co., 1974.

Hawkins, Clifton C. '"Race First Versus Class First": An Intellectual History of Afro-American Radicalism, 1911–1928'. Ph.D. dissertation, University of California, Davis, 2000.

Herbst, Susan. *Politics at the Margin: Historical Studies of Public Expression Outside the Mainstream*. Cambridge: Cambridge University Press, 1994.

Hobson, Barbara (ed.). *Recognition Struggles and Social Movements: Contested Identities, Agency and Power*. Cambridge: Cambridge University Press, 2003.

Hogan, Lawrence D. *A Black National News Service: The Associated Negro Press and Claude Barnett, 1919–1945*. Rutherford, Madison, Teaneck: Fairleigh Dickinson University Press; London, Toronto: Associated University Presses, 1984.

Hooker, James R. *Black Revolutionary: George Padmore's Path from Communism to Pan-Africanism*. New York: Praeger Publishers, 1967.

Howe, Stephen. *Anticolonialism in British Politics: The Left and the End of Empire, 1918–1964*. Oxford: Clarendon Press, 1993.

Johnson, James W. 'The Associated Negro Press: A Medium of International News and Information, 1919–1967'. Ph.D. dissertation, University of Missouri-Columbia, 1976.

Killingray, David (ed.) *Africans in Britain*. Ilford: Frank Cass and Company, 1994.

Langley, J. Ayodele. *Pan-Africanism and Nationalism in West Africa: 1900–1945*. Oxford: Clarendon Press, 1973.

Larson, Charles R. *The Ordeal of the African Writer*. London, New York: Zed Books, 2001.

Lewis, David Levering. *W. E. B. Du Bois: The Fight for Equality and the American Century, 1919–1963*. New York: Henry Holt and Company, 2000.

Murapa, Rukudzo. 'Padmore's Role in the African Liberation Movement'. Ph.D. dissertation, Northern Illinois University, 1974.

Murray-Brown, Jeremy. *Kenyatta*. Second edition. London: George Allen and Unwin, 1979.

Ogungbesan, Kolawole. *The Writing of Peter Abrahams*. New York: Africana Publishing Company, 1979.

Ottley, Roi. *No Green Pastures*. London: John Murray, 1952.

Polsgrove, Carol. *Divided Minds: Intellectuals and the Civil Rights Movement*. New York: W. W. Norton and Company, 2001.

Postgate, John and Mary. *A Stomach for Dissent: The Life of Raymond Postgate: 1896– 1971*. Keele: Keele University Press, 1994.

SELECT BIBLIOGRAPHY

Rathbone, Richard. *Nkrumah and the Chiefs*. Accra: F. Reimmer; Athens: Ohio University Press; Oxford: James Currey, 2000.

___ (ed.). *British Documents on the End of Empire: Ghana*. Parts I and II. London: HMSO, 1992.

Robinson, Cedric J. *Black Marxism: The Making of the Black Radical Tradition*. Chapel Hill, NC and London: University of North Carolina Press, 1983.

Rowley, Hazel. *Richard Wright: The Life and Times*. New York: Henry Holt, 2001.

Schwarz, Bill (ed.). *West Indian Intellectuals in Britain*. Manchester and New York: Manchester University Press, 2003.

Shaloff, Stanley. 'Press Controls and Sedition Proceedings in the Gold Coast, 1933–39', *African Affairs*, 71: 284 (July 1972), 241–63.

Shepperson, George and St Clair Drake. 'The Fifth Pan-African Conference, 1945 and the All African People's Congress, 1958', *Contributions in Black Studies*, 8 (1986–87), 35–66.

Sherwood, Marika. *Kwame Nkrumah: The Years Abroad, 1935–1947*. Legon, Ghana: Freedom Publications, 1996.

Singh, Kelvin. *Race and Class: Struggles in a Colonial State, Trinidad 1916–1945*. Calgary: University of Calgary Press and Kingston: The Press–University of West Indies, 1994.

Spitzer, Leo and LaRay Denzer. 'I. T. A. Wallace Johnson and the West African Youth League', *International Journal of African Historical Studies*, 6: 3 (1973), 413–52; 'Part II: The Sierra Leone Period, 1938–1945', 6: 4 (1973), 565–601.

Tignor, Robert L. *W. Arthur Lewis and the Birth of Development Economics*. Princeton and Oxford: Princeton University Press, 2006.

Turner, Joyce Moore.'Richard B. Moore and His Works', in W. Burghardt Turner and J. M. Turner (eds), *Richard B. Moore, Caribbean Militant in Harlem*. Bloomington: Indiana University Press; London: Pluto Press, 1992.

Urquhart, Brian. *Ralph Bunche: An American Life*. New York, London: W. W. Norton, 1993.

Von Eschen, Penny M. *Race Against Empire: Black Americans and Anticolonialism, 1936–1957*. Ithaca, NY and London: Cornell University Press, 1997.

Wilford, Hugh.'"Unwitting Assets?"': British Intellectuals and the Congress for Cultural Freedom', *Twentieth Century British History*, 11: 1 (2000), 42–60.

Wilson, Edward Thomas. *Russia and Black Africa before Second World War*. New York, London: Holmes and Meier, 1974.

Worcester, Kent. *C. L. R. James: A Political Biography*. Albany, NY: State University of New York Press, 1996.

Wuthnow, Robert. *Communities of Discourse: Ideology and Social Structure in the Reformation, the Enlightenment, and European Socialism*. Cambridge, MA and London: Harvard University Press, 1989.

Ziegler, Philip. *London at War, 1939–1945*. London: Pimlico, 2002.

INDEX

Abrahams, Daphne, 118
Abrahams, Dorothy, 60-1, 118
Abrahams, Peter, xi, xiii-xiv, 59-61, 70, 75-6, 78-9, 81-3, 104, 118-23, 131-8, 166-9
 Works:
 Dark Testament, 61, 83, 119
 Mine Boy, 83, 119
 Path of Thunder, The, 83, 119
 Return to Goli, 118-122, 137
 Song of the City, 83, 119
 Tell Freedom, 83
 Wild Conquest, 119
 Wreath for Udomo, A, 132-136, 161
Abyssinia *see* Ethiopia
Accra Evening News (also *Ghana Evening News*), 96-7, 111, 125, 149
Achebe, Chinua, 7, 40, 170
Adu, A.L., 159-60
Africa and the World, 31
African Bureau *see* International African Service Bureau
African Drum, 119-20
African Morning Post, 6, 70
African Press Agency, 104, 123,
African Sentinel, 32-3
African Standard, 46
Ako-Adjei, S., 70, 91-2, 96
All African People's Conference (Accra, 1958), 160
Allen, W.H., 61
Allen and Unwin (publishing firm), 12-14, 47, 61-4, 119, 169
Anderson, Benedict, xii
Anglo-American Caribbean Commission, 67-8
Ankrah, J. A., 166-7
Appiah, Joe, xvi, 70, 75, 82, 87, 92, 98, 107, 109, 126-7, 133, 148, 166

Appiah, Peggy, xvi
Asian Socialist Bureau, 140-1
Associated Negro Press, 66, 89
Atlantic Charter, 56-69
Attoh, K. Y., 107
Awolowo, Obafemi, 75
Awooner-Renner, Bankole, 75
Awoonor-Williams, F., 107
Azikiwe, Nnamdi, 1-6, 17-18, 30, 54, 56, 61-2, 70-1, 82, 88, 90, 97, 99-100, 114, 141, 151, 158, 166

Ballard, Arthur, 65
Banda, Hastings, 75, 128, 160
Bandung Conference, 147-8
banned publications, 27, 31-2, 97, 100-3
Baring, Sir Evelyn, 122
Barnes, Leonard, 65
Barnett, Claude, 66
de Beauvoir, Simone, 138
Berman, Bruce, 42
Blackman, Peter, 79
Bloom, Hyman, 108
Blyden, Edward Wilmot, xvi, 24
Boggs, Grace Lee, xvi, 130-1, 155-8, 165-6
Boggs, Jimmy, 155
Botsio, Kojo, 105
Bourdet, Claude, 149
Brace, Harcourt, 104
Briggs, Cyril, 1
British Broadcasting Corporation (BBC), 118-21
British Centre Against Imperialism, 39
Brockway, Fenner, 26-7, 39, 43, 53, 55, 86, 90, 103, 110, 166
Bunche, Ralph, 43, 77
Burma, 99

[181]

INDEX

Cain, Arthur, 76
Cary, Joyce, 62, 136, 138
censorship, xv–xvi, 55, 71, 100–3, 164, 169
Central Intelligence Agency (CIA), 147, 150–1, 162
Chamberlain, Neville, 43–4
Chatterjee, Partha, xiii, 147
Chicago Defender, 33, 38, 54–5, 69, 80, 90, 141
chieftaincy and chiefs' rule, 112–13, 138, 147–9
Churchill, Winston, 56–7
Clarke, Belfield, 60, 163
Cole, William E., 124–5
Colonial Office, 32, 34, 92, 100–2, 128, 133
Colonial Parliamentary Bulletin, 82
Common Wealth Review, 85
communism, xv–xvi, 1–10, 13, 60–1, 79, 82, 101, 105–8, 151, 145–6
Communist International, 1, 4, 26, 41, 107, 150
Communist Party (British), 12, 15, 30, 82
Conference of Independent African States (1958), 160
Congress for Cultural Freedom, 89, 147, 151
Constantine, Learie, 24
Convention People's Party (CPP), 97, 104–5, 107–8, 111, 113–14, 124–7, 148, 161–2
Controversy, 34, 37, 85; *see also* Left
Cowart, Blyden (George Padmore's daughter), xvi, 4
Cripps, Louise, 25–9, 37, 45
Cripps, Peggy, 148
Cripps, Sir Stafford, 28, 58, 64
Crisis, 1, 12, 38, 47, 54–5, 58, 66, 77, 89, 96, 105, 154
Crisp, Dorothy, 83, 119
Cunard, Nancy, 1, 2–6, 8, 13–14, 31, 56–61, 64, 164

Daily Comet, 71
Daily Mail (Gold Coast), 97

Daily Worker, 28, 41, 55, 61, 86, 103
Danquah, J. B., 92, 107, 110
Denmark, 26
de Silva, Joseph, 65–6
Dobson, Dennis, 65, 100, 111, 139, 148–51, 158, 164
Domingo, W. A., 62
Dover, Cedric, 79, 83, 104
Drake, St Clair, xv, 4, 29, 39, 41, 66, 81–2, 90–1, 96, 137, 160, 163, 166–7
Du Bois, W. E. B., xi, 69, 75, 80–1, 103–4, 112, 126, 138, 145, 164
du Sautoy, Peter, 136
Dzewu, Dzenkle, 125

Economist, The, 18
Economist Bookshop, 88
Edwards, Brent Hayes, xi
Emergency Powers (Defence) Act (1939), 46
Empire, 67, 86
Encounter, 151, 162
Ethiopia, 7, 11–12, 23, 25–6, 43, 80

Fabians, 34, 57, 92 140, 151, 161
Faber and Faber (publisher), 136
Fact, 38
Fanon, Frantz, 160, 165
federalism, 149, 160
Fifth Pan-African Congress *see* Pan-African Congress
Fight, 28
Firth, Raymond, 87

Gambia, 102
Gandhi, Mohandas, 58
Garvey, Amy Ashwood, 25, 60
Garvey, Marcus, 24, 60, 91, 145, 157
Ghana, 34, 112, 123, 152–62, 167–9; *see also* Gold Coast
Gittens, Joyce, 123
Gold Coast, 7–8, 30–3, 91–3, 96–101, 104–14, 122–40, 147–9, 152–6; *see also* Ghana
Goldwater, Walter, 164–5
Gollancz, Victor, 15, 80

[182]

INDEX

Griffith, G. T. N. *see* Makonnen, Ras
Griffiths, James, 100–3
Guardian of Trinidad, 24; *see also Manchester Guardian*
Guérin, Daniel, 150–1

Habermas, Jürgen, xii
Haile Selassie, 26
Harper and Brothers (publisher), 137
Harrison, William, 35
Hill, Herbert, 126–7
Hinden, Rita, 57, 140, 151, 161
Hitler, Adolf, 4, 6, 12, 15, 28, 43–4
Ho Chi Minh, 78
Hobson, J. A., 10
Hogarth Press, 10, 24, 58–9
Holmes, Ivar, 26, 79, 85
Hooker, James R., xv, 46, 86, 151, 164–5
Howe, Russell Warren, 162
Huiswoud, Otto, 1
Huxley, Elspeth, 36, 39

Independent Labour Party (ILP), 26–7, 34, 53–4, 65, 86, 90
India, 58, 92, 120, 147
International Affairs, 66
International African Friends of Ethiopia (IAFE), 25–6
International African Opinion, 34–6, 45–6, 164
International African Service Bureau (IASB), 30–47, 66–8, 76, 80
International Trade Union Committee of Negro Workers (ITUC-NW), 2, 4, 8, 30, 113

James, C. L. R., xiii, xv–xvi, 3, 6, 10, 17, 23–30, 34–38, 40–3, 70, 78, 81, 84, 98, 110, 114, 121, 129–31, 154–8, 163–9
Works:
Beyond the Boundary, 164
Black Jacobins, The, 36–7, 164
Case for West-Indian Self Governnment, The, 10, 24
History of Negro Revolt, A, 38, 165

Nkrumah and the Ghana Revolution, 155–8, 165
World Revolution, 27–9
Johnson, I. T. A. Wallace *see* Wallace Johnson, I. T. A.
Johnson-Forest Tendency, 130–1
Jones, Arthur Creech, 55, 76, 92, 102
Jones, Chris, 45
Joseph-Mitchell, M., 102
Josselson, Michael, 151
Joyce, Robert P., 128

Kaunda, Kenneth, 160
Keenleyside, Hugh, 161–2
Kell, Sir Vernon, 30
Kenya, 13–14, 39–40, 90, 100–2, 120–2, 131, 139–41, 170
Kenya African Union (KAU), 121–2
Kenyatta, Johnstone (Jomo), xi–xiv, 2–3, 6, 9, 14, 25–30, 34–43, 47, 55, 60, 66–7, 75, 82, 87, 90–1, 120–2, 133–5, 157, 160, 167–9
Works:
Facing Mount Kenya, 39–42
Kenya, The Land of Conflict, 67
Kikyu Central Association, 6, 55, 66
King, Kenneth, 167
Knopf (publisher), 136
Koinange, Mbiyu (Peter), 39, 41, 47, 90–91, 122, 130–1
Kolarz, Walter, 65
Kouyaté, Garan, xi, 2, 5–6
Kristol, Irving, 151

Labour Party, British, 5, 11, 18, 98, 102, 140–1, 151, 161, 169
Lamming, George, 133
Larson, Charles R., 170
Laval, Pierre, 12
League of Coloured Peoples, 33, 92, 102–3
League of Nations, 77
Leakey, L. S. B., 39
Left, 54, 58, 66; *see also Controversy*
Left Book Club, 15, 59
Lenin, V.I. (and Leninism), 6, 10, 65, 125, 130, 156–7, 165

[183]

INDEX

Lewis, Arthur, 33–4, 88, 129, 161–2
Leys, Norman, 57
Lindsay, Jack, 79
Listener, 16
Little, Kenneth, 88
Locke, Alain, 1, 16, 28–9, 44–5, 64–5, 67
Lugard, Lord, 17
Lumumba, Patrice, 160

Macdonald, Dwight, 78
McNair, John, 46
Makonnen, Ras, 2, 19, 25–6, 29, 33–6, 39, 42–7, 60, 66–7, 75–83, 87–91, 131, 159–62, 165–7
  Work:
  Pan-Africanism from Within, 166–7
Malinowski, Bronislaw, 28, 39, 41, 43
Manchester Guardian, 24, 80, 82, 130
Manchester Congress *see* Pan-African Congress
Markham, James, 111
Marx, Karl, 157
Mau Mau, 41, 121–2, 139
Mayfield, Julian, 166–7
Melucci, Alberto, xiii
Melville, Herman, 129, 168
Metropolitan Police, 30–1, 43, 76, 82
Miall, Bernard, 61
Milliard, Peter, 66
Milne, Van, 153
Moon, Parker Thomas, 10–11
Moore, Richard B., 1
Moral Rearmament, 150–1
Murapa, Rukudzo, 96
Murray-Brown, Jeremy, 67
Mussolini, Benito, 12, 15

Nation (Trinidad), 156
Nation (US), 138
National Association for the Advancement of Colored People (NAACP), US, 1, 12, 54, 69, 81, 104

National Council for Civil Liberties, UK, 102
nationalism, 100, 135–6, 145–6, 148, 160, 165
National Liberation Movement (NLM), 148–9, 153
Negro Welfare Association, 5, 12
Negro Worker, xv, 2–5, 8, 30
Negro World, 24, 60
Nehru, Jawaharlal, 99, 147
Nelson and Sons (publishing firm), 153–4, 158
New African, 82
New Leader, 17, 26–7, 34, 39, 45–6, 53–5, 58, 66, 75–6
New Statesman and Nation, 86
New York Amsterdam News, 19, 54–5
New York Times, 37
Ngugi wa Thiong'o, 170
Nigeria, 30, 71, 80, 99–101, 141, 149, 158, 160, 166
Nkrumah, Kwame, xi–xv, 70–1, 75, 81–2, 90–3, 96–101, 104–14, 122–8, 131–40, 146–70
  Works:
  Ghana: The Autobiography of Kwame Nkrumah, 151–4, 158
  Towards Colonial Freedom – Africa in the Struggle Against World Imperialism, 127
Nunn, G. N. N., 100, 151
Nurse, James Hubert Alfonso, 23
Nyerere, Julius, 160, 165

Ogungbesan, Kolawole, 83
Ollivierre, Cyril, 2–3, 29, 45
Ormsby Gore, William, 31–2
Orwell, George, 34
Osman, Yagoub, 79
Ottley, Roi, 89

Padley, Walter, 85–6,
Padmore, George
  Life:
  death, funeral and obituaries of, 162–3
  early life in Trinidad, 23–4

[184]

INDEX

financial circumstances of, 28–9
Gold Coast visit, 104–8
Ghana years, 159–62
health problems of, 47, 60, 162
marriage of, 4, 29
work in Communist International, 2–4
years in the United States, 1–2
Works:
Africa: Britain's Third Empire, 79, 98, 100–3, 106–7, 114, 149–50, 169
Africa and World Peace, 26, 28–9, 42, 58
Afrika unter dem Joch der Weissen, 15–16
Gold Coast Revolution, The, xiv, 111, 113, 123, 132, 156, 161, 169
Hands Off the Protectorates, 34
How Britain Rules Africa, 5–10, 13–19, 42, 88, 98, 169
How Russia Transformed Her Colonial Empire (with Dorothy Pizer), 62–5, 85–6, 88, 92,
Life and Struggles of Negro Toilers, The 2, 8, 30, 36
Pan-Africanism or Communism?, 145–51, 156, 158, 160, 163, 167
White Man's Duty, The (with Nancy Cunard), 58, 61, 67
Padmore, Julia (George's wife), 4, 29, 44
Pan-Africa, 79, 83, 86–90
Pan-African Bookshop, 88
Pan-African Congress (Fifth), xiv, 75–6, 81–3, 91, 98, 104
Pan-African Federation, 66, 69, 81–2
Pan-African Publishing Company (Panaf Service), 66
Parrish, Margot, 152
Patterson, William, 5
Peace Information Center, 104
Perham, Margery, 17–18, 57
Phillips, Anne, xiii
Phillips, Morgan, 140–1
Pittsburgh Courier, 38, 54–5, 89–90, 105, 141, 163

Pizer, Dorothy, xiv–xv, 29, 34, 37, 45, 57, 59, 64, 78, 83–5, 104, 106, 109, 113, 118, 123, 128–31, 137, 150–4, 158–65
Postgate, Raymond, 38
Powell, Erica, 152–4
Présence africaine, 150, 163
public sphere, xii–xiii, 169

Rathbone, Richard, 113
revolutionary sentiment, 28–9
Reynolds, Reginald, 87
Richards, Sir Arthur, 90
Richardson, Maurice, 9
Ridley, F. A., 65, 86, 100
Robeson, Paul, 29, 126
Roosevelt, Franklin D., 54
Rose, Paul, 140–1
Rotapfel-Verlag (publishing firm), 15–16
Routledge (publishing firm), 9–11
Rowley, Hazel, 124, 127

Saro Wiwa, Ken, 170
Sartre, Jean-Paul, 138
Sawyer, Eugene, 124
Schneider, Agnes, 126
Schuyler, George, 89, 163
Schwarz, Bill, xii
Secker and Warburg (publishing firm), 27–8, 39
Senghor, Leopold, 148
Sherwood, Marika, 82
Siedel, Lucy, 126
Sierra Leone, 33, 46, 56
Simnet, W. E., 63–4
Smith, C. A., 85–6
socialism in African states, 63, 158, 161, 165–6
Socialist Asia, 139–41, 151
Socialist Leader, 78, 83–6, 90, 92, 96, 100, 108
Sorensen, Reginald, 31
South Africa, 37–8, 119–20, 123, 132, 135, 169
Souvarine, Boris, 36, 42
Soviet Union, 62–5, 85–6, 158

[185]

INDEX

Soyinka, Wole, 170
Spengler, Oswald, 37
Stalin, Joseph (and Stalinism), 6, 24, 36, 42, 159, 161
Stock, Dinah, 39, 41, 47, 55, 87
Strauss, Harold, 136
Sudan, 79–80, 139, 162
surveillance, 4–5, 30–1, 43, 76, 82, 106–7, 139–41

Talking Drums, 107
Tanzania, 165
Theis, Otto, 8–9, 12, 14–16
Theophilus, Isaac, 30
Times, The, 17, 57
Times Literary Supplement, 17, 66, 86, 100, 130, 151
totalitarianism, 158–9
Toussaint L'Ouverture, 29, 36–7, 121
trade unions, 33, 68–9, 99–100, 149; *see also* International Trade Union Committee of Negro Workers
tribalism and tribal culture, 41, 132–5, 147–9, 158–61
Tribune, 64
Trinidad, 23, 56, 68, 156–7
Trotsky, Leon (and Trotskyism), 24–5, 28, 34, 45, 157
Truman, Harry (and Truman Doctrine), 89, 104
trusteeship status, 77–8

Uganda, 101–2, 141, 149, 152
United Asia, 147
United Gold Coast Convention, 92, 96. 107
United Nations, 77–8, 81, 120, 161–2
Universal Declaration of Human Rights, 102

Von Eschen, Penny, 89

Wallace Johnson, I. T. A., xi, 30–3, 38, 46, 68–9, 75–7, 81, 83
Wamala, Samwiri, 102
Warburg, Fredric, 27–8, 36, 39, 42–3
Ward, Arnold, 5
Washburn, Patrick S., 54
Wells, H. G., 64
West Africa, 82
West African National Secretariat (WANS), 81–2, 92
West African Pilot, 54, 56, 108
West African Students Union (WASU), 64, 66, 82, 87, 91, 113
West African Youth League, 33, 75
Williams, Eric, 56–7, 67–8, 88, 166
Wilson, Edward T., 2
Wilson, Edwin, xvi
Wishart (publishing firm), 8, 12, 14–15
women's contribution to literary and promotional activity, 27, 83–4, 87, 130–1
Woolf, Leonard, 10–11, 58–9
Woolf, Virginia, 10
Wright, Ellen, xv, 84, 159
Wright, Richard, xi–xv, 78–9, 83, 122–9, 133–9, 147–50, 154, 164, 169
  Works:
  Black Power, 122–9, 136–9
  Colour Curtain, The, 147–8

Young Men's Christian Association, 25

Zik Press, 151

EU authorised representative for GPSR:
Easy Access System Europe, Mustamäe tee 50,
10621 Tallinn, Estonia
gpsr.requests@easproject.com

www.ingramcontent.com/pod-product-compliance
Lightning Source LLC
Chambersburg PA
CBHW070943230426
43666CB00011B/2540